Rare and Scarce
Birds in
North East Scotland

Rare and Scarce Birds in North East Scotland

Written by
I. M. Phillips

Design and layout by
H. I. Scott (Pica Design)

Illustrations by
M. Langman & J. P. Smith

Printed by
Biddles Ltd.

Privately published

To Ken Shaw

They should be annual

Published by I. M. Phillips (1997)

© Text, I. M. Phillips
88 Langdykes Drive, Cove, Aberdeen AB12 3HW. Tel: 01224 897898

© Figures, H. I. Scott (Pica Design)
259 Union Grove, Aberdeen AB10 6SX. Tel: 01224 310199

© Illustrations, M. Langman
59 Sturcombe Avenue, Roselands, Paignton, Devon TQ4 7TD. Tel: 01803 528008

© Illustrations, J. P. Smith
157 Standon Road, Wincobank, Sheffield S9 1PH. Tel: 0114 2491378

ISBN 0 9531259 0 4

Contents

Acknowledgments

From the inception of the project in the autumn of 1992 many people have assisted and given encouragement. I would like to express my thanks to those people.

Particular thanks go to Andy Thorpe and Ken Shaw who read through the draft versions and made valuable and constructive comments for its improvement. The enthusiasm and encouragement from Ken helped me to push on when my own enthusiasm was fading. Many queries on local and Scottish rarity decisions were answered in full by Andy Webb (regional recorder) and full access to the 1996 database was made available prior to the 1996 bird report being compiled. To the Grampian Ringing Group, particularly Raymond Duncan and Rab Rae, for supplying ringing reports and searching out some elusive records. Several people made constructive comments on very early drafts of what was then called 'The Should be Annual' Annual, particularly Stuart Reeves, Brian Stewart, Graham Buchanan and Allen Knox. Also to Richard Schofield who first suggested that these records should be brought together in one place.

I would also like to thank all those people who searched out photographs of rarities taken in the North East Scotland region particularly Sam Alexander, Stuart Reeves, Andy Webb, Mark Sullivan and Raymond Duncan.

I am grateful to Harry Scott (Pica Design), for taking the basic text and data, and producing the finished article seen here.

If I have overlooked anyone who has assisted I apologise and extend my sincere thanks. Finally, the many rarities summarised within the text have to be found by someone. Those rarity hunters of the region who take time to find and identify rare and scarce species, then describe and submit those records, all deserve thanks.

Introduction

North East Scotland region

Elgin

Cullen

Banff

Fraserburgh

Buckie

Rattray Head

Loch of Strathbeg

Keith

Turriff

Peterhead

R. Spey

R. Deveron

Huntly

R. Ythan

Ellon

Meikle Loch

Cruden Bay

Tomintoul

Rhynie

Inverurie

Collieston

Newburgh

Corby Loch

Balmedie

R. Don

Loch of Skene

Blackdog

ABERDEEN

Lochs Davan & Kinord

R. Dee

Girdleness

Ballater

Aboyne

Banchory

Portlethen

Braemar

Loch Muick

Stonehaven

R. North Esk

Inverbervie

Edzell

Laurencekirk

N

St Cyrus

0   15   30

Montrose

Scale in kilometres

Area over 100 m	Area over 500 m	Regional boundary

Introduction

Like many areas in Britain, the North East Scotland region has had a tradition of recording the occurrence of rare and scarce species from the 1800s onwards. The majority of the early records relate to birds which were 'collected', that is to say shot. Many of the collectors were aware enough of the rarity value of these species to write short notes for journals published at that time. During the mid to late 1800s several attempts were made to bring together some of these records for small areas. MacGillivray wrote *The Natural History of Deeside and Braemar*, only published in 1855 after his death. Thomas Edward's *The Fauna of Banffshire* was published in Smiles' *Life of a Scotch Naturalist* in 1877, followed by Serle publishing a paper on the *Avi-Fauna of Buchan* in 1895.

The first regional avifauna, *The Vertebrate Fauna of Dee*, covered much of the current region and was written by Sim in 1903. This volume was an admirable attempt to publish the status of all the bird species that had occurred within the area in one place. One weakness of this work was the author's personal opinions of some of the records and also of some of the people reporting the records. Sim was particularly scathing in some of his remarks on the Banffshire naturalist Thomas Edward. *The Vertebrate Fauna of Dee* was a useful step forward, but it is not among the best of the regional *Vertebrate Fauna* series in Scotland.

After the turn of the century, records continued to be reported in the journals of the day, particularly *British Birds*. The publication of the journal of the Scottish Ornithologists' Club, *Scottish Birds*, starting in 1958, gave more space for records of Scottish interest.

The two volume work, *The Birds of Scotland* (Baxter and Rintoul 1953), attempted to bring together the status of all bird species that had occurred in Scotland. The records of the rare and scarce birds were covered fully, but again the authors exercised their own opinions on the validity of many records. Thom in *Birds in Scotland* (1986) largely followed Baxter and Rintoul in acceptance or rejection of early records.

It was not until the early 1980s that another attempt at a regional avifauna was attempted. This took the form of a year-round atlas using data from field work undertaken between January 1981 and December 1984. The results were published in 1990 as *The Birds of North East Scotland* (Buckland *et al.* 1990). This work still stands as the most valuable single text on the local status and distribution of birds in the region. The work included a smaller section on the rare and scarce birds that had occurred during the atlas period and some of the more important historical records.

When Sim published *The Vertebrate Fauna of Dee* (1903) there had been 243 species recorded in the North East Scotland region. This had increased to 251 when Baxter and Rintoul published *The Birds of Scotland* in 1953. The current list stands at 340, with Brünnich's Guillemot on category D3 (tideline corpses only), Yellow-legged Gull waiting on a decision by the British Ornithological Union Records Committee as to its status as a full species and Little Shearwater still under consideration by British Birds Records Committee.

With the increased interest in rare and scarce migrant and vagrant birds there is now a place for a fuller treatment of the rare and scarce species.

In putting together the data used in this book, it is almost inevitable that some errors have occurred. It would be useful if readers could inform the author of any inaccuracies or omissions so that the database can be altered accordingly.

A brief birder's site guide to North East Scotland

The North East Scotland recording area is nearly 7000 km², much of it remote and relatively inaccessible, especially in winter (Buckland *et al.* 1990). During migration periods much of the effort of local birders is concentrated along the extensive east coast. Any area of cover is worth checking during spring and autumn when there is a north easterly, easterly or south easterly wind and rain. The stretch of coast between Aberdeen and Rattray Head is the best known and gets a greater amount of coverage than the stretch south of Aberdeen to St Cyrus. This, along with the low number of active birders in the region, affords good opportunities to find your own migrants (rare or otherwise) without the 'hordes' associated with some areas of England.

Migrant sites

Girdleness (NJ 973053): a low lying promontory forming the southern side of the mouth of the River Dee in Aberdeen. The bulk of the site is taken by a golf course, surrounded by a tarmac public road. The embankments between the road and the river/sea are worth checking for migrants among the gorse, willow herb and occasional bush. The old Torry Battery (gun emplacements) and the ditch with gorse surrounds often produce good numbers of migrants in fall conditions. The allotments (private), at the north western edge of the golf course, can be viewed clearly from the outside and again hold migrants in fall conditions. The eastern point, by the lighthouse and foghorn, is probably the regions premier seawatching point for passage gulls, skuas and shearwaters.

Donmouth (NJ 954095): the estuary of the River Don on the north side of Aberdeen. Much of the area between the mouth and Balgownie Bridge is a local nature reserve and a public bird hide is present. The estuary has bushes along the river bank which may hold migrants. The estuary itself holds small numbers of waders and has had its fair share of passage rare and scarce waders. It is perhaps best known for the large gull roost in late autumn and winter which is well worth checking for rarer gulls.

Donmouth to Murcar (NJ 954095 to NJ 959120): the stretch of coastal dunes bordering a golf course are accessed from the north side of the River Don. This sandy coastal area holds large numbers of sea ducks in summer and winter and is the prime site for Surf Scoter and has good chances of turning up King Eider and rarer grebes and divers.

Balmedie Country Park (NJ 976180): an area of coastal dunes and bushes around two car parks accessed by a public road. An underwatched site still to achieve its full potential.

Ythanmouth and the River Ythan (NJ 999252): a huge area of tidal river estuary and dunes slacks most noted for its huge breeding colony of Common Eider and at least one regular King Eider. The area can be accessed from many points and a public hide is present at Waulkmill. The area is tremendous for passage waders and wildfowl. In the dune slacks south of the rivermouth are Foveran Bushes, a small group of bushes which frequently holds rare and scarce migrants. The dunes hold large flocks of Snow Buntings in winter with other species also possible.

Meikle Loch (NK 029308): accessed by an unlabelled track off the main road. Park sensibly in the limited space by the loch. Variable results are obtained here. Has been good for White-winged Black Tern in the past.

Cotehill Loch (NK 027293): a small loch viewed from the roadside (park sensibly). Worth checking as it can be done quickly.

Collieston area (NK 040283): Park by the church before the village and check the several areas of bushes by the roadside. Surprisingly productive. The viewpoint above the public carpark north of the bay is good for seawatching but is generally underwatched. Several good gardens can be overlooked from the streets in the village, but always be aware of public sensitivity.

Cruden Bay Woods (NK 092363): park in the public car park in Cruden Bay and walk the wooded area and the gully down toward the sea. This is one of the most extensive areas of cover on the east coast. The fields to the north of the gully (private land) are worth checking for finches and buntings. Always worth checking but often better in autumn than spring.

Annachie Lagoon (NK 107534): follow the road to the coast from St Fergus village and park behind the dunes. Walk north toward the oil terminal. A stream passes through the dunes here, often forming a lagoon when the sea closes the entrance with sand. Good for autumn waders and terns.

Rattray Head (NK 110577): follow the road to the old coast guard cottages and park. The small apparent amount of cover (gorse, weeds and willow herb) in this area can be very productive in fall conditions. A good seawatching point from the dunes but underwatched. South of the carpark, in fields behind the dunes, are the Rattray Flashes. When holding water this area is good for waders and wildfowl.

RSPB Loch of Strathbeg Nature Reserve (NK 074590): access from Crimond village (NK052567). Five hides overlooking the main loch and scrapes. Detailed instructions from reserve centre. Can be excellent for wildfowl, waders and raptors.

Fraserburgh (NJ 999676): park at Kinnaird Head car park west of the harbour. An excellent seawatching point in the right conditions. The outfalls here attract large numbers of gulls in winter.

Phingask Bay (NJ 975670): 1 mile west of Fraserburgh. A rocky bay, viewed from the roadside, with a huge gull roost in winter.

Banff and Macduff (NJ 685645): Two small harbours and the mouth of the River Deveron holding numbers of gulls in winter and sea duck offshore.

This list covers many of the regular coastal sites watched by local birders but is in no way meant to be fully comprehensive. Any coastal village such as Whinnyfold, Findon, Newtonhill or Muchalls has areas and gardens worth checking during migration time. Some sites such as Drums and Hatterseat are accessed by private roads and both are subject to landowner consent.

Notes on the Species accounts

The format chosen for the species accounts closely follows that of *Rare Birds in Britain and Ireland* by J. N. Dymond *et al.* (1989), *Rare Birds in Britain 1800-1990* by L. G. R. Evans (1994) and *Rare and Scarce Birds in Yorkshire* by A. Wilson and R. Slack (1996).

The systematic list follows the order of Dr K. H. Voous's *List of Recent Holarctic Bird Species* (1977).

The summary of the world range for each species is based mainly on information given in the above-mentioned sources, with additional data from *The New Atlas of Breeding Birds in Britain and Ireland* by Gibbons *et al.* (1993), the annual Rare Breeding Birds Panel Reports in *British Birds* and three volumes of *Rare Birds in Britain* for the years 1991 to 1993, by L. G. R. Evans.

The historical records have been taken from the pages of a number of journals, particularly the *Annals of Scottish Natural History*, *The Zoologist*, *British Birds*, *Proceedings of the Natural History Society of Glasgow*, the *Journal of the Buchan Field Club* and the *Proceedings of the Aberdeen Working Men's Natural History Society*. In addition *The Vertebrate Fauna of Dee* by Sim (1903) and *The Birds of the West of Scotland* by Gray (1871) brought together many of the older records. More recent information (from 1958) has been taken from *Scottish Birds*, the journal of the Scottish Ornithologists' Club.

The bulk of the recent records for the North East Scotland region have been taken from the local bird reports between 1974 and 1995. The data for 1996 come from the Regional Recorders' database to be used in compiling the 1996 report. The records from earlier than 1974 come from the annual Rarities Reports in *British Birds* and the *Scottish Bird Report* produced by the Scottish Ornithologists' Club.

The majority of records included within this book have been submitted to and accepted by the appropriate Rarities Committees. British rarities are the responsibility of the British Birds Rarities Committee (BBRC), with the Scottish Birds Rarities Committee (SBRC) considering species no longer considered by BBRC. The local North East Scotland Rarities Committee (NESRC) assesses locally rare and scarce species not considered by either of the two national committees.

Several species are included that recently ceased to be considered by any committee because they have become more regular (Yellow-browed Warbler and Reed Warbler). Also included are some species of interest to migrant finders, which have never required descriptions (Red-backed Shrike, Bluethroat, Wryneck etc).

Several species have been deliberately excluded from the book on the grounds of sensitivity as breeding species. These include Corncrake, Spotted Crake and Goshawk.

Most of the species' accounts for the scarce migrants cover the years 1974 to 1996. For mainly winter visitors, it is sensible to present data for winter periods rather than as annual totals in the graphs. The annual histograms present data of individuals seen in that year (or winter). The monthly or weekly histograms present data, from several years, on the arrival date of new individuals.

Distribution maps are included, where relevant, to show the spread of records across the region.

Species accounts

White-billed Diver *Gavia adamsii*

Breeds in the Arctic from western Siberia east to Canada. The majority of birds winter in coastal waters adjacent to breeding grounds but small numbers occur off north west Europe.

This species is a regular winter visitor to Scottish waters, particularly around the Northern Isles (Evans 1994).

There have been only six records from this region of this Arctic species, all between October and March. This pattern is typical of British records (Dymond *et al.* 1989). Of the four live records, three have been on the east coast with one on the north coast. The individual in March 1996 was seen by many appreciative local birders.

ALL RECORDS

1969 24 Mar **Rattray** found dead, now in British Museum, Tring. (Dr J.J.D.Greenwood, Dr B.B.Rae, *per* D.M.Burn) (*BB* 67: RR)

1974 21 Oct **Aberdeen** (A.G.Knox) (*BB* 68: RR)

1979 23 Feb **Banff Bay** juvenile (J.J.C.Hardy) (*BB* 73: RR)

1988 9 Oct **Peterhead** (M.Innes) (*BB* 82: RR)

1996 1 Feb **Portsoy** found dead, skull sent to Natural History Museum, London, for confirmation (A.D.Murdock) (subject to acceptance)

1996 24-30 Mar **Peterhead** (K.Gillon) (*BB* 90: RR)

White-billed Diver *by M. Langman*

Pied-billed Grebe *Podilymbus podiceps*

Breeds in Northern, Central and South America. The Northern American population winters south in the USA.

There has been only one record in North East Scotland of this American grebe, the second record for Scotland. The individual was photographed and appeared as plate 181 in the *Brit. Birds* Rarities Report for 1977 (Vol. 70).

ALL RECORDS

1977 9 Jan-27 Mar **Strathbeg** (J.Dunbar *et al.*) (*BB* V70: RR)

Red-necked Grebe *Podiceps grisegena*

Breeds in eastern Siberia, Alaska, western Canada, and Europe from Denmark and Hungary east to the Volga Basin. Most winter in coastal waters around the breeding areas. Much of the European population winters in the Baltic and North Seas.

There are good numbers of wintering birds in Scotland in most years, with the majority in the Forth estuary.

There are several records from the last century for the region. Edward (1854) said that it occurred on the Loch of Strathbeg as an occasional visitor and Gray (1871) noted only one, shot in Aberdeenshire on 2nd May 1867. Serle (1895) said he had seen this species at Peterhead and that one was shot near Fraserburgh in January 1895. Sim (1903) considered Red-necked Grebes to be slightly more common than Great Crested Grebes, with several 'obtained within our district', but he only gives details of four specimens, including the individual mentioned above by Gray.

There are few records for the early part of this century. Baxter and Rintoul (1953) only note its occurrence in this region from the Loch of Skene, but gave no dates.

Since 1960, Red-necked Grebes have been irregularly recorded in small numbers, largely from coastal locations. There is a marked variation in the number of records between years, as with the winters of 1978-79, 1980-81, 1981-82 and 1995-96 being particularly good years with between eight and nineteen birds present. These influxes must relate, in part, to severe cold weather on the near continent, forcing birds to cross the North Sea from the Baltic countries. Birds are rarely seen away from the sea, but have been recorded on the Loch of Strathbeg, Cults Reservoir, Loirston Loch, the River Dee and the Loch of Skene. The latter site is some 17km from the coast and constitutes the furthest inland record of this species.

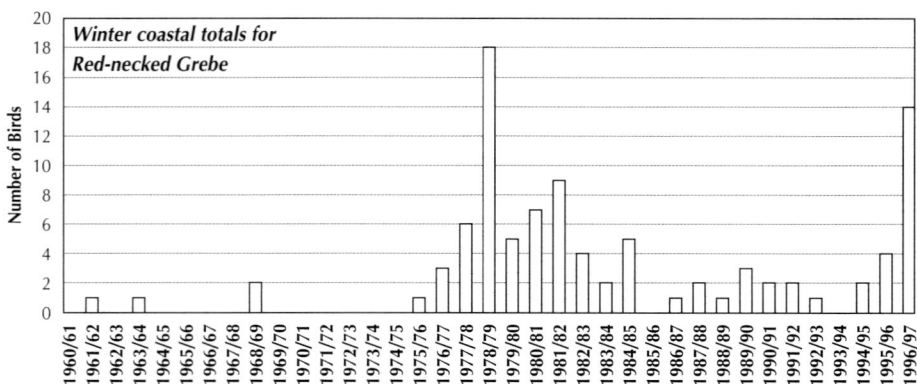

Winter coastal totals for Red-necked Grebe

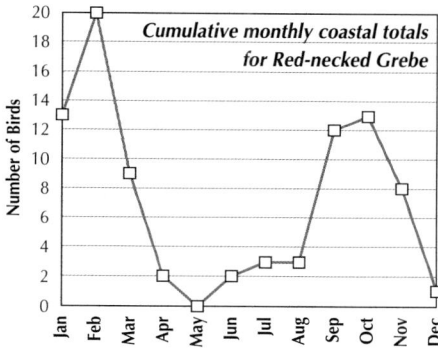

Cumulative monthly coastal totals for Red-necked Grebe

Red-necked Grebes have been reported in every month except May, although the majority of records fall between September and March. There is a decline in records after November, with few birds actually present in December. During an intensive seawatching study off Peterhead between 1978 and 1988 (Innes 1994) small numbers of birds (1–3 individuals) were regularly recorded passing close inshore during January–February and September–October. The conclusion reached was that it was impossible to separate birds on genuine passage from birds on feeding movements. Most records refer to single birds seen either flying just offshore or birds on the sea for one or two days.

Very occasionally birds linger for several days, with exceptional records in 1976 and 1977 of single birds apparently present off the Forvie-Ythan area from 27th July until 5th September and 21st June until 13th November respectively.

The bulk of the records come from Peterhead, boosted by the intensive seawatching study by Mike Innes between 1978 and 1988 (Innes 1994). The stretch of coast from Girdleness north to Collieston accounts for the majority of the remaining records. There are few records from the underwatched north coast.

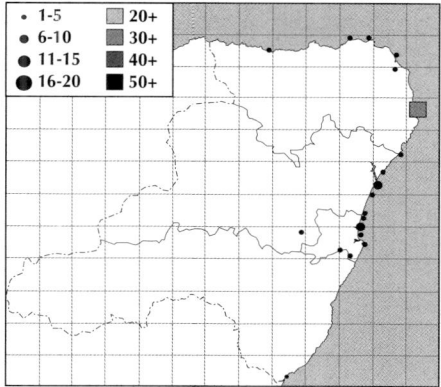

Red-necked Grebe sightings

Red-necked Grebe by M. Langman

Slavonian Grebe *Podiceps auritus*

Breeds throughout the boreal zone of the northern hemisphere, wintering in coastal waters of more temperate zones.

Slavonian Grebes have a very vulnerable foothold in Scotland as a breeding species, having first bred in 1908 (Crooke *et al.* 1993). The current population is only about 60 pairs, but varies considerably from year to year (Gibbons *et al.* 1993). There are only sporadic records of breeding or attempted breeding within the North East region due to a lack of suitable habitat.

There are records of Slavonian Grebes in the *Old Statistical Account of Scotland* (1791-99) and the *New Statistical Account of Scotland* (1845) from the parish of Banchory-Ternan. During the late 1800s they are noted only as occasional in Aberdeenshire (*Scot. Nat.* 1885-86). Sim (1903) noted only one record; that of a female shot at Brackley Castle, giving no date.

There are few further records until the 1960s, when a pair bred inland in 1960 and 1962 (*Scot. Birds* 1963). Since then birds have been seen occasionally in breeding habitat. From 1974 Slavonian Grebes have been recorded in every year except 1993. The number of birds seen in any one year varies from one to thirteen, and as with Red-necked Grebes, hard weather in winter on the near continent often results in influxes. Birds have been recorded in every month of the year with a peak in September-October. Summer records are fewer and often refer to birds present at inland sites.

The majority of records come from the Loch of Strathbeg, with birds most often present between September and November. Spring records from this location are scarce. Many records have come from Peterhead, predominantly of birds passing seawatching points between 1978 and 1988 (Innes 1994). Outside of these two locations, smaller numbers of birds are noted from coastal locations and small lochs close to the coast (Cotehill Loch, Corby Loch, Cults Reservoir and

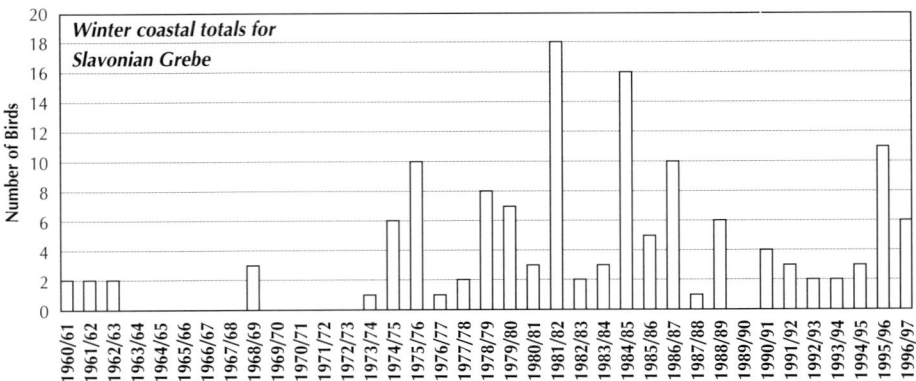

Winter coastal totals for Slavonian Grebe

Loirston Loch). The east coast accounts for the majority of records, with the area between Aberdeen and Collieston favoured. Fewer birds are seen on the north coast. Most records refer to single birds, although two birds have been present together at some times. The highest count was of five birds on the sea off Rattray Head on 25th October 1975 and four off St Cyrus on 25th October 1980. Birds occurring on the Loch of Strathbeg have been known to stay for up to two months. Away from the Loch of Strathbeg, the majority of records refer to birds staying for only one or two days.

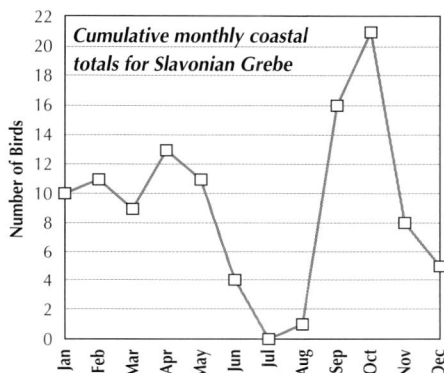

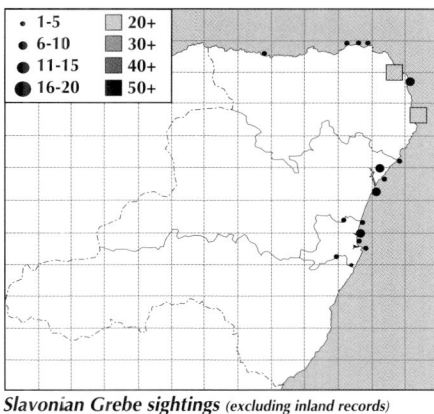

Cumulative monthly coastal totals for Slavonian Grebe

- 1-5
- 6-10
- 11-15
- 16-20
- 20+
- 30+
- 40+
- 50+

Slavonian Grebe sightings (excluding inland records)

Black-necked Grebe *Podiceps nigricollis*

Breeds locally through most of Europe and parts of southern Scandinavia. Also from southern Russia south to Afghanistan. The species is widespread in North America and there are isolated populations in south east China, southern Africa and South America (Harrison 1983).

The Black-necked Grebe is a scarce breeder in Britain, with the majority being in Scotland. The current breeding population fluctuates and is estimated to be between 15 and 40 pairs (Gibbons *et al.* 1993). There are no breeding records for the North East of Scotland. The wintering population is located primarily off southern England, with a few at favoured locations further north (Lack and Ferguson 1986).

The earliest record of this species for the region was one seen at Fyvie Loch in March 1893 (*Buchan Field Club*: 3) and Sim (1903) only records one shot on 2nd March 1898 at Strathbeg. There are no further records until the late 1950s when a single bird was seen on a small lochan on Forvie Moor on 16th April 1958 (*Scot. Birds* 1958). The next record was again from Forvie with a bird present between 10th and 14th May 1970 (*Scot. Birds* 1971). In the 21 years from 1974 to 1994, there were records of only 16

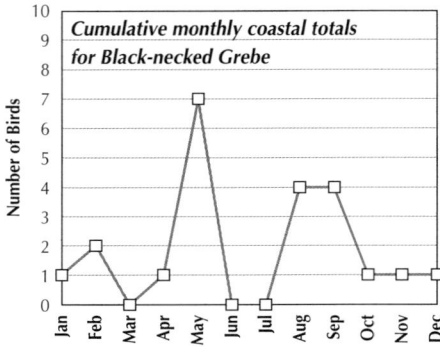

Cumulative monthly coastal totals for Black-necked Grebe

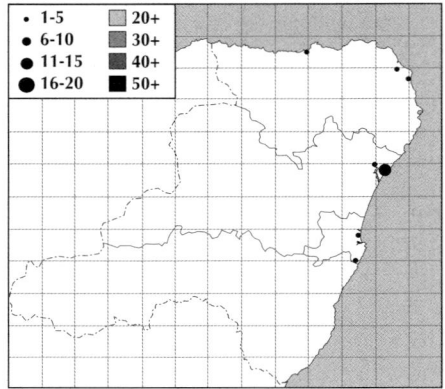

Black-necked Grebe sightings

birds, and there were no records in nine of these years. Single birds account for most of the records, with two birds seen in some years. The exceptions have been 1979, when three individuals were seen, and 1996 when two birds were recorded at two different sites at the same time. Records have come from all months except June and July. The majority of birds are seen in May or between August and September. Smaller numbers of birds are seen during the winter months. Freshwater bodies close to the coast account for most of the records with birds rarely seen on the sea. Meikle Loch is the most favoured site, accounting for nearly half of the records. The Loch of Strathbeg and the Ythan estuary are also favoured locations.

Black-necked Grebes
by M. Langman

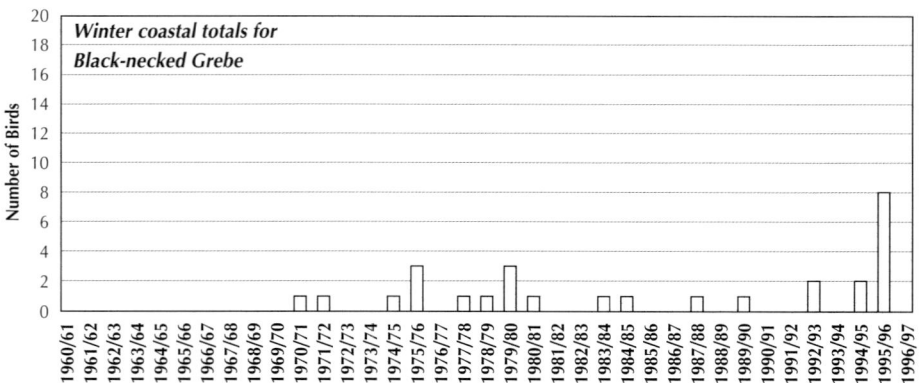

Winter coastal totals for Black-necked Grebe

    Rare and Scarce Birds in North East Scotland

Cory's Shearwater Calonectris diomedea

Breeds on the islands of the Mediterranean, Canaries, Salvage Islands, Madeira, Azores and Cape Verde Islands. After the breeding season birds disperse into the Atlantic, reaching the east coast of North America, southern and western coasts of Ireland, south west England and into the North Sea. Winters off South Africa.

Cory's Shearwaters are scarce in Scottish waters, with most autumn records from counties bordering the North Sea (Dymond *et al.* 1989).

The first record of this large shearwater for the region (and Scotland) was in 1947 when a single bird was seen at sea 1.5 miles north of Aberdeen (*Brit. Birds* Vol. 41). There have been a further 16 birds specifically identified as this species, of which 11 have occurred since 1989. This probably reflects the increased number of hours spent seawatching by a small number of observers rather than an increase in actual numbers of birds present in the northern North Sea. The seawatching point of Girdleness accounts for the majority of these records. Most records are of single birds, nearly all flying north off the east coast. There has been only one record from the north coast. Two birds were seen on seawatches on 2nd November 1970 and on 11th September 1989. In several years there have been more than one bird recorded, with three (or four) in 1970 and three in 1989. The best year on record for this species was 1995 when five birds were seen.

Of the 18 Cory's Shearwaters recorded, the majority occurred between early August and mid September. There are

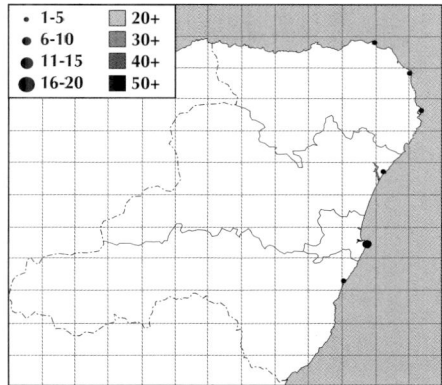

Cory's Shearwater sightings

Legend:
- 1-5
- 6-10
- 11-15
- 16-20
- 20+
- 30+
- 40+
- 50+

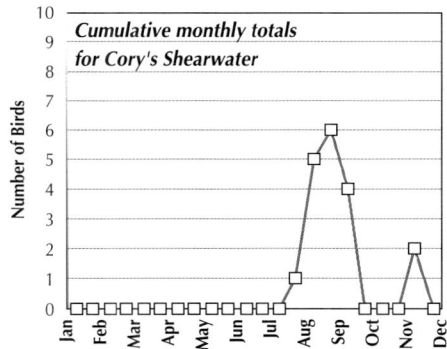

Cumulative monthly totals for Cory's Shearwater

two records for early November, both on the same day in 1970.

In recent years observers have become more aware of the identification features that allow separation of Cory's and Great Shearwaters.

ALL RECORDS

1947 10 Sept *at sea 1.5 miles north of Aberdeen* first Scottish record (BB: V41)

1970 21 Aug *Collieston* (Dr C.J.Feare *et al.*)

1970 21 Aug *Rattray* prob. same as above (M.R.Williams) (*BB* 64: RR)

1970 2 Nov *Rattray* (2) (M.R.Williams) (*BB* 65: RR)

1976 1 Sept *Kinnaird Head, Fraserburgh* (D.I.M.Wallace) (*BB* 70: RR)

1981 24 Aug *Peterhead* (M.Innes)

1989 10 Aug *Girdleness* (I.M.Phillips, S.A.Reeves)

1989 11 Sept *Newtonhill* (2) (K.D.Shaw, S.G.Addinall)

1990 24 July *Girdleness* (I.M.Phillips, S.A.Reeves)

1990 26 Aug *Newtonhill* (K.D.Shaw)

1991 26 Aug *Girdleness* (I.M.Phillips)

1995 8 Aug *Girdleness* (C.Cronin)

1995 9 Aug *Girdleness* (C.Cronin)

1995 11 Aug *Collieston* (T.W.Marshall)

1995 15 Aug *Girdleness* (I.M.Phillips)

1995 21 Aug *Girdleness* (I.M.Phillips)

1995 3 Sept *Girdleness* (I.M.Phillips)

1996 6 Sept *Girdleness* (I.M.Phillips)

Cory's Shearwaters
by M. Langman

Annual totals for Cory's Shearwater

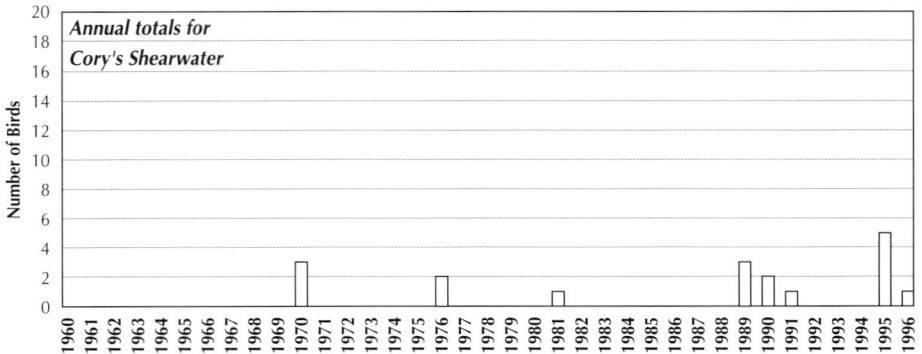

Great Shearwater *Puffinus gravis*

Breeds in the Tristan da Cunha Islands in the South Atlantic. Birds disperse northwards after the breeding season, along the east coast of North America and then across the Atlantic to the coasts of western Europe by autumn. The number present in British waters varies from year to year with most off the south west approaches. The number present in the North Sea is generally low and as such this species remains very scarce off the coasts of the region.

The first note of this species for the North East region was of at least six birds seen from the *F.R.S. Scotia* on 22nd September 1965. The vessel was between 8 and 11 miles south east of Girdleness at the time of the observations.

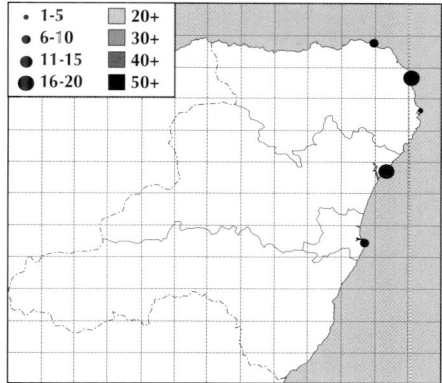

Great Shearwater sightings

Legend:
- 1-5
- 6-10
- 11-15
- 16-20
- 20+
- 30+
- 40+
- 50+

The first land based record for North East Scotland appears to have been four years later when, in 1969, eight passed Rattray Head on 3rd August. Two days later two more passed the same point.

There have been records for only a further 51 birds since 1970. Of these, 36 were recorded in the 1970s, with 11 in 1970 and 16 in 1976 (a period when there were large numbers seen nationally). There were only four birds seen in the 1980s and only three, to date, in the 1990s. This species remains very scarce in North East Scotland.

The majority of birds are seen between August and November, peaking in August and the first half of September. Outside of this period there has been a single record from June, another of a bird on the sea at Fraserburgh on 14th February 1981 with another here in February 1997. The east coast seawatching points of Rattray Head,

Collieston and Girdleness account for most of the records with only nine birds seen from Fraserburgh on the north coast.

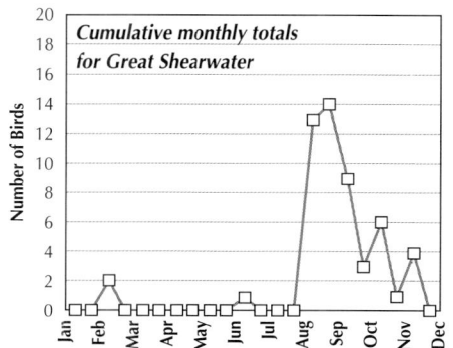

Cumulative monthly totals for Great Shearwater

ALL RECORDS

1969 3 Aug *Rattray* (8N)		

1969 3 Aug *Rattray* (8N)
1969 5 Aug *Rattray* (2)
1970 21 Aug *Collieston* (3N)
1970 21 Aug *Rattray* (3N)
1970 31 Oct *Rattray*
1970 2 Nov *Rattray* (4)
1971 16 Jun *Rattray*
1971 18 Sep *Collieston*
1973 5 Aug *Collieston*
1975 29 Sep *Girdleness*
1976 19 Aug *Collieston*
1976 28 Aug *Girdleness*
1976 29 Aug *Girdleness* (2N)
1976 29 Aug *Collieston*

1976 1 Sep *Fraserburgh*
1976 2 Sep *Fraserburgh*
1976 10 Sep *Fraserburgh* (3)
1976 1 Oct *Collieston* (6N)
1977 9 Aug *Collieston*
1977 7 Sep *Fraserburgh* (2)
1977 25 Sep *Collieston*
1979 30 Sep *Collieston*
1981 14 Feb *Fraserburgh* one on the sea
1981 21 Aug *Peterhead*
1981 10 Sep *Peterhead*
1989 2 Aug *Girdleness*
1995 27 Aug *Girdleness*
1995 29 Aug *Girdleness*
1997 2 Feb *Fraserburgh*

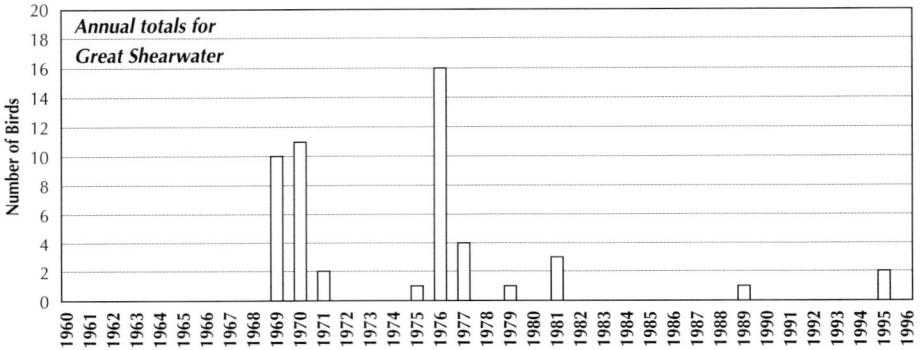

Annual totals for Great Shearwater (bar chart, Number of Birds vs years 1960–1996)

'Large Shearwater' sp.

There have been 22 records of unspecifically identified large shearwaters which were either Great Shearwater or Cory's Shearwater. Twenty of these records came in the late 1970s (with 11 in 1976 and 4 in 1977) and two in the early 1980s. These records are concentrated in the period late August to late October.

Mediterranean Shearwaters *by M. Langman*

Rare and Scarce Birds in North East Scotland

Mediterranean Shearwater *Puffinus yelkouan*

Breeds on the offshore islands of the eastern Mediterranean (nominate form* P. yelkouan*) and the Balearic Islands (subspecies* mauretanicus*). After the breeding season the* P. yelkouan *population disperses into the Black Sea, while the subspecies* P. y. mauretanicus *disperses into waters off north west Europe. Until recently both forms were considered to be con-specific with Manx Shearwater. The species was officially split from Manx Shearwater and added to the British List in 1991 (BOU 1991).

There have been only ten records of Mediterranean Shearwater (subspecies *P. y. mauretanicus*) mainly from the east coast (Peterhead 6 records, Girdleness 3 records) with a single record from the north coast (Fraserburgh). The majority of records come from the latter half of August and first half of September. Outside of this period there is only one record.

ALL RECORDS
1981 30 Aug ***Peterhead*** (M.Innes)
1982 20 Aug ***Peterhead*** (M.Innes)
1985 8 Sep ***Peterhead*** (M.Innes)
1987 28 Aug ***Peterhead*** (M.Innes)
1987 29 Aug ***Peterhead*** (2) (M.Innes)
1991 30 Aug ***Girdleness*** (A.G.Clarke, J.R.W.Gordon)
1992 10 Oct ***Fraserburgh*** (G.Buchanan, I.M.Phillips)
1994 12 Sep ***Girdleness*** (J.Oates, I.M.Phillips, M.S.Scott)
1996 7 Sep ***Girdleness*** (C.Cronin, I.M.Phillips)

Storm Petrel *Hydrobates pelagicus*

Breeds in the eastern North Atlantic and in the Mediterranean. Northern populations winter off Namibia and South Africa.

The numbers breeding in Britain and Ireland are estimated to be between 50,000 and 100,000 pairs, which represents between two-thirds to three-quarters of the world population (Gibbons *et al*. 1993). The nearest colonies to this region are in the Orkney and Shetland Islands.

Sim (1903) reported that 'This delicate little bird is frequently cast upon the coast of Dee, and during storms is conveyed far inland.' The status of this species continued as very rare throughout much of this century with few live records reported (except for fishermen who regularly saw these birds offshore).

The status changed considerably in the early 1980s, when tape-luring by ringers at sites along the east coast started. During the following years hundreds of birds were ringed during these sessions. The results of these sessions suggested that Storm Petrels are quite numerous close inshore during late summer (Buckland *et al*. 1990).

Seawatching records are generally very rare. Since 1975 one or two birds have been seen in most years from June through to late September. There have been several exceptional years when large numbers are reported over small periods of time. In 1987, 114 were seen from Peterhead in July and a further 47 in August. Smaller numbers were reported from other sites during this period. In 1988 a further 93 were seen off Peterhead. Both of these years were eclipsed in 1990 when 130 were seen off Fraserburgh on 18th August and then 131 were seen off Peterhead on 22nd September. The only other outstanding count was of 95 off Fraserburgh on 14th July 1993. It is unclear what particular conditions cause these large numbers to be seen inshore in daylight. It must be some peculiar combination of weather and hydrographics along with, possibly, food supply.

Storm Petrels by M. Langman

Leach's Petrel Oceanodroma leucorhoa

Breeds in the northern Pacific and Atlantic Oceans. In the Atlantic the main wintering areas are thought to be the Gulf of Guinea and off Brazil.

The main British breeding population is almost exclusively on the far north western islands, particularly the St Kilda group. In autumn the species is a regular passage bird along the west coast of Scotland particularly during westerly gales.

There are only three records of this species from the last century. Sim (1903) reports that a bird was found dead, inland at Milltimber in December 1876. In August 1884 a bird was caught alive (but later killed) in Aberdeen Harbour and another picked up dead at Rothie Norman.

In the early part of this century there are again only a few records. A bird was found dead on the beach at the Donmouth on 5th January 1908. In May 1909, a bird was found inland under the 'Mounth' near Durris.

There was a nationwide wreck of Leach's Petrels in the winter of 1952, but there were only three records from the North East region associated with it. A single bird was at Aberdeen, another was inland at Kemnay and yet another inland at Fasque, Fettercairn (*ASNH* 1953).

From 1976 there have been only 30 records of this species, the majority from tape-luring sessions (19) at Collieston and Girdleness. The best year for this species during these sessions was 1986, when 15 were seen or caught in nets at Girdleness and Collieston between 10th July and 10th August. Despite continued efforts at tape-luring petrels, no Leach's Petrels have been caught since 1989.

Seawatching records are much rarer and are less than annual. These generally refer to single birds in October and November, but two birds were seen at Fraserburgh in October, 1991. Peterhead, Girdleness and Fraserburgh account for the majority of birds seen on seawatches.

ALL RECENT RECORDS
1976 24 Oct *Forvie* dead
1978 5 Aug *Drums*
1985 31 Jul *Greg Ness* tape-lured
1985 5 Nov *Peterhead*
1985 7 Nov *Peterhead*
1986 10 Jul-10 Aug *Collieston and Girdleness* (15) seen or trapped
1987 27 Jul *Peterhead*
1987 3 Aug *Collieston* tape-lured
1987 9 Aug *Peterhead*
1988 19 Jul *Collieston* tape-lured
1988 9 Oct *Fraserburgh*
1988 9 Oct *Aberdeen*
1988 17 Oct *Aberdeen Harbour* picked up dead
1989 7 Aug *Collieston* tape-lured
1991 19 Oct *Fraserburgh* (2)

'Frigatebird' sp.

An unidentified frigatebird was seen off Forvie on 20th August 1960 (Mrs R.Maxwell, A.J.M.Smith) (*Brit. Birds* Vol. 55: RR).

Common Bittern *Botaurus stellaris*

Breeds from western Europe eastwards to the Sea of Japan. Partially migratory and dispersive outside the breeding season.

The current British population is estimated at only 16 pairs, largely confined to East Anglia with an isolated population in Lancashire (Gibbons *et al.* 1993). Continental birds arrive in Britain in winter, mainly December and January, with most arriving during periods of hard weather. It seems likely that the birds occurring in this region and other parts of Scotland are of continental origin.

The earliest record of Bittern is by Edward (*Naturalist* Vol. 4) who noted that it had occurred at the Loch of Strathbeg, with one having been shot in the autumn of 1824. There are sketchy references in the *New Statistical Account of Scotland* (1845) for the parishes of Banff (one shot in 1831), Banchory-Ternan (reported as *ardea stellaris*), Longside, Crimond (occasionally seen) and Peterhead. Sim (1903) thought, despite any real evidence, "...we are justified in saying that the Bittern is much less common throughout 'Dee' at the present time than it had been when there was double the amount of ground suitable to its wants than there is now; to which may be added the fact that to those of the last generation the name of the 'Mire Drum' was well known and perfectly understood." Following this Sim (1903) lists only nine records of birds between 1824 and 1899. These birds occurred at various sites from September to April.

In the early part of this century there are few records. One was killed and another seen near Aberdeen in January 1900 (*Brit. Birds* Vol. 1) and another was reported from St Combs in March 1937 (*Scot. Nat.* 1937-38).

Between 1970 and 1995 there were records of less than fourteen birds. The uncertainty is caused by the intermittent nature of sightings owing to the skulking nature of this species. For instance, in 1991, what was probably the same individual was seen at the Loch of Strathbeg on dates in January and February and what may have been the same bird on 18th to 23rd June.

Most records occur in the winter period between October and February, with January the peak month. There are records for May and June. The Loch of Strathbeg is currently the most favoured site, having held birds in five of the last seven years. Five records from the region refer to birds picked up as corpses.

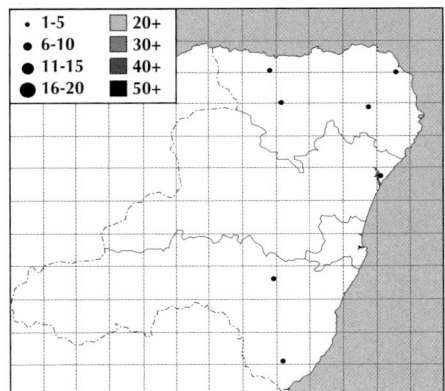

Bittern sightings

ALL RECENT RECORDS

1970 7 May *Laurencekirk* female killed by a car

1973 1 Jan-3 Feb *Loch of Pitfour*

1977 23 Jan *R. Deveron, Alvah* dead (*per.* W.Murray)

1980 25 Jan *Newburgh* hit wires, later released. (C.G.Hancock *et al.*)

1982 Jan *Drumlithie, nr Laurencekirk* dead

1987 29 Jan *Ythan* dead (R.Duncan)

1988 4 Oct *Strathbeg* (G.Evans)

1988 Dec *Kimmeskie, Banchory* dead (C.Simpson)

1989 Feb *Strathbeg* probably over-wintering bird from 1988 (J.Dunbar)

1989 May-Jun *R. Deveron,Turriff* (H.Gray)

1991 30 Jan *Strathbeg* (A.J.Leitch) also on 10th Feb (G.Christer, J.Dunbar)

1991 18-23 Jun *Strathbeg* (G.Christer *et al.*)

1992 5 Jan *Strathbeg* (J.D.Poyner)

1994 19 Nov *Strathbeg* seen intermittently until 27th (A.Sinclair, T.W.Marshall *et al.*)

1996 3 Jan-25 Feb *Strathbeg* (A.S.Leitch *et al.*)

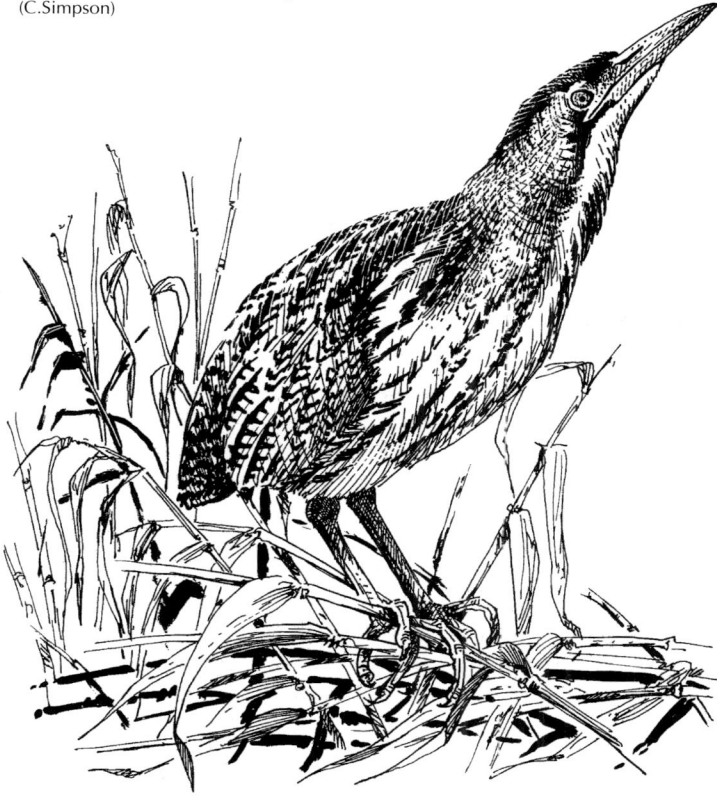

Common Bittern
by M. Langman

American Bittern *Botaurus lentiginosus*

Breeds in North America and winters in the southern United States and Central America.

There has been only one record for the North East, which was the third for Scotland. The date, November, is typical of British records of this species (Dymond *et al.* 1989)

ALL RECORDS

1854 Nov *Balgownie Links, Toll-Bar, Bridge of Don*

Little Bittern *Ixobrychus minutus*

Breeds across most of western and eastern Europe (except Scandinavia, Britain and Ireland). Extends east to Sinkiang. Also occurs in central and southern Africa and Australia. The European population winters in tropical Africa.

There are three old records mentioned in *The Vertebrate Fauna of Dee* (Sim 1903). The first flew on board a vessel entering Aberdeen Harbour on 21st October 1866 (in the company of a Water Rail). The remaining records are references to notes in *Birds of the West of Scotland* (Gray 1871), where one is reported to have been shot '...at the junction of the Don and the Ury below Keith Hall' on 28th May 1868 and an immature male shot on a marsh near Fintray House on 23rd September 1868.

There have been no records of this species this century.

Night Heron *Nycticorax nycticorax*

Breeds in the Netherlands, France, the Iberian Peninsula and north west Africa. The range extends eastwards to Japan. Also occurs in southern Africa and the Americas. The European population winters in Africa south of the Sahara to Cape Province.

There have been only two records of this small heron in North East Scotland. The most recent record in 1975, in early May, is typical of an overshooting continental migrant.

ALL RECORDS
1865 9 Jan *Mennie, Aberdeen* shot
1975 3-8 May *Newburgh* (M.A.Macdonald)
  (*BB* 69: RR)

Night Heron
by M. Langman

Plate 1. **Leach's** *Oceanodroma leucorhoa* and **Storm Petrel** *Hydrobates pelagicus*, Girdleness, July 1986 (*R.Duncan*)

Plate 2. **Glossy Ibis** *Plegadis falcinellus*, Strathbeg, November 1986 (*S.M.D.Alexander*)

Plate 3. Spoonbill *Platalea leucorodia*, Strathbeg, August 1996 (*I.M.C.Hastie*)

Plate 4. Small race Canada Geese *Branta canadensis*, Loch Skene area, December 1992 (*S.A.Reeves*)

Plate 5. **King Eider** *Somateria spectabilis*, Ythan, June 1987 (*S Young*)

Plate 6. **Common Crane** *Grus grus*, Rosehearty, Fraserburgh, June 1994 (*S.M.D.Alexander*)

Plate 7. Black-winged Stilt *Himantopus himantopus*, Meikle Loch, October 1984 (*M.Tasker*)

Plate 8. Greater Sand Plover *Charadrius leschenaultii*, Donmouth, August 1991 (*S.M.D.Alexander*)

Plate 9. **Least Sandpiper** *Calidris minutilla*, Rigifa Farm, August 1988 (*A.Webb*)

Plate 10. **White-rumped Sandpiper** *Calidris fuscicollis*, Annachie Lagoon, October 1995 (*S.A.Reeves*)

Plate 11. **Baird's Sandpiper** *Calidris bairdii*, Annachie Lagoon, September 1990 (*S.A.Reeves*)

Plate 12. **Lesser Yellowlegs** *Tringa flavipes*, Cults Pool, May 1992 (*S.A.Reeves*)

Plate 13. **Mediterranean Gull** *Larus melanocephalus*, Dyce, January 1994 (*S.M.D.Alexander*)

Plate 14. **Sabine's Gull** *Larus sabini*, Kinnaird Head, Fraserburgh, October 1996 (*S.A.Reeves*)

Plate 15. **Kumlien's Gull** *Larus glaucoides kumlieni*, Banff Harbour, February 1989 (*S. Young*)

Plate 16. **Ross's Gull** *Rhodostethia rosea*, Fraserburgh, January 1997 (*S. Young*)

Plate 17. Ivory Gull *Pagophila eburnea*, Cairnbulg - in care, January 1992 (*S.A.Reeves*)

Plate 18. Forster's Tern *Sterna forsteri*, Ythan, May 1995 (*M.A.Sullivan*)

Plate 19. **White-winged Black Tern** *Chlidonias leucopterus*, Meikle Loch, August 1987 (*A.Webb*)

Plate 20. **Snowy Owl** *Nyctea scandiaca*, St. Fergus, May 1991 (*A.Webb*)

Plate 21. **Bee-eater** *Merops apiaster*, Belhelvie, October 1995 (*I.M.Phillips*)

Plate 22. **Wryneck** *Jynx torquilla*, October 1987 (*R.Duncan*)

Plate 23. **Bluethroat** *Luscinia svecica*, Girdleness, May 1981 (*S.M.D.Alexander*)

Plate 24. **Isabelline Wheatear** *Oenanthe isabellina*, Girdleness, October 1979 (*S.M.D.Alexander*)

Plate 25. **American Robin** *Turdus migratorius*, Inverbervie, December 1988 (*S.M.D.Alexander*)

Plate 26. **Booted Warbler** *Hippolais caligata*, Newtonhill, October 1993 (*S.M.D.Alexander*)

Plate 27. **Barred Warbler** *Sylvia nisoria*, Balmedie, September 1995 (*R.Duncan*)

Plate 28. **Pallas's Warbler** *Phylloscopus proregulus*, Balmedie, November 1994 (*R.Duncan*)

Plate 29. **Red-breasted Flycatcher** *Ficedula parva*, November 1987 (*R.Duncan*)

Plate 30. **Red-backed Shrike** *Lanius collurio*, Donmouth, May 1997 (*I.M.C.Hastie*)

Plate 31. **Common Rosefinch** *Carpodacus erythrinus*, Balmedie, September 1993 (*R.Duncan*)

Plate 32. **Little Bunting** *Emberiza pusilla*, Rattray, May 1988 (*A.Webb*)

Little Egret *Egretta garzetta*

Breeds in north west Africa, the Iberian Peninsula, through the Mediterranean eastwards to southern Asia and Australia. Also occurs in southern Africa. Recent northward expansion has seen birds breeding in south west Britain, France and the Netherlands. The bulk of the European population winters in Africa, between the Sahara and Equatorial Africa. Between 50 and 75 birds now appear regularly to winter in southern England.

There have been eight records of this species for the North East region since the first in the early seventies. The six records in recent years are in line with the increased occurrence of this species in Britain. The records from 1993 and 1996 probably relate to single birds wandering around the region. Most records are from spring and early summer, which are typical of migrants overshooting from the near continent.

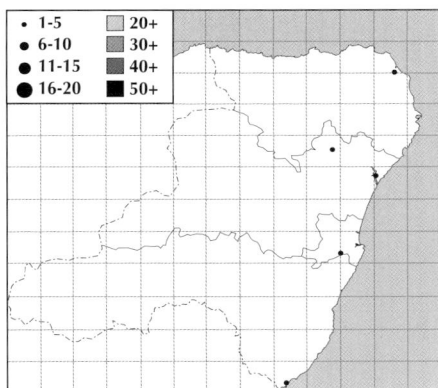

• 1-5	☐ 20+
• 6-10	☐ 30+
● 11-15	■ 40+
● 16-20	■ 50+

Little Egret sightings

ALL RECORDS

1974 22-29 May ***Strathbeg*** (J.Dunbar) (*BB* 68: RR)

1983 14 Jun ***Haddo House Lake*** (J.Malster)

1993 6 May ***Cults Pool*** adult breeding plumage (D.J.Bain)

1993 1-7 Jun ***Strathbeg*** adult breeding plumage (J.Dunbar, T.W.Marshall)

1995 6 May ***North Esk, Kinnaber*** (G.M.Addison *et al.*)

1996 15 May-3 Jun ***Ythan*** (S.Agnew)

1996 6-8 Jun ***Strathbeg*** (I.M.Phillips, K.D.Shaw)

1996 9 Jun-26 Aug ***Ythan*** (R.McGregor)

Little Egret
by M. Langman

Great White Egret *Egretta alba*

Breeds from Hungary eastwards to Japan and south to Australia. Also occurs in Africa south of the Sahara. Also present in North, Central and South America. A small but increasing population breeds in the Netherlands. The European population winters around the northern Mediterranean region.

Evans (1994) gave only 40 records of this species in Scotland up to the end of 1990.

There are no positive records of this species prior to the first accepted record in 1978. There is, however, a note in *The Vertebrate Fauna of Dee* (Sim, 1903) of 'A White Heron, supposed to be an Egret, was observed on the west side of the Loch of Strathbeg in the spring of 1816. It was seen for several days to frequent the same spot, but on being fired at once or twice it left and did not return.' There is also mention of a Great White Heron, again from the Loch of Strathbeg, in 1854 (*ASNH* Vol. 8: 369). The note originated in the *Proceedings of the Glasgow Natural History Society*, but neither Gray (1871) nor Sim (1903) mention this record.

There are three recent records, all in spring or early summer and probably relate to birds overshooting the small, but increasing, near continental breeding areas.

ALL RECORDS
1978 23-28 Jun **Strathbeg** (C.G.Hancock, A.R.Kitson, B.J.Stewart *et al.*) (*BB* 71: RR)
1989 21-22 Apr **Loirston Loch** (M.A.Sullivan *et al.*) (*BB* 83: RR)
1992 10-15 Jun **Ythan** (S.M. & W.G.Johnston *et al.*) (*BB* 86: RR)

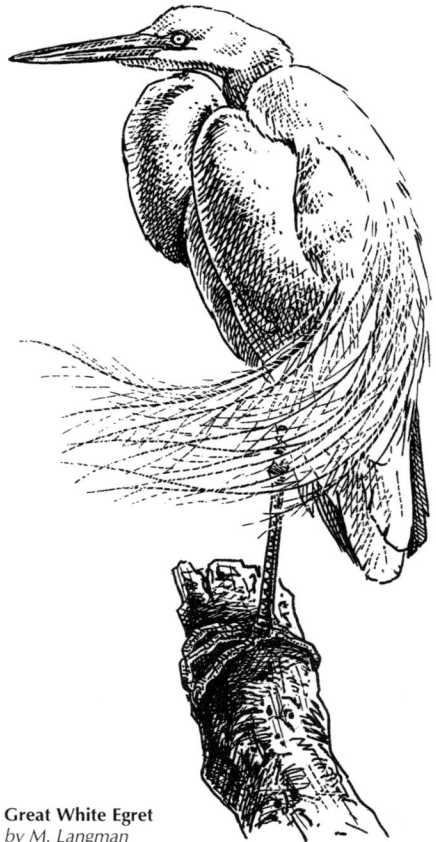

Great White Egret
by M. Langman

Purple Heron *Ardea purpurea*

Breeds from the Netherlands, France, the Iberian Peninsula and north west Africa eastwards to China and Indonesia. Also occur in southern Africa. The European population winters south of the Sahara in Africa.

The Purple Heron is only an irregular vagrant to Scotland, having been recorded in eight years between 1950 and 1983 (Thom 1986).

The first record of this species was reported in the *Zoologist* (1849) when a single bird was shot near Turriff (Parish of Monquhitter) in March 1847. Sim (1903) also makes note of this bird but thought the record was from the autumn. A second bird was shot near the Donmouth on 28th September 1872 (Sim 1903).

There have been two recent records (1992 and 1996), both in late spring which is typical of British records (Dymond *et al.* 1989). The 1996 bird at the Loch of Strathbeg was enjoyed by many local birders during its stay. These records are the farthest north this species has been recorded in mainland Scotland (Dymond *et al.* 1989, Evans 1991, 1992, 1993).

ALL RECENT RECORDS
1992 10 May **Corby Loch** immature (W.R.P.Bourne)
1996 10-13 Jun **Loch of Strathbeg** (C.Hamper, M.B.Cowie), (subject to acceptance by SBRC)

White Stork *Ciconia ciconia*

Breeds from the Iberian Penninsula across to the Middle East. The entire population winters in Africa, south of the Sahara.

This species has been annual in very small numbers in Scotland since 1975 (Thom 1986).

In the North East region there is only a single record from the 1800s, when a bird was shot on a moss in the parish of Lonmay during the severe winter of 1837-38. There are no further records until a bird was shot at Mintlaw on 2nd June 1924 (*Scot. Nat.* 1931-32).

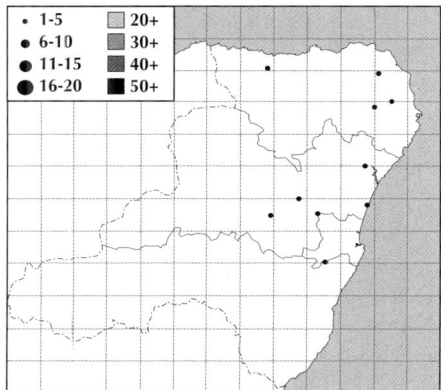

White Stork sightings

There have been only ten further records, probably of only seven individuals. All but one of these occurred in the late 1960s and 1970s. These records were typically between April and June and are consistent with the majority of British records (Dymond *et al.* 1989). There have been no records since 1982.

ALL RECORDS
1837-1838 Winter *Lonmay, nr Strathbeg* shot on a moss
1924 2 Jun *Mintlaw* shot (BB: V25, *Scot. Nat.* 1931)
1967 2 Jun *Inverurie* (A.J.M.Smith) (BB 61: RR)
1967 7-9 Jun *Ellon* (Dr G.M.Dunnet, R.Fordham, W.Murray) (BB 61: RR)
1969 15-20 Apr *Milltimber and Balmedie* poss. same bird at Potterton 17 Apr (*BB* 63: RR)
1971 11 May *Bridge of Alvah* (Mrs A.F.W.Sharp *et al.*) (*BB* 65: RR)
1975 11 May-20 Jun *Fintray* (*per* A.G.Knox) (*BB* 68: RR)
1977 27 Feb *Monymusk* (Mrs H.Duncan *per* A.G.Knox) (*BB* 70: RR)
1979 25 Apr/18 May *Banchory and Maryculter* (Miss M.Stevenson *per.* A.G.Knox) (*BB* 72: RR)
1982 16 Apr *Rora* (Mrs J.D.Breward) (*NESBR* 1982)

White Stork
by M. Langman

Glossy Ibis *Plegadis falcinellus*

The Glossy Ibis is a very discontinuous breeding species from the Balkans to southern Asia, Indonesia and Australia. Also occurs in southern Africa and the Caribbean. The majority of the European population winters south of the Sahara in Africa.

The earliest record for the region that can be attributed to this species occurs in the *New Statistical Account of Scotland* (1845) where '*ibis falcinellus*' is noted from Banchory-Ternan. The bird was also referred to as a Brazilian Curlew, the specimen having been shot on the Loch of Leys in September 1842.

Edward (1854) noted that it had occurred once on the Loch of Strathbeg but gave no details and Sim (1903) does not mention any from this site until 1902. Sim (1903) does record individuals shot on the moors of Crathes in 1844 (also noted by Baxter and Rintoul 1953), a male shot at the mouth of the Ythan on

4th October 1880 and another shot at the Loch of Strathbeg on 22nd October 1902. In 1907, an immature bird appeared at Watermill, Fraserburgh, around 'harvest time' (*Brit. Birds* Vol. 1) and in mid October 1920 two were seen near Kintore (*ASNH* 1921-22). Another was shot on 3rd May 1938 near Warthill (*ASNH* 1937-38).

There has been only one recent record, that of a long staying bird at the Loch of Strathbeg from September to November 1986. The remains of this bird were found in January 1987.

The records suggest that this species was a far more regular visitor to the region than is currently the situation. The paucity of recent records is in line with the Europe-wide decline of this species (Tucker and Heath 1994)

ALL RECORDS
1844 *Moors of Crathes, Banchory*
1880 4 Oct *Ythan-mouth* male shot on the mudflats
1902 22 Oct *Strathbeg*
1907 Autumn *Watermill, Fraserburgh* immature
1920 mid Oct *Kintore* (2)
1938 3 May *Warthill*
1986 27Sep - 23 Nov *Strathbeg* remains found Jan 1987 (R.J.Jones, S.Welch *et al.*) (*BB* 80: RR)

Spoonbill *Platalea leucorodia*

Breeds mainly in scattered sites in the Netherlands, France and Iberia eastwards to eastern Siberia. Also occurs in the Indian subcontinent. The European populations winter mainly in the Mediterranean, although some birds may winter farther north in mild winters.

Many colonies in eastern Europe are declining, but the more western colonies (Netherlands and Spain) have recently been expanding (Tucker and Heath 1994).

The first reference in the North East region for this species is by Thomas Edward (*Naturalist* Vol. 4, 1854) where he noted that it had occurred on two or three occasions at the Loch of Strathbeg. He gave no dates or supporting evidence for this statement. Sim (1903) only notes one further record, that of a bird shot on Aberdeen Links, but again no details or date were given.

Since 1970 there have been regular records of Spoonbills, with the Loch of

Strathbeg the most favoured location. The remaining records all come from the Ythan. Although not annual, there have been birds seen in the region in more years than not since 1970. Single birds are most regular but in 1972 two birds spent a week on the Ythan; in 1975 an adult and an immature were at Strathbeg and in 1996 three birds spent much of the summer at Strathbeg. The several colour-ringed birds reported from the region have all been from colonies in the Netherlands.

All records have occurred between 7th May and 31st August, with most in May and June. Several birds have stayed throughout the summer.

ALL RECENT RECORDS

1970 9-13 Jun *Strathbeg*
1970 24 Jun-24 Aug *Ythan*
1971 8 Jul *Ythan*
1972 7-15 Jun *Ythan* (2) 1 remained until 7 Aug
1974 15-20 May *Strathbeg*
1975 17-19, 31 May *Strathbeg* immature
1975 15 May-14 Jun *Strathbeg* adult, colour ringed *(a)* - South Flevoland, 1974.
1976 Autumn *Ythan* (2) (noted in *Scot. Birds*)
1977 2-4 Jul *Strathbeg* adult, colour ringed *(b)* as pullus in 1974 at Zwanenwater Callantsoog, the Netherlands
1977 9 Jul *Ythan* adult, colour ringed *(b)*
1978 23 Apr-25 Jun *Strathbeg* adult, colour ringed *(c)*

1978 1-2 Jul *Ythan* adult, colour ringed *(c)*
1981 10 Jun *Strathbeg*
1984 22-25 Jul *Strathbeg*
1986 6 Jul *Ythan*
1988 7-22 May *Strathbeg*
1991 27 Jun-27 Aug *Strathbeg*
1992 26May-31Aug *Strathbeg*
1992 29 May *Ythan*
1993 18-28 Jul *Strathbeg*
1996 3 Jun-3 Sep *Strathbeg* (3) one colour ringed *(d)*, two stayed until 14 August

(a-d denote individual colour-ringed birds)

Bewick's Swan *Cygnus columbianus bewickii*

Breeds across almost the full breadth of high-Arctic Siberia. The population east of the Taimyr Peninsula migrates south west through the White Sea and Baltic, wintering chiefly in Denmark, the Netherlands and southern Britain.

The earliest note of this species is by Edward (1854) who noted that the species was of rare occurrence at the Loch of Strathbeg, with specimens obtained in 1814 and 1826. Subsequently they were noted as 'occasional or periodical, but rare' for Aberdeenshire (*Scot. Nat.* 1885–86). Despite these statements Sim (1903) wrote 'There is no record, so far as I know, of this species having been identified as a visitor to Dee, except for the somewhat misty statement of Edward.' Similarly Baxter and Rintoul (1953) gave no records for 'Dee'.

The record of six birds at Rattray Head in February 1955 is probably the first acceptable record for the region (*Scot. Nat.* 1954–55). Picozzi (in Buckland *et al.* 1990) noted that in the 1950s, small numbers of Bewick's Swans were recorded on the dune slacks south of

Rattray and at Pittenheath. This was the last place in Scotland regularly to hold birds at that time.

Despite the increase in observer awareness and an increase in the number of birds wintering in Scotland (average of 91 in Scotland between 1980 and 1984, particularly Caerlaverock, with up to 70 birds (Thom 1986)) Bewick's Swans remain very scarce in this region.

Since the winter of 1969/70 there have been records in most winters of between 1 and 10 birds. In the winters of 1986/87 there were probably fifteen birds and in 1990/91 there were up to nineteen birds reported. There may be some overlap of records with birds feeding in one area and roosting in another. Many of the records are of small groups of birds closely associating with flocks of

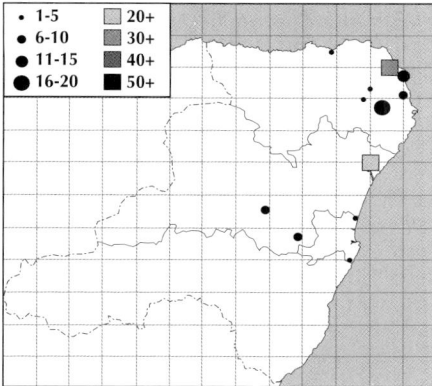

Symbol	Range	Symbol	Range
•	1-5	▢	20+
●	6-10	▨	30+
●	11-15	▩	40+
⬤	16-20	■	50+

Bewick's Swan sightings

ALL RECORDS

1955 6 Feb **Rattray** (6) first record
(*Scot. Nat.* 1954-55)

1955 28 Dec **Rattray** (5) also 1st Mar 1956
(BB: V52 1959)

1964 19 Feb **Strathbeg** (4)

1964 12 Oct **Pitfour**

1965 Jan **Pitfour**

1965 7 Feb **Pittenheath**

1969 25 Sep **Strathbeg** (3)

1969 10 Dec **Strathbeg** (3)

1971 17 Jan **Strathbeg** (6)

1972 5 Mar **Strathbeg** (3)

1974 21 Feb **Birsemore**

1975 12 Jan **Skene** (5)

1975 14 Sep **Pitfour**

1975 8 Dec **Strathbeg**

1976 13 Feb **New Aberdour** (3)

1976 15 Feb **Skene** (3)

1976 6 May **Strathbeg**

1977 9 Jan **Strathbeg**

1979 17-20 Mar **Monymusk**

1979 1 Nov **Longside**

1979 7 Dec **Monymusk** (8)

1980 9 Nov **Strathbeg** (6)

1980 22 Nov **Strathbeg** (1)

1980 25-26 Nov **Strathbeg** (2)

1981 26 Nov **Strathbeg** (2)

1981 2 Dec **Ythan** (1)

1983 30 Nov **Strathbeg** (1)

1984 17 Nov **Middlemuir nr Newburgh** (4)

1986 14 Dec **Blackhill** (6)

1987 3 Jan **Ythan** (9)

1989 27 Mar **Logie Buchan** (2)

1990 24-29 Oct **Loirston** (4)

1990 5 Nov **Murcar** (5N) poss same at
Inverquhomery 14-21 Nov

1990 17-26 Nov **Longside** (6)

1990 6-13 Dec **Strathbeg** (8 max)

1991 6 Jan **Loirston Loch** (4)

1992 8 Jan **Longside** (3)

1992 29 Jan **St Fergus** (6)

1992 1-2 Mar **St Fergus** (6) probably same
as above

1993 9-19 Dec **Longside** (3) with 7 on 10th,
8 on 12th, also seen at Rora Moss from 16-19 Dec

1994 11 Dec **Longside - Inverquhomery**
12 - 19th, 24-31st

1996 13 Jan-17 Feb **Pitscow Sand Pit, Mintlaw**

1996 23-28 Feb **Strathbeg**

1996 12-13 Oct **Strathbeg**

Whooper Swans. These groups are generally only of between one and five birds, but a party of nine were seen in the Ythan area in 1987. Most birds are seen in the north east corner of the region around the Loch of Strathbeg-Rattray-St Fergus district and the Ythan area. Smaller numbers of birds are seen in the middle reaches of the region, around Monymusk and the Loch of Skene.

Thom (1986) noted that there were no records for Kincardine and this is still the case.

The majority of birds arrive in November or December, but in some years birds arrive later in January and February.

A Darvic-ringed bird present at Longside, near Peterhead, in December 1993, had been ringed at Martin Mere in Lancashire in January 1991 and had been seen on the Dutch Polders in March 1993.

Bean Goose *Anser fabalis*

Breeds in scattered pockets from Scandinavia east to the Bering Sea in eastern Asia. The western races winter in the lowlands of Europe.

Bean Geese were at one time the most abundant of the grey geese in Scotland, but around the turn of the century their numbers declined greatly (Thom 1986). The earliest reference to this species for North East Scotland was by Edward (1854) who noted that the species 'is yearly met with and at times very plentiful.' Sim (1903) noted that the species was 'a regular visitor to the Loch of Strathbeg and other sheets of water within Dee, but owing to their extreme watchfulness, very few are obtained.' He further noted that during the months of September and October flocks were to be seen or heard passing south over Aberdeen, and again, less frequently, in the spring.

During the 1880s the situation appears to have been changing somewhat and Bean Geese were reported from Aberdeenshire only as 'a rare winter visitor', although Drummond Hay believed they had been confused with Pink-footed Geese (*Scot. Nat.* 1885-86).

Berry (1939) described the status of the Bean Goose in the North East as only an uncommon passage migrant, with small flocks wintering in a few locations. There are few further significant reports until January 1963, when a single bird was shot from a group of 28 similar birds at Cruden Bay. Thom (1986) noted an unusually large influx around the Slains Lochs in October/December 1968 with a peak of 107 on 23 November.

Numbers have never again reached these levels.

The majority of records occur between October and March, but birds have been seen as early as September (1994, although this bird might have been of feral origin) and as late as May (1976). Since the winter of 1969/70, there have been records in all but eight of the winter periods with between one and five birds regularly. Up to nine birds were seen in the winters of 1970/71, 1972/73 and 1974/75. The winters between 1975/76 and 1977/78 had between 17 and 24 birds present.

The areas around Strathbeg-Rattray and the Slains Lochs-Ythan area are currently the most favoured. Few records occur away from these areas. Ogilvie (1978) mentions Deeside as a regular haunt but the only recent record from that area appears to be two shot near Aboyne on 13th January 1979.

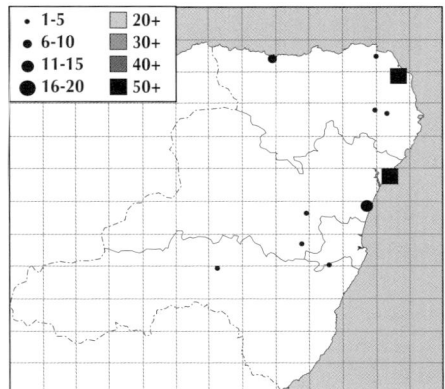

Bean Goose sightings

Bean Geese are easily overlooked amongst the large flocks of Pink-footed Geese now wintering in the region. This is further hampered by agricultural changes which have pushed many flocks away from previously favoured areas which were easily viewed from roads without disturbance (Buckland *et al.* 1990).

The majority of records refer to the nominate race *Anser fabalis fabalis*, but three records (of four birds) were of the small tundra race *A. f. rossicus*.

ALL RECORDS OF *A. f. rossicus*
1972 13 Jan ***Aboyne*** (2) shot (R.E.F.Hislop)
1993 13 Mar ***Loch of Strathbeg*** (J.D.Poyner, P.Bloor, C.Jones)
1996 7-12 Feb ***Milltimber*** (A.W.Thorpe *et al.*)

Snow Goose *Anser caerulescens*

Breeds in Arctic North America. Birds of the race A. c. atlanticus (Greater Snow Goose) winter along the Atlantic coast of North America between Maryland and North Carolina.

In Britain the status of this species is confused by escapes or feral birds. The Snow Goose is one of the most widely kept species in wildfowl collections, with at least 169 free-flying individuals noted in 1993 and an additional 41 birds on the islands of Mull, Coll and Tiree (Evans 1995). Almost all of the feral birds are Lesser Snow Geese, except for about six birds in Orkney (Scott 1992). Despite this, many of the records of this species in the region have occurred with wintering flocks of Pink-footed Geese and White-fronted Geese, and may be genuine vagrants.

The first record of this species for the North East region came in 1958, when a party of three were at the Loch of Strathbeg on 22nd October. There were few further records until the mid 1970s when published records became more regular. The exact number of birds present in any one winter period is often difficult to assess; individuals can wander widely among the large numbers of wintering grey geese. In most years between one and three birds are seen, but in both 1986/87 and 1988/89 there may have been eight individuals present. Since the winter of 1975/76, there have been records of birds in every winter period except the most recent ones, 1993/94, 1994/95 and 1995/96.

The majority of records from the region refer to white-phase birds (34 since 1975), probably Greater Snow Geese, but there are several records of intermediate (8 since 1975) and blue-phase birds (13 since 1975). In May 1989, there were six Blue Snow Geese together at the Loch of Strathbeg, but this was exceptional and most reports are of single birds or two birds together.

Canada Goose *Branta canadensis*

Breeds across the whole of northern North America from the Aleutian Islands and Alaska east to the Atlantic coast. These birds winter across the whole of southern North America, north on the Pacific coast to British Columbia and south to Mexico (Madge and Burn 1988). There are feral populations in Britain, Sweden and the Netherlands, primarily of the larger races.

The earliest record comes from Edward (1854) who noted 'A bird thought to be of this species, was obtained on that part of the Loch (of Strathbeg) which lies nearest to Rattray, during the winter of 1819'. Sim (1903) was very sceptical of this record, but noted that two were shot from a flock of seven near Strathbeg on 24th August 1883. Possibly on the strength of this, they were noted as 'occasional or periodical' for Aberdeenshire (*Scot. Nat.* 1885-86). There are few other early records of this species and Baxter and Rintoul (1953) make no reference for this region.

The feral British population numbered 20,000 birds by 1976 (Buckland *et al.* 1990) few of which breed in Scotland. During the 1960s birds from the Yorkshire area started to migrate north to moult in the Beauly Firth near Inverness. Birds from the English Midlands also appear to have joined this trend and over 800 birds now moult there. As this trend developed the number of records for the North East of Scotland increased. Most records are of birds flying north in May or June, often inland between Aboyne and Ballater, but also along the coast. Fewer birds are seen in August or September when they return from the Beauly Firth (Buckland *et al.* 1990).

Some small flocks summer and one or two birds have been seen in winter. Unfortunately there have been birds released onto several fishing ponds in the region over recent years and these birds are breeding. As these are full-winged birds, some may inevitably wander around the region.

There have been two winter records of small dark race Canada Geese typical of the northern migratory races, and these may have been genuine vagrants.

1979 13 April **Ythan** (M.V.Bell)
1983 18 Dec **Fetterangus** (M.V.Bell)

The most stunning record of this species came in 1992, when two small race birds appeared at the Dinnet Lochs on 17th November (J.Parkin). One of these birds was neck-collared and had been ringed in Maryland, USA, on 10th February 1992 as a second year male. The birds regularly roosted on the Dinnet Lochs until mid-December. Away from this area the birds were regularly seen during late 1992 around the Muir of Fowlis (M.Watson *et al.*) and the Loch of Skene area until 24th January (G.Allen, J.Oates *et al.*). These birds were unfortunately shot by a local shooter. The collared bird represented the first proven occurrence of a wild North American Canada Goose in Britain.

Mandarin Duck *Aix galericulata*

The breeding range is fragmented between eastern Siberia and Japan. Habitat loss has caused much depletion of the native population. Birds winter in the lowlands of eastern China and Japan.

A feral population has been established primarily in southern England. There have however, been Mandarins on the River Tay in Perth since the early 1960s, with numbers fluctuating between 22 and 65 (Thom 1986).

The first record occurred in the region in 1976 when a male was seen on the River Don. Since this time there have been sporadic records of between one and three birds. The majority of records come from the River Deveron (Bridge of Alvah and Banff), the River Dee (from Banchory-Devenick to the Bridge of Dee) and from the River Don (Kintore and the Donmouth). Only four records have occurred away from these areas. Surprisingly one has been seen well inland on Loch Davan.

ALL RECORDS

1976 26 Apr **Don** male (P.R.Gordon)
1981 30 Nov-6 Dec **Banchory-Devenick** (B.J.Stewart)
1984 1 Apr **Kintore** a pair on the Don (T.D.H.Merrie, B.J.Stewart)
1988 21 Jun **Loch Davan** eclipse male (M.Marquiss)
1989 3-13 Apr **Bridge of Dee** male (B.J.Stewart, W.Marshall *et al.*)
1989 16 Sep **Bridge of Dee** male (A.Duncan)
1989 17 Sep **Loch of Skene** (P.Doyle, A.Duncan)
1990 31 Mar-30 Apr **Bridge of Alvah** (3) males with 2 poss. of this group seen on the Deveron on 12 May (R.Leverton)
1990 23 Dec **Old Deer** male (M.Innes)
1991 May-Jun **Haddo House** (J.Malster)
1991 21 Apr-31 May **Donmouth** male and female (S.M.D.Alexander, N.Picozzi, P.D.Bloor *et al.*)
1993 2 Apr **Banff** (J.D.Poyner, J.Dunbar)
1994 9 Jul **Bridge of Alvah** (2) (T.Bowditch)
1996 7-18 May **Mill Lade, Stoneywood Mill** female
1996 29 Sep-20 Oct **Kinloch** (W.Dunlop)
1996 19 Oct **Banchory-Devenick** (D.Bain)

American Wigeon *Anas americana*

Breeds in North America with small numbers breeding in Iceland. Winters in the southern United States and south to northern Columbia.

There had been only 52 birds reported from Scotland, until the end of 1990, with the majority from Shetland and Highland region (Evans 1994).

There is an old record from the Burn of Boyndie when a male was shot in January 1841. Baxter and Rintoul (1953) make no reference to this bird.

In the North East region there have been only 11 records, of 12 birds, all but one relating to drakes. The majority of these records are of single birds with the exception of a drake and sub–adult drake on the Loch of Skene in November 1992.

The Loch of Skene and the Loch of Strathbeg are currently the most favoured locations for this species, as both hold high numbers of wintering Wigeon and are used as staging posts by migrating wildfowl. The Loch of Skene tends to hold wintering birds, whereas the Loch of Strathbeg gets birds on passage in spring and early summer.

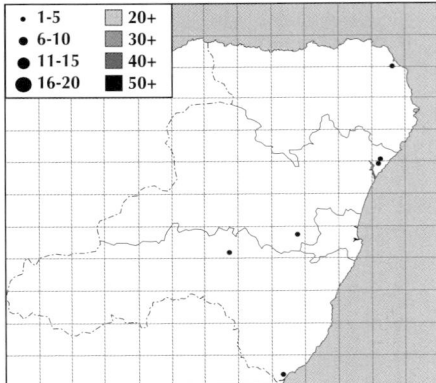

• 1-5		20+	
• 6-10		30+	
● 11-15		40+	
● 16-20		■ 50+	

American Wigeon sightings

ALL RECORDS

1957 4-5 May *Meikle Loch*

1972 15-23 Apr *Auchlossan* male (R.H.Dennis, N.Picozzi, D.P.Willis *et al.*) (BB: RR 1972)

1974 21-22 Mar *nr Loch of Strathbeg* female (D.I.M.Wallace) (*BB* 72: RR)

1989 16-17 Jul *Cotehill Loch* eclipse male (K.D.Shaw, J.L.Swallow, A.Webb *et al.*) (*BB* 83: RR)

1989 26 Jul-13 Aug *Kinnaber, River North Esk* immature male (G.M.Addison, M.S.Scott) (*BB* 83: RR)

1992 6-8 Jun *Strathbeg* adult male (*BB* 86: RR) (P.D.Bloor, I.M.Phillips *et al.*)

1992 14Nov-19Dec *Skene* male (G.F.Allen, J.Oates) with sub-adult male on 22 Nov (I.M.Phillips, K.D.Shaw *et al.*) (*BB* 87 & V88: RR)

1994 6-15 Nov *Skene* male (G.F.Allen, I.M.Phillips *et al.*)

1995 28 Oct *Skene* (G.F.Allen *et al.*)

1996 20 Mar-20 Apr *Strathbeg* (A.Leitch, T.W.Marshall) (subject to acceptance)

The records of a drake on Loiriston Loch in 1993 and 1994 relate to the same bird which was trapped and ringed and showed characteristics of a hybrid Wigeon (*Anus penelope*) x American Wigeon (R.Duncan, J.Duncan, I.M.Phillips, K.D.Shaw *et al.*) (*Birding World* Vol. 7: 116–117).

American Wigeon with Wigeon *by M. Langman*

Green-winged Teal *Anas crecca carolinensis*

Breeds in North America and winters in the southern USA south to Honduras and the West Indies.

There have been only seven records of this Nearctic subspecies in the North East region. The Loch of Strathbeg, which holds large numbers of wintering Teal (*Anas crecca*), accounts for all but one record. The recent records from consecutive years (1993–1996) at this location may in fact relate to just one returning individual.

ALL RECORDS

1957 31 Mar-20 Apr *Forvie* (W.Crawford *et al.*)
1978 4 Mar *Strathbeg* (A.R.Kitson)
1993 3-5 June *Strathbeg* (T.W.Marshall *et al.*)
1993 4-19 Dec *Strathbeg* (J.Dunbar, J.D.Poyner)
1994 7 Jan-20 Feb *Strathbeg* presumed same as above (T.W.Marshall *et al.*)
1995 14 Jan *Strathbeg* presumed returning bird.
1996 20 Jan-2 Dec *Strathbeg* presumed returning bird

Blue-winged Teal *Anas discors*

Breeds in North America and winters in the southern United States south to Peru and northern Brazil.

The majority of Scottish records come from the Hebrides, Orkney and Shetland (Evans 1994).

There have been three records (of probably only two birds), of this Nearctic species within this region. One in June and one in September.

ALL RECORDS

1980 2 Jun *Rattray* male (M.Innes)
1984 16 Sep *Fraserburgh/Sandhaven* female or eclipse male (K.Duncan, R.Smith) possibly the same bird shot at Strathbeg 19 Sep (*per.* R.H.Hogg)

Blue-winged Teal *by M. Langman*

Red-crested Pochard *Netta rufina*

The main breeding area is from south east Europe eastward to north western China and Mongolia. There are scattered populations in western Europe. Winters from the Mediterranean to the Indian subcontinent.

The closest breeding colony is in the Netherlands and it seems likely that the records from at least 1960 refer to genuine immigrants. The decline in this population has resulted in fewer autumn records in south east England (Lack 1986). Subsequent records may also relate to wild birds, as they have all occurred in autumn and early winter. Cramp and Simmons (1977) noted the period February–March and October–November as the periods of movement of continental birds. Despite this, the ever increasing English feral population may account for some or all of the records.

There have been only four records of five birds in North East Scotland.

ALL RECORDS
1960 Jan **Skene** (2) females
1982 31 Oct **Strathbeg** female, also on 12 Nov (J.Dunbar)
1985 9 Aug **Strathbeg** female (J.Dunbar)
1996 29 Oct-4 Nov **Strathbeg** male (A.Leitch)

Ring-necked Duck *Aythya collaris*

Breeds in North America, chiefly southern Canada and adjacent USA. The species has been increasing and extending eastwards in recent decades. Winters in the coastal lowlands of the USA and as far south as Costa Rica.

The first Scottish record was at Loch Morar, Inverness, in 1963, but it took another six years for the second record to occur. This latter record was at the mouth of the River Don, in Aberdeen. Despite the increase in Scottish records since 1977, there have been only two further records for North East Scotland.

ALL RECORDS
1969 16 Feb **Donmouth** male, 2nd Scottish Record (M.J.H.Cook) (*BB* 62: RR)
1989 4 Nov **Meikle Loch** female (C.Barton, J.R.W.Gordon *et al.*) (*BB* 83: RR)
1992 10-14 May **Strathbeg** male (J.D.Poyner *et al.*) (*BB* 86: RR)

Ferruginous Duck *Aythya nyroca*

Breeds from south west and central Europe eastwards to western China and Mongolia. Birds winter from southern Spain, north west Africa, Sudan and Ethiopia eastwards to northern India.

There is an early record of what may be this species in the *New Statistical Account of Scotland* (1845). A 'white-eye or castaneous duck' is noted from the parish of Banff. Sim (1903) makes only a sceptical reference to a report by Edward (*Naturalist* Vol. 4) that the species had 'occurred' at Strathbeg, giving no further details. These early, unauthenticated records must be considered of doubtful reliability (Thom 1986).

In November 1931, a drake was reported from the Donmouth in Aberdeen. In the editor's note accompanying the record it is reported that this is the fifth record for Scotland and the farthest north (*Scot. Nat.* 1931-32).

There has been only one further record for the region, a female at the Loch of Strathbeg in March 1977. Following a review of records this was noted as the sixth record for Scotland (*Scottish Bird Report* 1977).

ALL RECORDS
1931 22 Nov **Donmouth** male (C.H.Usher)
1977 12-27 Mar **Strathbeg** female (P.M.Ellis *et al.*) also on 20 Nov and 18 Dec (J.Dunbar)

King Eider *Somateria spectabilis*

Breeds around the Arctic coasts. European birds winter off northern Norway.

Within Britain the King Eider is a rare, but regular visitor. The majority of records have been from the Shetland Isles, but Highland and Grampian also account for good numbers of birds. In North East Scotland the majority of records have been of single birds associating with large flocks of Common Eiders. This has resulted in many records of long staying individuals, particularly during the summer months, and probably involves some returning birds.

Since the first record in 1951, King Eiders have been regularly seen off the coast of North East Scotland and have been almost annual throughout the late seventies until the present. In most years the first reports come in late April and early May, although there are some March records. Throughout the summer months the majority of records are of single birds, particularly the easily identified drakes. In several years up to two drakes have been reported. The situation is confused by many observers not taking careful notes on individuals to prove the presence of additional birds.

The number of records tends to fall off during the moult period (from July–September) when the species is less obtrusive among large moulting flocks of Common Eiders (although King Eider moult appears to commence later than that of Common Eider). There are several records of males in eclipse plumage during October and November, with a few records of adult-plumaged birds in December and January. It has been assumed that, in most years, the 'regular' drake from the Ythan winters in the Tay estuary.

The best year to date for this species was 1989 when between three and six birds were present in the region, and included two females. Records of females are less frequent but one was seen in 1975 and two in 1989.

The majority of records come from the Ythan estuary, which holds large numbers of breeding Common Eiders. There are regular reports from the east coast area between the Donmouth and Blackdog, which also holds large numbers of Common Eiders and other seaducks, particularly during the moult period. Smaller flocks of Common Eiders at Girdleness have also produced several records of King Eiders. There has been only one record for the north coast, a sub-adult drake at Sandend in May 1992.

King Eider *by M. Langman*

Steller's Eider *Polysticta stelleri*

Breeds in Arctic Russia, Alaska and north west Canada. European birds winter off northern Norway and some in the southern Baltic.

There has been only one record of this extremely rare vagrant. It was the seventh record for Britain and the fifth for Scotland.

ALL RECORDS
1970 8 Nov *Rattray* male (M.R.Williams)
(*BB* 63: RR)

Surf Scoter *Melanitta perspicillata*

Breeds in northern North America. Birds winter in the Pacific and on the Atlantic coast of North America, extending as far south as North Carolina.

Most records of this species in Britain have been in Scotland, with Grampian, Highland and Lothian the most productive areas. In the North East Scotland region the bulk of the records have been from the stretch of coast between the Donmouth and Blackdog, an area where large flocks of Common Scoter (2,000+) and Velvet Scoter (100+) build up from late June until October. There have been only two records from the north coast, both from around Fraserburgh Bay (1978 and 1996).

The first record for the North East region appears to be of one off Aberdeenshire in November 1855 (Harting 1901, in Naylor 1996). There are no further records until 1971.

Since 1971, this species was recorded less than annually into the early 1980s and then more regularly from the late 1980s until the present. The majority of records refer to single drakes, but at least two drakes were present in eight years between 1971 and 1996. The best year for this species was 1991, when six birds were present together off Murcar (K.D.Shaw, S.A.Reeves). Most records fall between mid–June and late–July, but birds have been seen as early as April and as late as November. This is another species which, as it demands time and effort searching through large flocks of seaducks, inspires few observers.

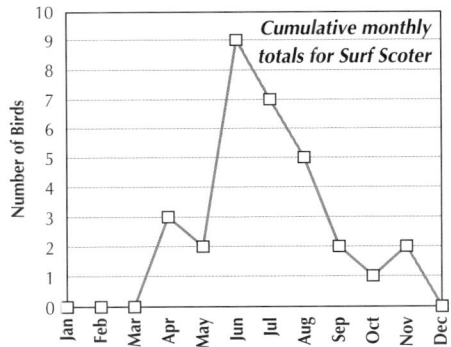

Cumulative monthly totals for Surf Scoter

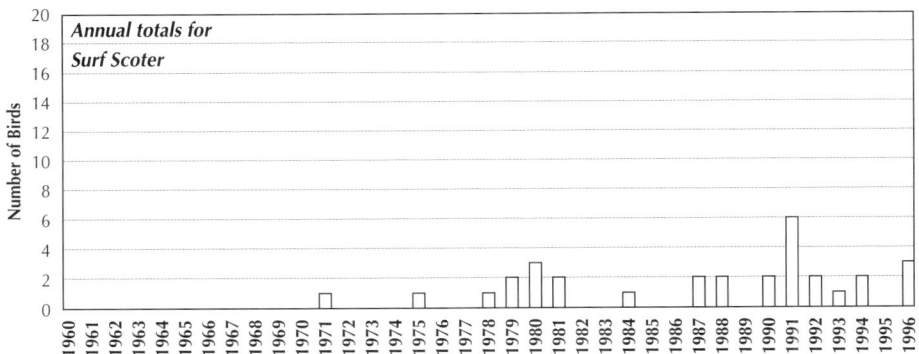

Annual totals for Surf Scoter

Honey Buzzard _Pernis apivorus_

Breeds from western Europe eastwards to the boreal zone of Asia. Winters in Africa.

Honey Buzzards are rare, localised breeders in Britain and scarce passage migrants. The sites of breeding birds are generally kept secret and the total British population is uncertain. The Rare Birds Breeding Panel documents an increasing British population of 28 pairs (Ogilvie _et al._ 1996).

The Honey Buzzard has long been a rare breeder in Scotland, with Aberdeenshire among the few recorded localities. MacGillivray (1855) referred to a nest having been found in the woods at Abergeldy (Aberdeenshire) and in 1867 a pair bred at Ballogie, but the birds were unfortunately shot. Sim (1903) records that 'the stomachs of both contained bees and honey. The nest with two eggs was found'.

Passage birds are also noted with the earliest record in the _New Statistical Account of Scotland_ (1845) of 'ring-tailed buzzard' from the parish of Fyvie, which may relate to this species. Gray (1871) further noted a bird shot in 1868 in Aberdeenshire. For both Aberdeenshire and Kincardineshire the species is noted as 'occasional but rare' (_Scot. Nat._ 1885-86).

The Vertebrate Fauna of Dee (Sim (1903)) lists 16 birds between 1864 and 1902, with a further three birds recorded by Serle (1895). These birds were mainly in September, with fewer June and July records. This prompted Sim (1903) to note that 'there seems no doubt that the bird is most frequently seen and obtained during autumnal migration'.

1864 Sept _Crimmonmogate_
1867 Sept _Deeside_ (_Free Press_, Jan 8th 1867)
1868 NA _Ballogie_
1869 Jul _nr Fyvie_ for eight days (_Avi-Fauna of Buchan_)
1874 NA _Ballogie_ 'seen'
1875 NA _Culter House_ killed
1889 NA _Pitfour_ shot (_Avi-Fauna of Buchan_)
1898 19 Sep _Kinmundy_ shot, immature (_Avi-Fauna of Buchan_, addenda)
1890 24 Sep _Crimmonmogate_ female shot
1892 NA _Pitfour_ trapped tearing up a bee's nest
1893 3 Jul _Haddo House_ shot
1896 21 Sep _Durris_ killed
1896 24 Sep _Urie_ male killed
1897 17 Jul _Pitfour_ shot
1898 15 Sep _Kinmundy_ shot, bird of the year
1901 23 Sep _Port Errol_ shot
1901 30 Sep _Ardlethen_ shot
1902 25 Sep _Crimmonmogate_ killed by Lord Carnegie
1902 21 Jun _Fyvie_ killed

There are two further notes from the early part of this century:

1912 May _nr Aberdeen_ shot, now in Univ. Museum (_Scot. Nat._ 1915)
1913 15 Aug _Kemnay_ shot (_Scot. Nat._ 1914)

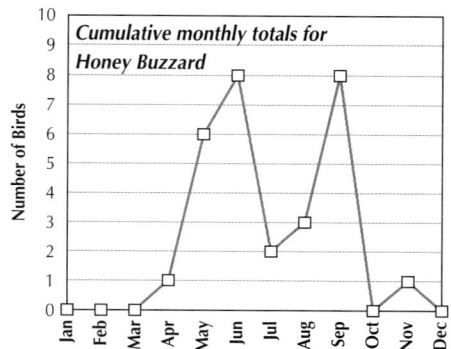

Cumulative monthly totals for Honey Buzzard

Baxter and Rintoul (1953) wrote that in Scotland, 'Aberdeen is the county where most records occur'. They gave no further details, but must have considered the aforementioned records.

More recent records have continued the trend of 'occasional but rare' with the species less than annual. Most records are of single birds on passage during May and June, August and September. In some years, however, there have been several birds seen, with five in 1976 and possibly seven in 1981. These years include those birds at inland sites with breeding suspected. Proof of breeding has not been obtained from any site in recent years.

ALL RECENT RECORDS

1963 3 Sep *Rattray*
1974 13 Jun *Deeside*
1975 Autumn *Deeside*
1976 31 May *St Cyrus*
1976 12 Jun *New Deer* female, dead
1976 1 Aug *Deeside*
1976 19 Sep *Methlick*
1976 Nov *Loch Tilt*
1977 24 Apr *Site details withheld*
1977 1 Jun *Site details withheld* (2)
no evidence of breeding
1980 12 Jul *Deeside*
1980 8 Sep *Strathbeg*
1980 20 Sep *Fowlsheugh*
1981 9 May *Deeside*
1981 30 May *Site withheld* (4) together
1981 4 Jun *Strathbeg*
1981 21 Sep *Donmouth* one in off the sea
1983 30 Sep *Strathbeg*
1984 8 June *Gight* emaciated bird which died
the next day
1988 20 Jun *Glen Dye*
1988 3 Jul *Cairngorm/Ben MacDhui Plateau*
1992 30 Aug *Girdleness* in off the sea
1992 31 Aug *Strathbeg*
1994 25 Jun *Peterhead* in off the sea
1994 10 Sept *Drums*

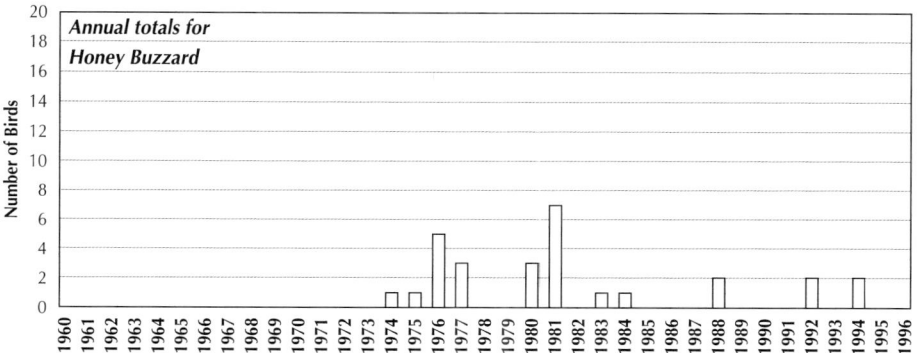

Honey Buzzard *by M. Langman*

Black Kite *Milvus migrans*

Breeds in Europe (except the north west), Asia, Africa and Australia. The European birds winter in Africa south of the Sahara.

Black Kites are still very rare in Scotland, with only ten birds recorded between 1901 and 1993. The majority of these records have been from Orkney, with only five mainland Scottish records. Of these three birds have occurred in North East Scotland, all in spring, and a fourth was in the Cabrach Hills (Moray and Nairn) bordering the region.

ALL RECORDS

1901 18 Apr *Aberdeen* male shot within the city boundary. Its stomach contained a few small feathers only. The second record for the British Isles (*BB* 1 & *ASNH* 1901, 133)

1979 30 May *Strathbeg* (J.Dunbar) (*BB* 72: RR)

1995 3-5 May *Girdleness* poss. same Meikle and Peterhead (J.R.W.Gordon, P.Bloor, T.W.Marshall, C.Coles, T.Donaldson) (subject to acceptance)

Black Kite
by M. Langman

Red Kite *Milvus milvus*

The Red Kite has almost its entire world population in Europe, with just a few tens of pairs in Morocco (Tucker and Heath 1994). The remnant British population was confined to Wales.

In 1989 an experimental programme was set up to see if viable breeding populations could be set up in England and Scotland using young birds from Spain and Sweden, where there were healthy populations, and from failed nests in Wales. Since 1989, 93 birds have been released in Scotland and 73 in England. So far the programme has been successful, with breeding taking place in Scotland and England.

The Red Kite used to breed in North East Scotland and may have been quite widespread. In the *Old Statistical Account of Scotland* (1791-99) the Gled was only said to be resident in Birse (1793), and two years later at Braemar, Crathie and Alford (although many parishes had sketchy write ups for the local natural history). In 1794, Kites occurred at Kirkmichael, Banffshire (Baxter and Rintoul 1953). Sir Hugh Gladstone mentioned 'Swallow-tailed Gleds' from the vicinity of Loch Skene in 1837, but also stated they had now gone.

By the mid 1800s there were still several references for the region attributable to Red Kite within the *New Statistical Account of Scotland* (1845) where '*Milvus vulgaris*' was noted as occurring from Banff (not common) and Strathdon (rarer than Buzzard), with '*Falco milvus*' noted from Strachan, Bervie, Lumphanan, Methlick and Crimond. The species was noted as abundant for Fordoun in Kincardineshire. A short time before 1857 a male was shot about four miles from Banff, and Edward (1857) says they used to be common in that neighbourhood.

MacGillivray (1855) says of the Kite in Aberdeenshire, that it was 'not very uncommon in the upper tracts. It nestles there in trees. Extremely rare to the east of Glen Muick.' Colonel Drummond Hay also said that the Kite was pretty common on Deeside about 1866.

However, by the time of Gray (1871) it was thought that 'At present it is doubtful if it breeds in more than three counties in Scotland, namely, Inverness, Perth and Aberdeen'. Fifteen years later they are noted only as occasional for Aberdeenshire (*Scot. Nat.* 1885-86). Writing in 1903, Sim stated, ' Within the past thirty-five years the Kite has become extremely scarce in 'Dee', and it is now very doubtful if a single pair is to be found breeding within the district. In 1865 six were seen by Mr A. Gill, nailed to a door at Monaltrie, Ballater; and in 1867 I saw five with Mr Brown, Micras, near Crathie, all locally killed specimens'. He further noted 'In the *Aberdeen Free Press*, Dec 13th, 1872, it is reported that a Kite was killed at Balmoral in July 1871. This bird has been occasionally observed about Braemar....up to 1890'. It was apparent that the Kite was becoming scarcer and during the 19th century it was so much persecuted as to be exterminated as a breeding bird. Baxter and Rintoul (1953) stated that the principal feature of the disappearance of the Kite in Scotland was the rapidity with which this was effected. The second half of the last century saw the virtual extirpation of the Kite from Scotland.

With the British breeding population confined to Wales since 1890 (Holloway 1996) records from North East Scotland became very scarce in the early part of this century. An unfortunate occurrence was the capture and death of a Kite 'inadvertently caught and killed in a trap set for vermin' on 18th April 1929 near Glen Dye in the parish of Strachan (*Scot. Nat.* 1929-30). This bird may have been a migrant from the continent.

Between 1929 and 1989 there were only seven records (eight birds) with the majority in coastal locations between late December and mid-June.

Records have understandably increased after the 1989 JNCC/RSPB re-introduction scheme started in northern Scotland and southern England. The released birds were wing-tagged and so the majority of recent records could easily be traced to this scheme. The bulk of the records occur from September to May and are generally from inland locations. So far few birds have summered, but it must surely be only a matter of time before the Red Kite breeds again within North East Scotland.

RECENT RECORDS PRIOR TO RELEASE SCHEME
1958 13 Feb *Old Aberdeen* (*BB* 53: RR)
1969 15 Apr *Kinnaber* (2)
1974 13 Jun *Cockbridge* (*NESBR* 1974)
1975 6-7 Jun *Strathbeg* (*NESBR* 1975)
1978 28 Dec *Sandend* (*NESBR* 1978)
1980 10 Mar *Strathbeg* (*NESBR* 1980)
1988 11-28 May *Kemnay* (*NESBR* 1988)

White-tailed Eagle *Haliaeetus albicilla*

Breeds in Iceland and from Scandinavia and Germany eastwards to north and east Asia. Small numbers re-introduced in western Scotland. Some Scandinavian and German birds winter in the Netherlands and north east France.

Definite records of this species breeding in Aberdeenshire are few. In the *Old Statistical Account of Scotland* (1791-99) White-tailed Eagles were said to be 'now rare' at Birse. There were still records of this species in the *New Statistical Account of Scotland* (1845) with *falco albicilla* from Banchory-Ternan and Strachan, and *falco haliaetus* from Peterhead. MacGillivray (1855) recorded them as breeding at Braemar, and Adams (1859) in the *Birds of Banchory-Ternan* noted them 'not so rare as the former' when comparing them with Golden Eagle. Sim (1903) said 'That the Sea Eagle was resident and bred within our confines is indisputable....In our day....it is certainly the less abundant of the two', and added that he knew of no recent nesting of the species and noted that 'the bird itself must now be looked upon as a rare straggler'. The only record he referred to was of one which struck Girdleness Lighthouse a few years before 1853. It was described as a young bird in its first winter plumage, but Baxter and Rintoul (1953) thought this to be a very unusual occurrence.

There are also old records of White-tailed Eagles nesting on the Pennan Rocks and cliffs near Troup Head, Banff (Baxter and Rintoul 1953). Sim (1903) was somewhat dismissive of the records from Pennan.

Apart from a single record in 1942 of an emaciated bird in Kincardineshire (*Brit. Birds* Vol. 36-37), most records this century have occurred in the 1990s and largely relate to wing-tagged birds from the west coast re-introduction scheme. A single record of an untagged bird (Rattray, December 1991) may have been a genuine vagrant from Scandinavia.

ALL RECENT RECORDS
1942 mid June *Kincardineshire* one alive but injured
(**1976** 11 Apr *Newburgh* eagle poss. this species)
1991/2 23Nov-26Feb *Braemar* second year bird (Ringers Conference)

1991 8 Dec *Rattray* second year bird with no wing tags (G.Christer, J.Dunbar)
1994 7 May *Glen Muick* two immature birds (R.Bramhall, T.Donaldson, M.Thornton, C.Coles)
1994 13 May *Fowlsheugh* wing-tagged (*per.* K.D.Shaw)
1994 27 May *Glenbeg* immature (B.L.Cosnette)
1995 19 Oct *Tillypronie* (I.Francis)
1996 30 April *Drumoak* poss. same *Westhill* (P.Cosgrove, G.Anderson)

Marsh Harrier *Circus aeruginosus*

Breeds in the Western Palearctic south to the Mediterranean and Levant, east to central Asia. Birds in western Europe winter in the Mediterranean region and Africa, south of the Sahara.

The bulk of the British breeding population is confined to East Anglia but birds summer in a wider number of locations. The current population is estimated at 129 females (due to polygamous males, the number of pairs is not quoted, Ogilvie *et al.* 1996).

There are some early records in the *New Statistical Account of Scotland* (1845) with *falco aeruginosus* reported from Banchory-Ternan and Strachan. An editor's note in McGillivray's *The Natural History of Deeside and Braemar* (1855) states that Dr Adams had seen Marsh Harrier in the neighbourhood of Banchory-Ternan. The species was subsequently described as a 'doubtful visitor, insufficiently identified for Aberdeenshire (*Scot. Nat.* 1885-86). Sim (1903) records only a male shot on 12th May 1881, at the Dinnet Lochs.

The species' status has changed considerably in recent years. Baxter and Rintoul (1953) noted only seven records for the whole of Scotland in the early half

of this century, but numbers have increased throughout Scotland since the 1950s (Thom 1986). In North East Scotland records, have become more regular since the early 1960s, and annual since 1974.

The majority of birds arrive between late April and June, with most arrivals in May. Single birds have been seen in February and March. Few new birds are then reported until August and September, but numbers are significantly lower than spring. There have also been single records from October and two from November.

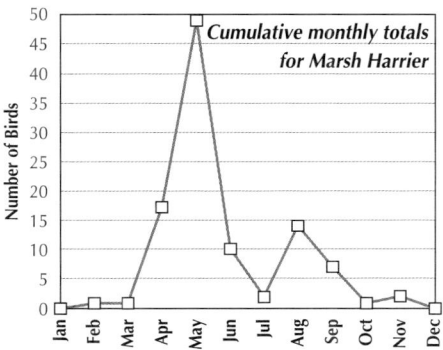

Cumulative monthly totals for Marsh Harrier

The actual number of birds present in any one year is difficult to assess, especially when multiple immatures, females and males are present at one site over a period of time. Since 1989, between five and ten birds have been recorded in every year. The Loch of Strathbeg is by far and away the premier site for this species, with many birds staying for extended periods of time. Several birds have summered at this location and stick carrying has been seen in more than one year. Breeding has not yet been proven, and young fledged birds have never been seen. With the number of birds regularly occurring at this site in spring and summer, the first successful breeding record cannot be too far away. Away from Strathbeg there are considerably fewer records from a number of sites along the east coast and a scattering of records from inland locations.

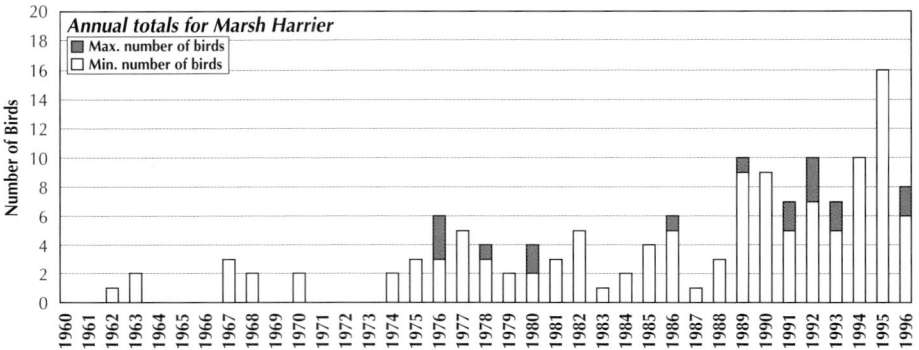

Annual totals for Marsh Harrier
■ Max. number of birds
□ Min. number of birds

Montagu's Harrier *Circus pygargus*

Breeds in southern and central Europe eastwards to central Asia. European birds winter in the Sahel region of sub-Saharan Africa. The British breeding population is small, with between six and 12 pairs in any year (Gibbons et al. 1993).

This species is extremely rare in Scotland, with only six records noted by Thom (1986) between 1950 and 1980. There have been only four records of this species in North East Scotland, all in late May or early June, which is typical of migrants in Britain.

ALL RECORDS

1963 26 May **Ythan** female found dead after collision with overhead wires

1969 NA **South Kincardineshire** shot

1991 3-4 Jun **Ythan** first year male (M.Kimber)

1993 24 May **Boddam, Peterhead** male (W.Dunlop)

Rough-legged Buzzard *Buteo lagopus*

This species has a circumpolar breeding range. Birds in the western Palearctic winter from the Baltic southwards to central and south eastern Europe. Small numbers winter in eastern Britain. Most reaching Scotland are probably of Scandinavian origin.

There are only a few records of this species from the last century. The paper *Avi-Fauna in Buchan* notes three shot at Troup in 1870, one seen at Gourdas in the autumn of 1877 and one trapped at Ardlogie in March 1884 (Serle 1895). In the 1880s they were noted as 'occasional or periodical, but not quite regular visitors' for Aberdeenshire and Kincardineshire (*Scot. Nat.* 1885-86). Sim (1903) in the *Vertebrate Fauna of Dee* notes the species '...is merely an irregular autumn visitor to Dee. In some seasons a good many are killed, while others may pass and no Buzzards be seen.'

Similarly the early part of this century saw only a scattering of records. One was caught at Fasque, Kincardineshire on 3rd November 1903 and another on 5th April 1904 at Fordoun (*TAWMNH Soc.* 1901-06). Baxter and Rintoul (1953) noted that '...in Aberdeen and SE Sutherland it is more or less regular on passage, but appears not to stay the winter', but gave no further details.

From the winter of 1972/73, between one and six birds were reported annually, until the winter of 1983/84 when there were no records. In the following ten winters there were records in only six winter periods, with only one or two birds in any one year. Birds tend to arrive from mid-October, with most in November. Wintering birds have now been reported in several years. As these are often at under-watched inland locations it is difficult to say during which month they arrived, indeed they may be just wandering individuals. It is also probable that this species is under-recorded, particularly in the remoter inland areas, with many going unnoticed among the resident (and increasing) Buzzard *Buteo buteo* population. There is

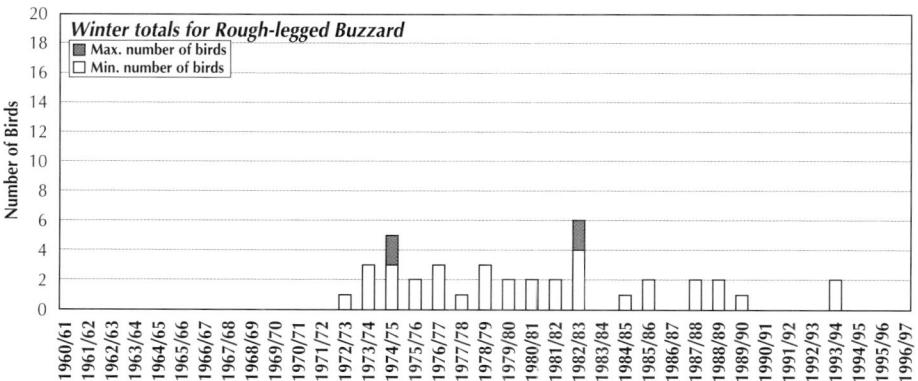

Winter totals for Rough-legged Buzzard

an increase in records during April, which suggests birds passing through the region on their return migration. There have been two records of birds during the summer. One at the Loch of Strathbeg on 21st June 1981, and another at the Tor of Troup on 29th July 1988.

The region is situated on the northern edge of the species' wintering range in Britain, but does still tend to register the large influxes seen elsewhere in eastern Britain. The winter of 1974/75 saw up to 250 birds in eastern England during October (Lack and Ferguson 1986), with between three and five recorded in this area. Similarly in 1982/83 a smaller influx into Britain produced between four and six birds in the region. This was not repeated for the large arrival of birds into Britain in the autumn of 1994, when no autumn records were received in the area.

Wintering birds tend to favour the upland regions, and although no one site holds birds every winter, Glen Dye has been particularly favoured. The Ballater

to Braemar region has also held birds in a number of years. During the winter of 1988/89 a bird was present on the coastal moorland at the Forvie Nature Reserve, and in 1993 a second-winter bird stayed on the coast at Cairnbulg Castle from 12th December until 22nd March 1994, allowing many people to catch up with this elusive species.

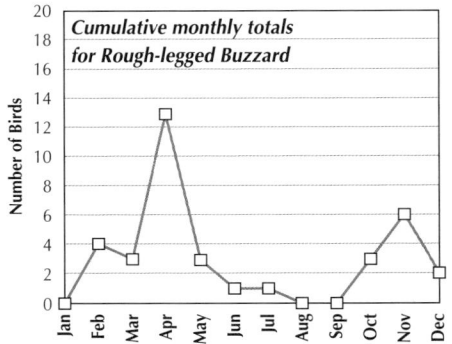

Cumulative monthly totals for Rough-legged Buzzard

Rough-legged Buzzard
by J. P. Smith

Spotted Eagle *Aquila clanga*

Breeds in north east Europe eastwards across Siberia. Winters in Turkey, Egypt and Ethiopia, discontinuously east to south east Asia.

There have been only about 10 records of this species for Britain, all but two in the last century (Dymond *et al.* 1989).

One is said to have been shot in Aberdeenshire on 20th September 1861 by the then Speaker of the House of Commons. Baxter and Rintoul (1953) investigated this occurrence and concluded that the specimen was in the City Museum, Leeds. The bird was unfortunately unlabelled. However, a note appeared in the appendix of the *Phil. and Lit. Soc. Annual Report* (of Leeds) in 1880-1881, referring to this bird as part of a collection acquired on loan at that time from S.W.Milner. Further investigation found that, unfortunately, the bulk of the collection was destroyed by a bomb in May 1941 and the specimen was lost at that time (A.Norris, Assistant Curator, Leeds City Museum *pers comm.*). This record is described as a 'probable' in the B.O.U's *Status of Birds in Britain and Ireland*.

Lesser Kestrel *Falco naumanni*

Breeds from Iberia and north west Africa eastwards into Asia. Winters in Africa.

There have been only 17 accepted records of this species in Britain, and only six since 1958 (Wilson and Slack 1996). There has been only one record for this area, that of a female shot at Boyndlie in the parish of Crimond on 25th October 1897. This was the first record for Scotland.

Lesser Kestrel
by M. Langman

Red-footed Falcon *Falco vespertinus*

Breeds from Poland and Romania east to Siberia. Winters in southern Africa.

There had been only 52 birds of this species recorded in Scotland up to the end of 1990, the majority from the Northern Isles (Evans 1994).

Sim (1903) makes note of a female shot at the Hill of Fiddes, Foveran, on 29th May 1866 and another shot at Crimmonmogate on 7th May 1897. Baxter and Rintoul (1953) noted the aforementioned records, but also an earlier one of a bird shot at Udny on 26th May 1856.

In the early part of this century there was only one further record. A bird was shot at Aboyne on 17th October 1913. There have been four subsequent records of this beautiful falcon, all of single birds.

Most records have occurred in May, a pattern typical of this species' occurrence in Britain. There have been single records for June, July and October. The last record was in 1992 when a first-summer female was present at Kirkton, near St Fergus. The species' habit of dropping onto its prey from a perch led to this bird being injured by passing traffic; it was taken into care and later released.

ALL RECORDS

1856 26 May **Udny** shot

1866 29 May **Hill of Fiddes, Foveran** shot, its stomach contained a mouse and two beetles

1897 7 May **Crimmonmogate** shot, its stomach filled with shrew-mice

1913 17 Oct **Aboyne** shot

1975 20 Jun **Crimond** male (J.Dunbar) (*BB* 68: RR)

1978 20-21 Jul **Balmedie** immature female (M.A.S.Beaman, A.Cruikshank) (BB: RR 1978)

1985 29-30 May **Auchmacoy, Ellon** male (S.Pritchard) (*BB* 79: RR)

1992 31 May-13 Jun **Kirkton nr St Fergus** (A.G.Clarke, J.R.W.Gordon *et al.*) (*BB* 86: RR)

Red-footed Falcon
by J. P. Smith

Hobby *Falco subbuteo*

Breeds in southern Britain and most of Europe and temperate parts of Asia. The European population winters in southern Africa.

The British population appears to be increasing, from an estimated 65 pairs in 1973 to an estimated population of 500-900 pairs in 1989-91 (Gibbons *et al*. 1993). The majority of these are in England, south of the Humber, but it is increasing in the north and recently bred in Scotland.

The earliest notes for this species occur in the *New Statistical Account of Scotland* (1845), where it is mentioned from Strachan, Banchory-Ternan and Fyvie.

In *The Birds of Western Scotland*, Gray (1871) makes reference to several records for this area. One had been killed 'some 23 years ago' near the town of Banff, and, in the autumn of the 'same year', 'an immature' captured at sea off Aberdeenshire. Sim (1903) in *The Vertebrate Fauna of Dee* also notes this bird as the first record for Dee in 1863.

FURTHER RECORDS WERE GIVEN BY SIM (1903) AS FOLLOWS
1868 Autumn *Kittybrewster* found dead
1868 Autumn *Broad Hill, Aberdeen* shot
1870 May *Fraserburgh* killed
1870 5 Jul *Fraserburgh* shot
1897 15 Jul *Pitfour* shot
1898 1 Jun *Aden* killed

Sim (1903) also notes a statement by Gray (1871) that '...in Glen Dye....the Hobby has for some years been known to breed', but added that this required confirmation.

Baxter and Rintoul (1953) reported 'As an occasional visitor the Hobby has occurred in....Kincardine, Aberdeen and Banff. The county from which we have most records is Aberdeen', but did not expand this with any details.

Since the late 1960s the Hobby has remained a scarce visitor to Scotland. Although annual in small numbers, Thom (1986) thought its occurrence justified it being classified as a vagrant. In North East Scotland there have been records in 20 out of 32 years since 1965. In most years only single, short-staying birds are reported. In 1995 an immature female spent a week in late July at a sand quarry near Dyce, hunting Sand Martins *Riparia riparia*. Two birds have been seen in several years (1974, 1978, 1984, 1993, 1994 and 1996). The best year was 1977, when four individuals were seen.

Most records occur between May and September, with moderate peaks in June and September indicating light passage through the region.

Cumulative monthly totals for Hobby

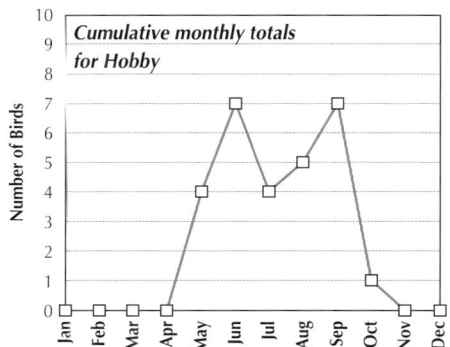

Gyr Falcon *Falco rusticolus*

Breeds circumpolar in the Arctic, wintering south to southern Norway, Finland, Siberia and Canada (to about 50°N).

Pennant (1772) refers to this species in the Appendix to his *Tour of Scotland*, where he says 'The Gyr Falcon has been shot in Aberdeen'. Sim (1903) also refers to this record.

There is a record of Norwegian Falcon in the *New Statistical Account of Scotland* (1845) from the parish of Fyvie. The only other record for the last century, given by Sim (1903), is one shot near Fraserburgh in March 1871. There is another record from the last century, of a bird shot at St Fergus Sands, Banffshire on 4th April 1888 (*Brit. Birds* Vol. 5, in Naylor, 1996).

There is only one record for the early part of this century, one obtained in Strathdon on 3rd March 1906 (*TAWMNH Soc.* 1901-06).

There were no other records until 1973, when a bird was found dead in Glen Tanar. The first recent, live bird was a grey phase individual in Strathdon. This bird was seen well by a member of the Raptor Study Group and a local gamekeeper. In 1992, a white bird was seen well on Bennachie on 28th November, but adverse weather the following day prevented its relocation by the numerous birders who searched for it.

An intermediate morph was seen at the Linn of Quoich in April 1995.

Two birds have been brought ashore from oil installation platforms and released. The first was in January 1975 and the second in November 1982.

ALL RECENT RECORDS

1906 3 Mar **Strathdon** shot (*TAWMNHS* Trans V1: 1901-06)

1973 18 Apr **Glen Tanar** found dead (N.Picozzi) (*BB* 67: RR)

1990 21 Apr **Strathdon** a grey phase bird (D.Calder, B.L.Cosnette) (*BB* 85: RR)

1992 28 Nov **Bennachie** (D.J.G.Gill) (*BB* 86: RR)

1993 14 Apr **Ben Macdui area** (I.T.Rowlands et al.) (*BB* 87: RR)

1995 24 Apr **Glen Quoich** (J.Bowler, J.Hunter) (*BB* 89: RR)

Gyr Falcon
by M. Langman

Common Crane *Grus grus*

Breeds in Scandinavia and Germany eastwards across Siberia, discontinuously south to Turkey. (Very small number of birds in UK). The European population winters from France to north and north east Africa, Turkey and south west Iran.

Baxter and Rintoul (1953) stated that many early records may have been confused with herons as they were often called cranes in Scotland. They considered the following records to be authentic. The earliest record of this species is made by Gray (1871) when he reports an immature shot on the banks of the Dee at the end of May in 1851. Sim (1903) adds that the bird was 'in a field eight miles up the River Dee'. A second bird was seen on 21st November 1868, being chased 'by a great number of Rooks and Jackdaws' in the vicinity of Gourdas (Serle 1895).

There is an apparent gap in records of almost 100 years. In recent times there have been 14 records of up to 18 birds between 1962 and 1994. Most records are of single birds, but two were at Kemnay in August and September of 1962, two were seen at the Loch of Strathbeg in August and September of 1977, and three were at Maryculter in December 1976. Many birds have stayed for several days and even weeks, but a bird that arrived in April 1978 stayed in the area for almost a year before departing.

Most records occur in spring and early summer, but there have been records for every month.

ALL RECENT RECORDS

1962 14 Aug-16 Sep **Kemnay** (2) (A.Anderson, D.Jenkins, M.Jenkins) (*BB* 55: RR)

1966 15-23 Oct **Newburgh** immature (Dr G.M.Dunnet, H.Milne, W.Murray) (*BB* 59: RR)

1976 17 Apr **Newburgh** in flight (C.J.Spray) (*BB* 70: RR)

1976 21-23 Dec **Maryculter** (3) (W.Stewart) (*BB* 70: RR)

1977 22-26 Mar **New Pitsligo** immature (T.Hodd) (*BB* 70: RR)

1977 24Aug-25Sep **Strathbeg** (2) (J.Dunbar, Dr A.G.Knox) (*BB* 70: RR)

1978 26 Apr **Ythan** adult stayed in the Collieston/Ythan/Forvie area until 13 April 1979 (D.J.Butler, C.D.Scott *et al.*) (BB: RR 1979)

1987 12 Sep **Newburgh** in flight (K.Duncan, A.J.Leitch, M.Kimber, R.Rae)

1988 14 Apr **Banff** (R.D.S.Scott)

1988 18-25 Apr **Scotstown** possibly same as above. Then moved between Ythan and Scotstown until 27 Sep., many observers

1989 15 May **Leask** (T.W.Marshall, R.Neilson)

1989 16 June **Strathbeg** (S.Cooter, J.Dunbar)

1994 28 May **Ythan** in flight, (A.Taylor) later possibly same Rosehearty, 5th-13th June (K.Buchan, A.Webb)

1996 14 May **Blackdog-Millden** (2) (C.Kindley)

1996 7 Sept-31 Oct **Sandhaven** also Strathbeg (C.Cronin, I.M.Phillips *et al.*)

1996 19 Oct **Collieston** (S.Alexander, N.Picozzi)

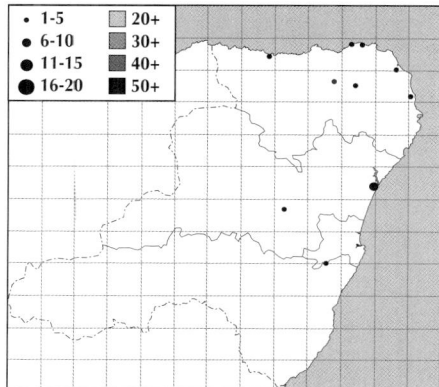

Legend:
- 1-5
- 6-10
- 11-15
- 16-20
- 20+
- 30+
- 40+
- 50+

Common Crane sightings

Little Bustard *Tetrax tetrax*

Breeds in France, Iberia and north west Africa eastward to Kazakhstan. Birds from northern France may winter in Iberia.

Sim (1903) in his *Vertebrate Fauna of Dee* notes two early records:

1873 13 Nov **Fingask, Oldmeldrum** shot-female
1889 10 Dec **Culter** killed

This century there have been a further two records:

1912 1 Jan **Gallaton, nr Stonehaven** shot on a farm. It had frequented a turnip field for about a fortnight. (*BB* 5) Specimen in Lundin Links Museum (*Scot. Nat.* 1937).
1935 3 Jan **Pitfour Estate nr Peterhead** female shot, weighed 1 lb 8 ozs (*BB* 29) (*Scot. Nat.* 1937).

The four records have all occurred during the winter months (November to January) and this is typical of this species in the British Isles (Dymond *et al.* 1989). The records for the region all came when the species was much commoner on the continent, yet there were still less than ten records for Scotland. The contraction of the breeding range has resulted in fewer reaching Britain since 1958 and there have been only two further records in Scotland (Evans 1994).

Little Bustard
by M. Langman

Houbara Bustard *Chlamydotis undulata*

Breeds in Israel and eastern Turkey east to Mongolia. Also north Africa and Canary Islands. The African and Canary populations are mainly resident, but the population in the southern regions of the former Soviet Republics winters in the Persian Gulf area.

There has been only one record of this species, identified as the eastern subspecies *C. u. macqueenii*. It was the first for Scotland and fourth for Britain. Sim (1903) notes the record under MacQueen's Bustard as being of a male, but most authors refer to it as being a female, including Dymond *et al.* (1989).

ALL RECORDS
1898 24 Oct **Pitfour, nr St Fergus** female shot
The only Scottish record occurred after 10 days of severe NE gales

Black-winged Stilt *Himantopus himantopus*

Breeds in southern Eurasia, Australia, Africa, and the Americas. The European population winters mainly in Africa south of the Sahara.

There is a record given by Gray (1871) of a bird seen on the Tile Burn, near the Donmouth, on 15th September 1867. The observer viewed the bird with binoculars at a range of 130yds, and noted 'under a clear sun....the legs orange, iris beautiful red.' Sim (1903) notes that the details of this record were 'charmingly exact. The Stilts eye is under a quarter of an inch in diameter. Let anyone view an eye four times that size placed at the same distance, and see if he can say if it is 'beautiful red' or any other colour, especially under a clear sun!'. Baxter and Rintoul (1953) considered this to be 'less well authenticated' than some others.

There has been only one recent record of this species. This was only the fourth record for Scotland this century.

ALL RECORDS
1984 14 Oct **Ythan** subsequently at Meikle from 16 Oct to 3 Nov. The remains were found at Cotehill. (I.C.McLeod) (*BB* 77: RR)

Avocet *Recurvirostra avosetta*

Breeds locally from western Europe and Africa eastwards to central Asia. Most of the Asian population moves south in winter. European birds are partially migratory and African birds largely sedentary.

Birds ceased to breed in Britain around 1837 and it was not until 100 years later in the early 1940s that re-colonisation started. The current British population is estimated at 400-500 pairs (Gibbons *et al*. 1993).

Edward (1854) noted that it had occurred on Strathbeg, giving no details. Sim (1903) thought that this record was 'too vague to be of any value', but added that there had been one record, of a bird shot on Old Aberdeen Links in 1841.

There have been ten records of 12 birds since 1969. These records have been spread throughout several months, with most in the first half of the year. The Ythan has accounted for seven records (eight birds) and the Loch of Strathbeg for two records (three birds).

ALL RECORDS
1841 NA *Old Aberdeen Links*
1969 23-26 Mar **Ythan**
1979 17 Apr **Ythan** (J.H.Sykes)
1980 17 Feb **Ythan** (R.W.Furness)
1984 27 Mar **Ythan** (2) (*per* A.G.Knox)
1986 19-22 Jan **Strathbeg** (T.W.Marshall, J.Dunbar)
1986 6-8 Jul **Ythan** (A.Simmons, E.Simmons *et al*.)
1987 24-31 Oct **Cults** (B.J.Stewart *et al*.)
1990 19-21 Apr **Ythan** (T.W.Marshall *et al*.)
1993 7 May **Strathbeg** (2) (J.D.Poyner, J.Dunbar, D.J.C.Gill) also on Ythan 8th May (G.Ruthven, W.G.Johnson, S.M.Johnson *et al*.)
1994 4-14 Dec **Ythan** (R.McGregor)

'Pratincole' sp.

An unidentified Pratincole was seen at Meikle Loch on 12th August, 1972 (R.H.Hogg).

Black-winged Pratincole *Glareola nordmanni*

Breeds from Romania east to central Asia. Winters in central and southern Africa.

There has been only one record of this species in North East Scotland. It was the second for Scotland where there has been only one subsequent record (near Dundee in August 1996).

ALL RECORDS
1976 11 Jul **Strathbeg** (R.Cardno, S.Cutts, J.Dunbar) (*BB* 70: RR) (*Scot. Birds* V10)

Little Ringed Plover *Charadrius dubius*

Breeds widely across Europe from Fenno-Scandia south to the Mediterranean and east across Russia to south east Asia. European birds winter in central Africa.

This species only started to breed in Britain in 1938, since which time it has expanded, with the present population estimated at between 825 and 1,070 pairs (Gibbons *et al.* 1993). The bulk of the population lies south of a line from the Teesmouth to the Mersey, although there are pairs in Northumberland and Cumbria. Breeding has occurred in Scotland on at least three or four occasions in recent years.

The first record is given by Sim (1903) who records an adult male which was caught alive in the Aberdeen fishmarket on 17th May 1894; it was given to Sim and preserved by him. This is possibly the first record for Scotland (Baxter and Rintoul 1953).

There were no subsequent records until a bird was seen at Auchmacoy in May 1977. With the documented northward spread of this species in England (Gibbons *et al.* 1993) it is perhaps not surprising that since 1991 the species has been more than annual in its occurrence. What was, perhaps, surprising was that in 1995 a pair bred in the region, raising three chicks. This was the farthest north this species had been recorded breeding in Britain. Breeding was attempted again in 1996, but the attempt failed.

The majority of birds have arrived in May, with fewer arriving in June and July. There are few reports of birds after July. The favoured sites for this species are the Loch of Strathbeg/Rattray area and the Donmouth. There have been two records of birds on passage at Girdleness (1992 and 1996). The best year to date for this species was 1996, when seven birds were seen during the year, with three together in May at Rattray.

Killdeer
by M. Langman

Killdeer *Charadrius vociferus*

Breeds in North America, the West Indies and Peru. Winters from the USA south to Peru.

The earliest record for Scotland (and Britain) is of one shot at Peterhead in 1867. The specimen was not identified until 1904, when it was found wrongly labelled as a Ringed Plover *Charadrius hiaticula* in a museum drawer (*ASNH* 1904: 247). The record is accepted by the BOU and Sharrock and Sharrock (1976), although Thom (1986) suggested the record be regarded with some suspicion. There have been only ten further records in Scotland.

There is only one recent record of this species. A single bird was seen at the Loch of Strathbeg on the 13th April 1995.

ALL RECENT RECORDS
1995 13-15 Apr *Loch of Strathbeg* (W.Dunlop, P.Webster *et al.*) (*BB* 89: RR)

Kentish Plover *Charadrius alexandrinus*

Breeds in western Europe and North Africa eastwards to Korea. The European birds winter as far south as northern Africa.

There were only seven records of this species in Scotland between 1949 and 1983 (Thom 1986). The second record for Scotland was on the Ythan in May 1962, and there have been two subsequent records in the North East. All the records have been single spring birds between the 30th April and 14th May.

ALL RECORDS
1962 3-4 May **Ythan** (A.G.Gordon, W.E.Pool)
1981 10-14 May **Ythan** (K.B.Shepherd *et al.*)
1984 30 April **Rattray** (T.W.Marshall)

Kentish Plover
by M. Langman

Greater Sand Plover *Charadrius leschenaultii*

Breeds from Turkey eastwards to Mongolia. Winters in the eastern Mediterranean, the Red Sea and coastal areas of southern and eastern Africa, and from southern Asia to Australia.

The first Scottish record was in 1979, with a second in 1982. The only record for the North East region was in 1991 and was the third record for Scotland (10th British). The bird was an adult male in almost full summer plumage.

ALL RECORDS
1991 18-19 Aug **Donmouth** (G.Smith, D.J.Bain, K.D.Shaw *et al.*) (*BB* 85: RR)

American Golden Plover Pluvialis dominica

Breeds in North America, wintering from Central America south to Argentina.

There had been only 31 Scottish records this century (up to 1994), the majority from Shetland, Orkney and the Western Isles (Evans 1994 and Rogers et al. 1991-94). There had been only four mainland records during this period.

In line with the rarity of this species in Scotland, there has been only one record for the North East Scotland region. The bird was an adult in full summer plumage, and appeared on the Ythan with a small number of Golden Plovers in July 1995. It spent a few days on the island at the mouth of the Tarty Burn, and was seen by many observers.

ALL RECORDS
1995 9-16 July **Ythan** (M.Darling, A.O'Connor, A.Murray) (*BB* 89: RR)

Temminck's Stint Calidris temminckii

Breeds from northern Scandinavia eastwards across northern Siberia. Winters in western and central Africa and south Asia.

The Temminck's Stint is a regular, though scarce migrant in Scotland. Records have increased markedly since 1973 (Thom 1986) and it has established itself as a breeding species, albeit in very small numbers (Gibbons et al. 1993).

Sim (1903) reports only three specimens for 'Dee', all in the last century:

1871 August ***Old Aberdeen Links***
1872 June ***Old Aberdeen***
1891 5 Sept ***Colly Burn, near Peterhead***

There were no further records until 1975, when there were six records of eight birds. This included three together at Meikle Loch on 26th August. Subsequently there were three birds in 1976, seven in 1977 (including an inland record) and two in 1978. There was then a gap of six years before the next record in 1985. This was followed by three further blank years, before three were reported in 1989, and one each in 1991, 1992 and 1993. Again this was followed by three blank years.

The majority of records have been in the last two weeks of May, with smaller

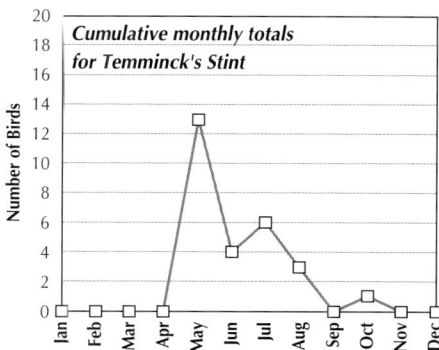

Cumulative monthly totals for Temminck's Stint

numbers in June, July and August. There has been one unusually late bird, in October 1976. All but one of the records have been of single birds. The only multiple record was of three together at Meikle Loch in August 1975.

The Loch of Strathbeg, the Donmouth and Meikle Loch are the most favoured localities for this species, with scattered records from seven other sites.

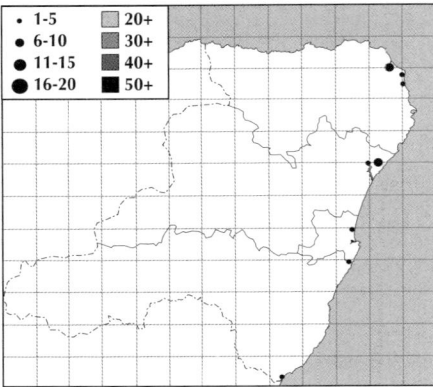

Temminck's Stint sightings

Legend:
- 1-5
- 6-10
- 11-15
- 16-20
- 20+
- 30+
- 40+
- 50+

ALL RECENT RECORDS

1975 13 May *Auchmacoy*
1975 26 May *Strathbeg*
1975 29 May *Meikle*
1975 18-25 Jul *Meikle*
1975 31 May *St Cyrus*
1975 26 Aug *Meikle* (3)
1976 3 Jun *Strathbeg* also 8th and 10th
1976 26-27 Jul *Meikle*
1976 4 Oct *Donmouth*
1977 2 Jun *Meikle*
1977 8 Jun *Strathbeg*
1977 28 Jun *Rattray*
1977 3 Jul *Meikle*
1977 15 Jul *Meikle*
1977 21 Jul *Ythan*
1977 July *Inland*
1978 29 May *St Fergus*
1978 30 May *Strathbeg*
1985 30-31 May *Donmouth*
1989 13-14 May *Donmouth*
1989 19 May *Rigifa*
1989 20 May *Strathbeg*
1991 31 May *Strathbeg*
1992 30May-2Jun *Strathbeg*
1993 11 May *Strathbeg*

Baird's Sandpiper
by M. Langman

Least Sandpiper *Calidris minutilla*

Breeds in northern North America, wintering from the USA to Brazil.

There were only two previous Scottish records of this diminutive wader before the Cove record. This bird appeared on a small, temporarily flooded area of a field.

ALL RECORDS

1988 31 Jul-4 Aug *Rigifa Farm, Cove*
(J.L.Swallow, J.McKee, K.D.Shaw) (*BB* 82: RR)

White-rumped Sandpiper *Calidris fuscicollis*

Breeds in northern North America, wintering in southern South America.

There have been 34 records of this species in Scotland up to the end of 1994 (Evans 1994, Rogers *et al.* 1992, 1993, 1994, 1995). The majority have been in Orkney and Lothian.

There have been four records for the North East region, all between July and mid–September. This pattern is consistent with this species' occurrence in Britain (Dymond *et al.* 1989).

ALL RECORDS

1985 31 Aug *Ythan* (Dr M.V.Bell) (*BB* 78: RR)
1985 12-13 Sep *Rattray* (D.C.Butcher, R.A.Schofield, S.T.Spencer) (*BB* 78: RR)
1993 4 Jul *Strathbeg* adult (P.Bloor, J.D.Poyner, S.A.Reeves *et al.*) (*BB* 87: RR)
1995 30-31 Jul *Annachie Lagoon* adult (I.M.Phillips, S.A.Reeves) (*BB* 89: RR)

Baird's Sandpiper *Calidris bairdii*

Breeds from north east Siberia eastwards across northern North America to north west Greenland. Winters to the south of Ecuador in South America.

There have been only 19 records of this species from Scotland up to the end of 1994 (Evans 1994, Rogers *et al.* 1992, 1993, 1994, 1995). Of these three have been in North East Scotland. The first was in 1982 at Rattray, and this was followed eight years later by a juvenile at Annachie Lagoon in 1990. Remarkably a second bird joined this one at Annachie on 15th, the first multiple occurrence of this species in Scotland. All three birds arrived in September, which is typical for juveniles of this species in Britain.

ALL RECORDS

1982 26 Sep *Rattray* juvenile (C.R.McKay, L.Steele) (*BB* 78: RR)
1990 6 Sep *Annachie Lagoon, St Fergus* joined by a second juvenile on the 15 Sep. Two present until 17 Sep, with only 1 on 18 Sep. (G.Christer, D.Smith, C.Westlake *et al.*) (C.Barton, A.G.Clarke *et al.*) (*BB* 84: RR)

Pectoral Sandpiper *Calidris melanotos*

Breeds in north east Siberia and northern North America. Winters in southern South America.

Thom (1986) notes the first record for Scotland as one shot in Caithness in 1928. There is an earlier record for the North East region given by Gray (1871) and Sim (1903). Both authors report an immature bird shot at the Donmouth in Aberdeen on 2nd October 1867. There are no further records for this region until 1973. Although this species has been annual in Scotland in very small numbers since 1973, it has been less than annual in this region. In the 24 years since 1973, there have been records in 13 years. In most years a single record is usual, but in 1977 and 1993 there were two birds seen, and in 1990 and 1992, three birds were recorded, including two together at Strathbeg in 1992.

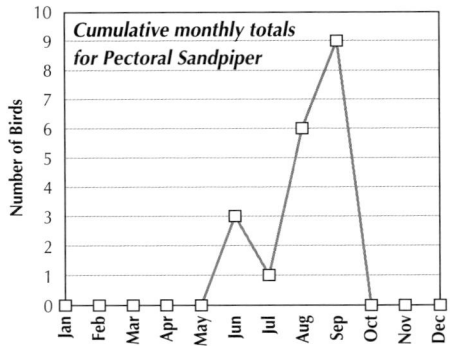

Cumulative monthly totals for Pectoral Sandpiper

The majority of birds occur between late August and late September, although there have been records in June and July. This is consistent with the species' occurrence in Britain.

Pectoral Sandpiper *by J. P. Smith*

The Loch of Strathbeg has accounted for 11 of the 17 records in the North East. The only other site to have more than a single record is Meikle Loch. This pattern of occurrence on coastal freshwater bodies is to be expected of this species.

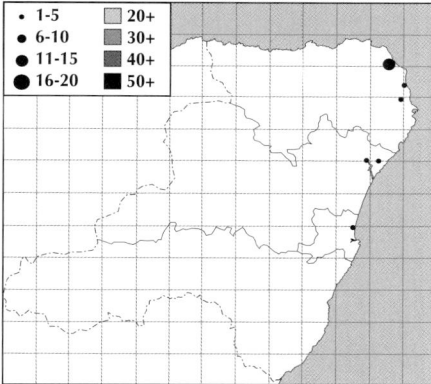

Pectoral Sandpiper sightings

ALL RECORDS

1867 2 Oct **Donmouth** an immature bird, shot
1973 21-25 Sep **Strathbeg**
1974 17 Sep **Strathbeg**
1976 10 Sep **Meikle**
1977 21 Aug **Strathbeg**
1977 3 Sep **Meikle**
1978 30 Sep **Donmouth**
1982 21 Sep **Ythan**
1982 25-29 Sep **Meikle** probably the above bird
1986 28 Sep **Ythan**
1989 26-28 Jun **Strathbeg**
1990 6-10 Jun **Strathbeg**
1990 4 Aug **Strathbeg** juvenile
1990 1-2 Sep **Annachie Lagoon** juvenile
1991 25-27 Aug **Kinloch**
1992 11 Jun **Strathbeg**
1992 19-20 Aug **Strathbeg** (2) one remained until 21 Aug
1993 21-22 Jul **Strathbeg** adult
1993 29 Aug **Strathbeg** juvenile
1996 28 Sept-4 Oct **Kinloch** juvenile

Broad-billed Sandpiper *Limicola falcinellus*

Breeds from Scandinavia eastwards to Siberia. Winters in south Asia and Australasia. European birds winter along the coasts from the Arabian peninsula and East Africa to western India, and possibly in the eastern Mediterranean (Tucker and Heath 1994).

It is perhaps surprising that this species, which breeds as close as northern Scandinavia, has only been recorded 22 times in Scotland. The majority of these records are from the eastern counties in May and June.

There have been only two records of this species from North East Scotland, both in the last week of May. The first record, in 1974, occurred in the south of the region, on the Angus border.

ALL RECORDS

1974 25 May **River North Esk Mouth** (N K.Atkinson) (*BB* 68: RR)
1988 30 May-3 Jun **Ythan** (A.Simmons *et al.*) (*BB* 82: RR)

Buff-breasted Sandpiper *Tryngites subruficollis*

Breeds in Alaska and north west Canada, wintering in northern Argentina and Uruguay.

The first reliable record for Scotland was in 1957, when a bird occurred in Lanarkshire (Thom 1986). There were only three further records in Scotland up to 1970, but since 1971 they have been almost annual.

There is a single record from last century reported by Sim (1903). This involved a specimen shot on the Ythan in the 'second week of August, 1862'.

There were no further records until 1977, when remarkably three birds appeared together at the Loch of Strathbeg. There have been only two subsequent records of this species.

ALL RECENT RECORDS
1977 18 Sep *Strathbeg* (3) (C.Rutter, M.J.Whitehouse) (*BB* 71: RR)
1989 10-14 Sep *Ythan* (S.M.Parsons, E.A.Parsons, B.J.Stewart)
1993 4 Sep *Strathbeg* (J.Dick, T.W.Marshall, I.M.Phillips, S.A.Reeves)

Great Snipe *Gallinago media*

Breeds in Scandinavia and from Poland eastwards to western Siberia. Winters in Africa, south of the Sahara.

Baxter and Rintoul (1953) note around 50 records of this species for Scotland, the majority of which BBRC find unacceptable (Thom 1986). Between 1958 and 1994 there were only 28 birds recorded in Scotland, all bar one from Orkney, Shetland and Fair Isle.

The earliest record of this species occurs in the *New Statistical Account of Scotland* (1845) where a possible specimen is noted from Banff. Sim (1903) notes it to be an occasional visitor to Dee, but mentions only three records. A bird was '...sent from Strathbeg along with some other birds...' around 1839 or 1840. One was shot at Aberdour but no date is given and a further bird was 'obtained' on the estate of Durris in October 1870. This last bird was described as a fine adult

male (*ASNH* Vol. 1: 154). There is another record of a bird shot in Aberdeenshire in late October 1878 (*Field* 1878: 548, in Naylor 1996). Sim (1903) makes no reference to this bird.

There are similarly few records for this century. One is reported to have been shot at the mouth of the Ythan, 5th September 1905 (*Zool.* 1905: 466, Witherby and Ticehurst 1907-08, *TAWMNH Soc.* 1901-06). A further record was of one at Drum, Aberdeenshire on 3rd November 1922 (*Scot. Nat.* 1923-24).

An intriguing record involves a bird in 1934. A Mr Carnie stated that while 'visiting a friend in Cheshire....he received from a game dealer in

Manchester a specimen of this bird, which after skinning, examining and sexing he sent for preservation. On enquiries we learned that it had been consigned with other game from I.M.Chalmers, Kinloch, St Fergus, Peterhead. It was received on 19th September and from its fresh condition could only have been killed about two days previously. The bird weighed 8 and one half ounces and proved to be a male.' The bird had been shot near Peterhead (*Scot. Nat.* 1935).

'Dowitcher' sp.

There has been one record of a bird not specifically assigned to either Long-billed Dowitcher or Short-billed Dowitcher.

ALL RECORDS
1971 12 Oct *Mouth of the North Esk*

Long-billed Dowitcher *Limnodromus scolopaceus*

Breeds in north east Siberia and north west Alaska. Winters in the United States and Central America.

The first record for Scotland occurred in Fife in 1867. Subsequently there have been only 22 specifically identified as this species in Scotland, all between 1969 and 1994 (Evans 1994, Rogers *et al.* 1992, 1993, 1994 and 1995).

There have been only two records of this Nearctic species in the North East region, one in spring and one in autumn.

ALL RECORDS
1980 11-12 May *Meikle Loch* (M.V.Bell, R.Elliot et al.) (*BB* 74: RR)
1995 22 Oct-21 Feb *North Esk, St Cyrus* (R Goater, M.S.Scott) (*BB* 89: RR)

Long-billed Dowitcher *by M. Langman*

**Hudsonian Godwit
with Black-tailed Godwits**
by M. Langman

Hudsonian Godwit *Limosa haemastica*

Breeds in northern North America. Winters in Argentina.

There has been only one record of this American wader, the first for Scotland and only the fourth for Britain.

ALL RECORDS
1988 26 Sept *Slains area, nr Collieston*
(J.Cooper, R.Duncan) (*BB* 83: RR)

Eskimo Curlew *Numenius borealis*

Breeds in northern Canada. Winters in the extreme south of Brazil south to Argentina.

There have been only seven records of this species in Britain, three of which occurred in the North East region. These records are all from the mid to late 1800s.

This species is now almost extinct and is unlikely to occur again.

ALL RECORDS
1855 6 Sep *Durris Estate, Kincardineshire* shot
1878 28 Sep *Slains, Aberdeenshire* shot
1880 21 Sep *Forest of Birse, Aberdeenshire*

Marsh Sandpiper *Tringa stagnatilis*

Breeds from Bulgaria and Romania, discontinuously east through Kazakhstan and eastern Asia. Winters in Africa, south of the Sahara, in southern Asia and Australia.

There have been only six Scottish records of this elegant wader, with only a single record for the North East region.

ALL RECORDS
1990 15-16 May *Cotehill Loch* also on Meikle Loch (C.Barton, A.G.Clarke *et al.*) (*BB* 86: RR)

Greater Yellowlegs *Tringa melanoleuca*

Breeds in northern North America. Winters in the United States south to southern South America.

There have been only five records of this species in Scotland. The single record for the North East region was the second for Scotland and the first for the Scottish mainland. The bird was in first-winter plumage, and was initially found on the Ythan in October 1957. Unfortunately the bird was later found dead.

ALL RECORDS
1957 25 Oct *Ythan* (J.G.Harrison)

Lesser Yellowlegs *Tringa flavipes*

Breeds in northern North America. Winters in the United States south to southern South America.

There have been only 21 records of this species in Scotland, since the first in 1910. There have been six records of, probably, only five individuals in the North East region. Surprisingly, there have been two records in each of three years. Four records were in autumn and one in spring. The majority of records are of short-staying birds, but in 1980 an individual spent three and a half months, from 17th January to 23rd April, at Cairnbulg, near Fraserburgh.

ALL RECORDS
1978 29 Sep *Rattray* immature (S.Howie, T.D.H.Merrie) (*BB* 73: RR)
1978 7 Oct *Ythan* immature (R.J.Miller) (*BB* 73: RR)
1980 17 Jan-23 Apr *Cairnbulg, nr Fraserburgh* (R.B.Cardno, J.Dunbar, S.Palmer) (*BB* 74: RR)
1980 6 Aug *Ythan* (S.North) (*BB* 74: RR)
1992 18-19 May *Cults Pool, Aberdeen* (D.J.Bain, L.T.A.Brain, K.D.Shaw *et al.*) (*BB* 86: RR)
1992 15 Aug *Strathbeg* (J.Dunbar, J.D.Poyner) (*BB* 86: RR)

Wilson's Phalarope *Phalaropus tricolor*

Breeds in North America. Winters in South America from Peru south to Argentina and Chile.

The first record for Britain occurred in Fife in 1954 and since that date there have been only 24 further records of this species in Scotland.

There has been only one record of this trans-Atlantic vagrant in the North East region, a single bird found on Cotehill Loch on 17th September 1984.

ALL RECORDS
1984 17-22 Sep *Cotehill Loch* (G.F.Bell, A.Nichol, A.Stalker *et al.*) (*BB* 78: RR)

Red-necked Phalarope *Phalaropus lobatus*

Breeds throughout the Arctic regions. The majority of the Western Palearctic population is held by Iceland and Sweden. There is a small breeding population in Shetland. European birds winter in the Arabian Sea.

Historical reports of this species are few, although Harvie-Brown (1906) and others considered that the species may have had a wide mainland distribution up to the early 19th century (Holloway 1996). In the paper *The Birds of Aberdeen and Links* (*Scot. Nat.* 1885-86) they were described as 'occasional to Aberdeenshire' and in *The Vertebrate Fauna of Dee* (Sim 1903) only four specimens are noted between 1846 and 1870.

1846 NA *Aberdeen*
1853 27 Oct *Fraserburgh* shot, female
1870 15 Sep *Old Aberdeen Links* shot
1870 18 Sep *Old Aberdeen Links* shot

In more recent times, despite there being a small British breeding population on Shetland, the number of records for this species in the region is still small. There were only nine birds between 1976 and 1996.

The majority of records have been in September (five birds), with three in June, and one in April.

ALL RECENT RECORDS
1976 10 Sep *Donmouth*
1978 12 Jun *Strathbeg*
1979 25 Apr *Fraserburgh*
1979 30 Jun *Meikle*
1979 1-3 Sep *Donmouth*
1980 27-28 Sep *Meikle*
1984 30 Jun *Meikle* adult female
1991 14 Sep *Ythan* (2) with 1 still present on 15th

Grey Phalarope *Phalaropus fulicarius*

Breeds circumpolar within the Arctic Circle. The major wintering grounds are at sea off Chile and western Africa.

The earliest note for the region is by Edward (1854) in his *Birds of Strathbeg*. He notes that it had occurred there as a rare visitor but gave no specific records. In the paper on *The Birds of Aberdeen and Links* (*Scot. Nat.* 1885–86) they were reported as only occasional. Sim (1903) gives only two records;

1866 1 Nov *Tileburn, nr Donmouth* killed
1876 23-24 Dec *Oldtown Links, Aberdeen* (1) killed during gales

There is a further single record for the early part of this century.

1903 8 Dec *Aberdeen harbour* caught (*TAWMNH Soc.* V11: 901-06)

Between 1960 and 1996 there have been only 14 records of 15 birds. All but one of the records fall, typically, between August and February. There has been one record from May. Most records refer to single birds, but two were present on the Ythan on 28 August, 1979. No one site has had significantly more records than any other, but birds have been recorded in three of the last four years from Fraserburgh.

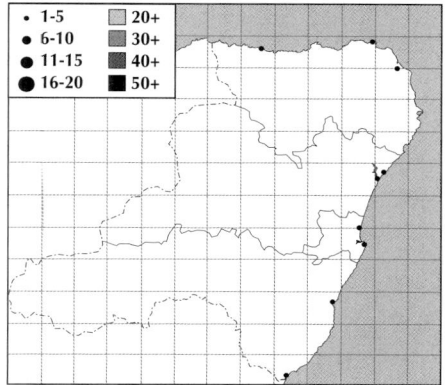

• 1-5		☐ 20+	
• 6-10		☐ 30+	
● 11-15		■ 40+	
● 16-20		■ 50+	

Grey Phalarope sightings

ALL RECENT RECORDS

1960 29 Aug *Donmouth* one resting on the sand with terns
1975 19 May *Kinnaber* female
1977 31 Jul *Strathbeg*
1978 3 Dec-7 Jan *Whitehills*
1979 17-20 Feb *Collieston*
1979 28 Aug *Ythan* (2)
1988 4 Dec *Fraserburgh*
1989 11-13 Aug *Waulkmill, Ythan*
1990 18-24 Sep *Strathbeg*
1991 29 Oct *Girdleness*
1993 18-23 Jan *Fraserburgh*
1995 22 Jan *Stonehaven*
1995 4 Feb *Fraserburgh*
1996 12-21 Jan *Fraserburgh*
1996 17-20 Nov *Fraserburgh*

Grey Phalarope *by M. Langman*

Long-tailed Skua *Stercorarius longicaudus*

A circumpolar breeder in the high Arctic. Winters in the Atlantic and eastern Pacific.

In the British Isles the Long-tailed Skua is a scarce passage migrant. The species was an official national rarity until 1979, based on an average of less than 100 records per year. During the late 1970s the status of this species was changed when spring movements were discovered off the Western Isles. A record 1,340 were recorded moving north off Balranald, North Uist between 12th and 21st May 1991 (Davenport 1992). Away from this site, spring records are scarce. Movements of birds in the autumn are more regular, particularly from North Sea coasts, peaking in September (Dymond *et al.* 1989).

The earliest records of this species are given by Sim (1903) under the name Buffon's Skua. A bird was shot inland on Bennachie in 1880, another at Netherdale on the Deveron in 1881 and the last killed at Fyvie on 2nd October 1890.

There are similarly few records for the early part of this century. A bird was shot at New Pitsligo in May 1903, and another shot at the Mains of Auchreddie, New Deer, on 19th May 1913. Surprisingly, these are the only spring records for this region.

During the 1970s and early 1980s small numbers of birds were seen in all but four years. The best year of this period was 1976 when 12 birds were seen. Numbers increased dramatically from the late 1980s. In 1988, 15 birds were seen from seawatching points but a flock of 32 was seen from a boat just off Aberdeen. This was a small portion of the 1,358 birds recorded in Britain that year. This was followed by unprecedented numbers seen in 1991. There were 193 birds off seawatching points in the North East region (more than all previous years added together), dominated by records from Girdleness. Several of these birds

Long-tailed Skua *by M. Langman*

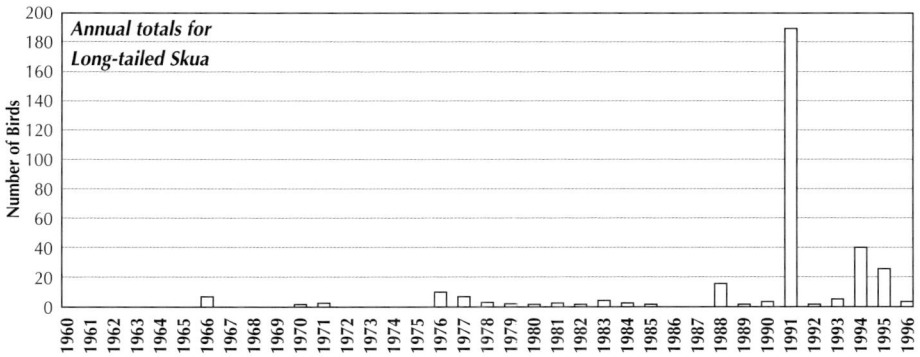

Annual totals for Long-tailed Skua

were seen to pass inland up the River Dee. This was again part of huge numbers in British waters (5,350 birds recorded). Three years later in 1994 there was another influx with 43 birds seen in the region. Surprisingly this was followed by another influx in 1995 when more than 25 birds were seen.

The reasons behind these recent huge influxes into the North Sea, and the variation from year to year, must be complex. Speculation often revolves around the breeding cycles of the Lemming *Lemmus lemmus*, which forms a major part of the diet of Long-tailed Skuas. A good breeding season for the Skuas must be an important factor in the eventual numbers seen in the North Sea, but the North East records have been largely of adult birds, with very few juveniles noted during the large passage movements. It is likely, therefore, that weather and even hydrographic conditions also play a part in why the birds enter the North Sea in large numbers in some years.

The last two weeks of August and the first two weeks of September are the most productive for this species, although records from late September and early October are not unusual. There have been small numbers of records from June, July and November. The premier site for this species is Girdleness, with most seawatchers congregating here during passage periods. Moderate numbers of birds have been seen from Fraserburgh and Peterhead.

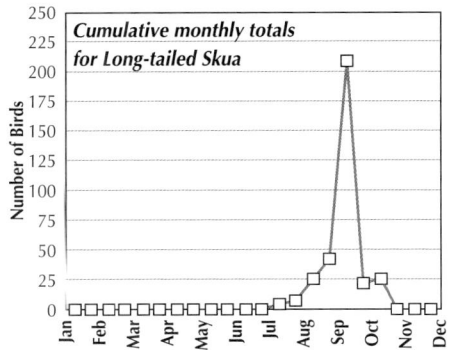

Cumulative monthly totals for Long-tailed Skua

Mediterranean Gull _Larus melanocephalus_

A localised breeder in Europe, principally around the Black Sea coasts and sporadically as far north as the Baltic Sea and British Isles. There is an established population in the Netherlands. Birds winter around the Mediterranean, Black Sea, the Atlantic and North Sea (Tucker and Heath 1994).

This species was first recorded in Scotland in 1957, when two individuals frequented Fair Isle. The next two records for Scotland came from the North East region, with individuals in 1972 and 1975, both from Girdleness. Since 1975 the species has been annual in Scotland in increasing numbers. There have been records of this species in the North East region every year since 1981.

The actual number of birds that have occurred in the region is complicated by long staying, wandering and/or returning individuals. The Donmouth in Aberdeen is by far and away the most regular site. The first record from this site was in 1982-83 when an adult and a first-winter roosted here. Since this time at least one bird has been present in the roost every winter. This bird is probably responsible for many of the records from Girdleness and possibly even the bird in Dyce in 1993. Careful ageing of individuals is important in assessing the number of birds present in any one year, and to date a maximum of three individuals have been present in any one year.

Away from Aberdeen, birds of varying ages have been seen at several sites, including Banff in the north west of the region, Fraserburgh and Peterhead. Inland records have occurred at Kemnay (1988), Loch of Skene (1993 and 1996),

Mediterranean Gull _by M. Langman_

Ord Dam (1993) and Dyce (1991 and 1993-94). An adult bird was seen in the large Common Gull colony in the Correen Hills in 1988, but breeding was not attempted/proven.

Records are concentrated in the winter period between October and March, with fewer records in April and only two from May.

Sabine's Gull *Larus sabini*

Breeds in Greenland, Arctic North America and north east Siberia. Winters at sea off western Africa and the Pacific coast of the Americas.

There are several old records for Scotland from the last century (Baxter and Rintoul 1953). There were only seven in the first part of this century, but since 1972 the species has been annual in Scotland in small numbers (Thom 1986).

The first record for the region was as recent as 1976, when a single bird passed Fraserburgh in October. In the following three years a further five records came from this site, with none elsewhere in the region. This hold was broken during the 1980s when three records came from Peterhead and singles from Rattray and Girdleness. There have been only five records of probably six birds in the 1990s.

Most records have been of single birds seen on seawatches, but a moulting bird was found among roosting Common Gulls on the Ythan in 1990 and an adult and juvenile were at Fraserburgh on 25 October 1996.

The majority of birds are seen in September and October, with single records in June, July and November.

ALL RECORDS
1976 28 Oct *Fraserburgh*
1977 7 Sep *Fraserburgh*
1977 31 Oct *Fraserburgh*
1978 15 Oct *Fraserburgh*
1978 18 Oct *Fraserburgh*
1979 11 Jan *Fraserburgh*
1984 2 Sep *Peterhead* juvenile
1984 17 Nov *Peterhead* juvenile
1987 17 Sep *Peterhead* juvenile
1987 26 Sep *Girdleness* juvenile, found by the observers looking for the Ross's Gull
1987 22 Oct *Rattray* adult
1990 19 Sep *Peterhead* juvenile
1990 30 Sep *Waulkmill, Ythan* an adult moulting from summer to winter plumage was in the gull roost
1995 9-12 June *Girdleness* first-summer
1995 6 Jul *Girdleness* adult
1996 17-31 Oct *Kinnaird* juvenile with adult on 25th

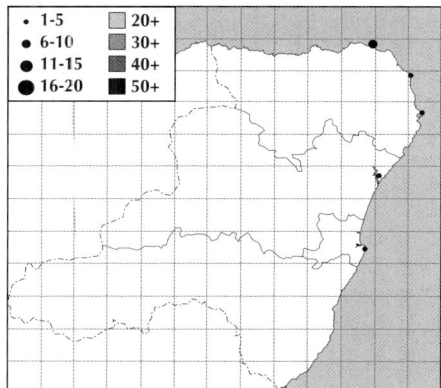

- 1-5   □ 20+
- 6-10   □ 30+
- 11-15 ■ 40+
- 16-20 ■ 50+

Sabine's Gull sightings

Ring-billed Gull Larus delawarensis

Breeds in North America, primarily around the Great Lakes and Canadian Prairies. Winters in the coastal areas of the USA and Mexico.

The discovery of a second-winter bird on the Ythan in 1976, was not only the first for the region but also for Scotland. Since 1981 there has been an increase in records of this species in Scotland, although this has not been on the scale of the rest of Britain.

There have been only six records for the North East region, the majority in either January or February.

ALL RECORDS

1976 14 Feb **Ythan** second winter (R.H.Hogg) (*BB* 70: RR)
1992 8 Jan **Donmouth** first winter (P.D.Bloor)
1993 6 Feb **Murcar** adult (G.M.Buchanan)
1995 29 Jul **Donmouth** second winter (C.Cronin)
1996 2 Nov **Donmouth** adult winter (S.Sharp, A.Hachenberg, J.Barker) (subject to acceptance)
1997 18 Feb **Strathbeg** adult winter (T.W.Marshall)

Kumlein's Gull Larus glaucoides kumleinii

Breeds in north east Canada. This subspecies is largely sedentary, but small numbers winter along the Atlantic coasts of North America.

There had been only seven accepted records of this subspecies in Britain up to the end of 1993 (Evans 1994, Rogers *et al.* 1991, 1992, 1993). In 1994 at least six were seen in Shetland. Since the first record for the North East in 1985 there have been annual records, of probably the same adult individual, from the Banff–MacDuff area during the winter months.

ALL RECORDS OF INITIAL SIGHTINGS

1985 17 Mar **Banff, MacDuff**
1986 15-20 Mar **Banff, MacDuff**
1986 25-26 Dec **Banff, MacDuff**
1987 14 Mar **Banff, MacDuff**
1987 30 Dec **Banff, MacDuff**
1988 5 April **Banff, MacDuff**
1989 12 April **Banff, MacDuff**
1990 5 Jan **Banff, MacDuff**
1991 5 Jan **Banff, MacDuff**
1993 23 Mar **Banff, MacDuff**
1994 4 Jan **Banff, MacDuff**
1995 7 Jan **Banff, MacDuff**

Ross's Gull *Rhodostethia rosea*

Breeds in north east Siberia, wintering in the Arctic Ocean.

The first Scottish record was on Shetland in 1936, and since then fewer than 30 have been recorded in Scotland. There have been three records of five birds in the North East region, all adults. The first was a single adult in September 1987, one of the earliest autumn records in Britain. The second record in 1993 was unprecedented, with the first multiple record of Ross's Gulls in Britain. Between 18th and 30th January three individuals were present, although only two were ever seen flying together.

ALL RECORDS

1987 26-28 Sep *Girdleness* (K.D.Shaw, K.A.Shaw *et al.*)

1993 18-30 Jan *Fraserburgh* 3 individuals, last record 30 Jan (A.G.Clarke, P.S.Crockett, A.W.Thorpe, R.Noble-Nesbitt) (*BB* 87: RR)

1997 31 Jan-10 Feb *Fraserburgh* (K.Buchan) (subject to acceptance)

Ross's Gulls *by M. Langman*

Ivory Gull *Pagophila eburnea*

Breeds throughout the Arctic and winters in the Arctic Ocean.

This species of the high Arctic is a rare visitor to Scotland and Evans (1994) notes only 42 'authenticated' records up to 1959, and only a further 23 until the end of 1990 in Scotland.

There are several records for the North East region from the last century (not considered by Evans 1994). The earliest note occurs in the *Zoologist* Vol. 5, of a bird shot at Banff in January 1847. This bird had apparently been seen in the company of two Iceland Gulls for several weeks. Gray (1871) noted that Thomas Edward listed one from Gardenstown in December 1860. Sim (1903) records ten birds killed in the area, including four killed on the Ythan in 1894:

1874 17 Nov **Aberdeen Harbour** (2) immature, shot
1894 9 Nov **Rosehearty** immature, shot
1894 December **Ythan** (4) killed
1895 13 Jan **Fraserburgh** adult, 'caught'
1896 January **Pennan** immature, killed

The only record from the early part of this century was of a bird obtained near Banff around 1908 (A.Knox *pers. comm.*).

Baxter and Rintoul (1953) commented that 'more occurrences have been recorded from the east than from the west and Aberdeen is the mainland county whence most of the records come'.

There have been only two recent records of this species in the area. The first was amazingly first seen coming to scraps of bread, with Black-headed Gulls, in a Westhill garden in January 1976. The bird was trapped, ringed and released. The last record referred to a bird picked up, unfortunately with only one wing, on the beach at Cairnbulg in 1991. The bird was taken into care and later died.

ALL RECENT RECORDS
1976 29 Dec-3 Jan **Westhill** (R.Rae *et al.*)
(*BB* 71: RR)
1991 29 Dec **Cairnbulg** first-winter picked up injured (L.T.A.Brain, Mrs M.Buchan *et al.*)
(*BB* 86: RR)

Ivory Gull
by M. Langman

Caspian Tern *Sterna caspia*

Breeds on the Baltic and Black Sea coasts, Tunisia and discontinuously east to Manchuria and south to southern Africa, Australia and New Zealand. Also present in North America. The western Palearctic population winters mainly in west Africa. The population in Scandinavia around the Baltic is currently declining (Tucker and Heath 1994).

The first record for Scotland was as recent as 1968, and since then there have been only 17 birds in Scotland up to the end of 1994 (Evans 1994, Rogers *et al.* 1991, 1992, 1993, 1994). The first record for the North East was at the Loch of Strathbeg in 1974. This was the fourth for Scotland, and at that time the farthest north the species had been recorded in Britain. Remarkably a single bird was seen at the Ythan in 1975 and 1976. These are the only records for the region and may have related to a returning individual.

The records were between June and August, which is typical of this species in Britain.

ALL RECORDS
1974 13 Aug ***Strathbeg*** 4th Scottish record (J.Dunbar) (*BB* 68: RR)
1975 25 Jun ***Ythan*** 5th Scottish record (A.H.Cuthbert) (*BB* 69: RR)
1976 25 Jul ***Ythan*** 7th Scottish record (P.M.Ellis, C.J.Spray, L.Steele) (*BB* 71: RR)

Roseate Tern *Sterna dougallii*

Breeds in north west Europe, southern Africa and through the Indian Ocean as far as Australasia. Also in the Americas. The small European population winters off north west Africa.

The current British population is estimated at fewer than 90 pairs and is in steady decline (Gibbons *et al.* 1993). The closest, regular breeding birds to this region are in the Firth of Forth, yet this species remains very scarce in the North East.

There is a single record by Thomas Edward (1854), who reports having shot a bird at Strathbeg in 1849. Sim (1903) thought that this record required confirmation and gave no other records for the region. There are few records for the early part of this century, and it is not until the late 1960s and 1970s that this species was reported with any regularity. Between 1968 and 1994, only 33 birds were reported, and they are less than annual. In any year it unusual for more than two birds to be seen and most records are of single birds on passage, with two birds reported on four occasions. Four birds were at the Loch of Strathbeg in 1979. In 1975 there were five birds seen and in 1979 up to nine birds were recorded.

All records have fallen between May and early September, with small peaks in May and August. There is no one site that this species favours, with records coming most often from sites holding numbers of breeding Common *Sterna hirundo* and Arctic Terns *Sterna paradisaea* such as the Ythan area, St Fergus, St Cyrus and the Strathbeg area.

Breeding has been suspected on at least two occasions, and an adult and two juveniles were seen at the St Fergus ternery in July 1989. In several springs, birds have also been seen at the St Cyrus ternery.

There has been only one inland record of this species, referring to a corpse in a Peregrine eyrie in May 1975.

Forster's Tern *Sterna forsteri*

Breeds on freshwater marshes in North America, from the prairies of Canada, Maryland and Wisconsin in the north, to California and Texas in the south. Birds winter along the Pacific coast from California to Guatamala, and on the Atlantic coast from Virginia to the Gulf of Mexico.

The first record of this species in Scotland came in October–November 1985, when a first-winter bird appeared off Musselburgh. Strangely the second record for Scotland was also a first-winter at Musselburgh in December 1994. This bird stayed into 1995 and is thought to be the individual that appeared on the Ythan as a first-summer bird in May 1995. As such this became the first bird to summer in Scotland (last seen on 1st August) and was the farthest north this species had been recorded in Britain.

ALL RECORDS
1995 3 May-1 Aug *Ythan* first-summer (P.Doyle, R.McGregor *et al.*) (*BB* 89: RR)

Bridled Tern *Sterna anaethetus*

Breeds in the Caribbean and Central America, west Africa, and from the Red Sea through the Indian Ocean to Australia.

There have been only three records of this species in Scotland, the bird from the Ythan on 2nd August 1988 being the second. This bird is thought to have been the one seen in Northumberland during July, and then again in late August (Evans 1994).

ALL RECORDS
1988 2 Aug *Ythan* (A.J.M.Smith) (*BB* 83: RR)

Black Tern *Chlidonias niger*

Breeds on freshwater marshes throughout western Eurasia, from southern Sweden and France eastwards. Winters in tropical Africa.

Sim (1903) notes only two records for the last century. One was shot on the Ythan in October 1866, and another in summer plumage was shot at the Donmouth in April 1867. There is also an undated record from the Donmouth (*Scot. Nat.* 1885-86).

There are few notes for the early part of this century. A full summer bird was seen on the River Deveron, above Huntly, on 9th May 1945 (*Brit. Birds* Vol. 38). Baxter and Rintoul (1953) noted 'this tern occurs chiefly in southern Scotland....but has been noted in....Kincardine and Aberdeen...', giving no further details.

Since 1963 this species has been seen regularly in the North East region. Numbers vary greatly from year to year, with no records in some years and a maximum of 18 in 1971. There are records from late April through to mid-October. Spring passage is generally less pronounced than autumn, with a small peak of records in early May. Autumn passage is noted from late July, peaking markedly in August and early September.

The majority of records are of one or two birds, mainly from coastal locations.

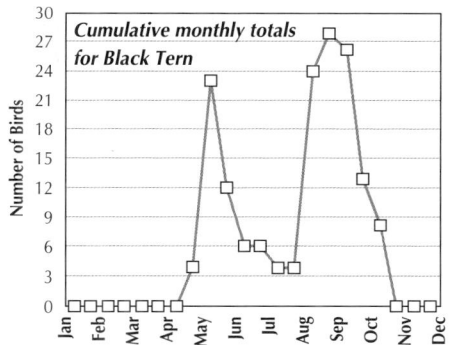

Cumulative monthly totals for Black Tern

Black Terns
by M. Langman

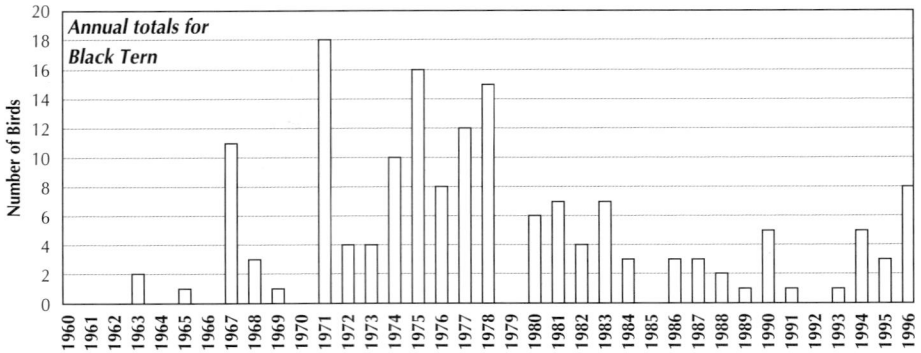

Annual totals for Black Tern

Small flocks of between three and five birds are noted in some years (five at Cruden Bay in 1967, five at Gourdon in 1974 and five at Strathbeg in 1975). The largest flock, numbering eight birds, was surprisingly reported from Loch Davan, 40 miles inland, on 7th May 1971.

Birds may appear anywhere along the coast, particularly the east coast, or on freshwater bodies close to the coast.

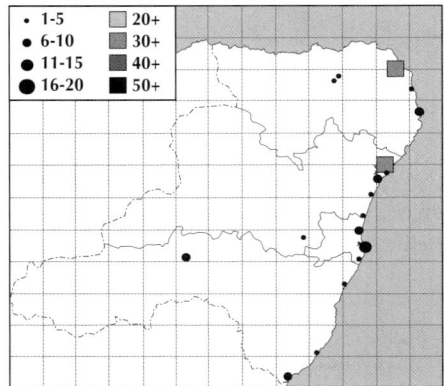

Black Tern sightings

White-winged Black Tern Chlidonias leucopterus

Breeds in Hungary and Bulgaria, eastwards through Asia to China. The western Palearctic population winters in Africa south of the Sahara.

Since the first record for Scotland in 1964, there had been only 17 reports up to the end of 1983 (Thom 1986). The first record for the North East region was in 1967 (one of four in Scotland that year), and there have been six subsequent records in the area. The majority of these have been in spring. There has been one record for July and one in September. All records have been of single adult birds, except for a probable second-summer bird at Meikle Loch in 1989.

ALL RECORDS

1967 21-28 Jun **Meikle** (R.Donaldson et al.) (BB 61: RR)

1973 26 Sep **Ythan** (M.J.Grigson, A.Parker) (BB 67: RR)

1975 25 May **Meikle** (M.A.Macdonald et al.) (BB 69: RR)

1987 23-26 May **Meikle** (A.Webb et al.) (BB 81: RR)

1989 25-26 Jun **Meikle** (R.D.Steele et al.) (BB 83: RR)

1991 14-22 Jul **Annachie lagoon** adult (T.W.Marshall et al.) (BB 85: RR)

1992 23 May **Strathbeg** (K.Munday et al.) (BB 86: RR)

Brünnich's Guillemot Uria lomvia

Breeds on Arctic coasts and islands, wintering at sea in the same areas.

This species is extremely rare in Britain, with Scotland having had the majority of records. Live birds are even rarer: most reports have been of tideline corpses.

The first record for the North East region is given by Sim (1903). He recorded that it 'had been found in June 1893, amongst a number of Common Guillemots that had got caught and were drowned in the Salmon nets at Belhelvie.' This record is not amongst those considered as acceptable by later authors (Thom 1986).

There have been three recent records of tideline corpses. Two records were in winter, while the 1978 bird occurred in July and was found 'freshly dead'.

ALL RECENT RECORDS
1978 14 Jul **St Cyrus** retained in Dundee Museum
1979 25 Feb **Rattray** head and upper neck in Aberdeen University Museum
1981 25 Jan **Johnshaven**

Pallas's Sandgrouse Syrrhaptes paradoxus

Breeds from the Kirgiz and Aral-Caspian steppes east to Manchuria. Partially migratory, wintering in south of the breeding range. Occasionally irruptive.

In the last century there were two notable influxes of this species, the first in 1863 and the second in 1888. In both years good numbers of birds were present in the North East region.

Gray (1871) records that in 1863, 15 were seen near Stonehaven on 25th May. There were also records for Aberdeen Links (*TAWMNH Soc.* 1906–16). Sim (1903) reported that a number of specimens were obtained in this irruption, but that by the end of the summer '...those of them that had escaped being shot had again taken their departure'.

The irruption in May 1888 was on a larger scale, with an estimated 2,000 birds reaching Scotland during this irruption (Thom 1986). Sim (1903) noted 'vast numbers landed on the eastern coast of Scotland – the county of Aberdeen being specially favoured...' This was also reported by Baxter and Rintoul (1953) who said '...they were numerous in many places, they were specially abundant in Aberdeenshire...'

Sim (1903) recorded that they took up residence on sandy ground between Mennie and the Sands of Forvie, with birds also present on the back bar at the Loch of Strathbeg. Many birds were seen and obtained throughout the whole of the eastern side of the region, most being taken just after the arrival. Many were seen in the parish of Fyvie, and identity was proved on 26th May when two males and four females were shot from a flock of about 50 birds on the Waggle Hill, Monquhitter. Sim (1903) reported that 'as the season wore on, the birds collected in packs upon such ground as that mentioned above'. By the autumn all the birds had departed this region.

Scops Owl *Otus scops*

Breeds in France, Iberia and north west Africa east to Japan and Indonesia. Much of the European population winters in Africa south of the Sahara.

There are only two records of this species for the North East region. The first record was of a female found dead at Kintore on 2nd September 1891. Its stomach was crammed with earwigs and beetles (Sim 1903). The second record was of a bird caught on a trawler, 25 miles off the Aberdeenshire coast. This record is included for interest but is not considered for the North East List.

ALL RECORDS
1891 2 Sep *Kintore* female found dead
(**1900** Oct caught on a trawler 25 miles off the Aberdeenshire coast)

Snowy Owl *Nyctea scandiaca*

Breeds in the Arctic, from Iceland and Scandinavia east to Siberia, Alaska, Canada and Greenland. Partially migratory and occasionally erupts southward. Has bred in Shetland in small numbers.

Snowy Owls have been known to visit Scotland, in small numbers and at irregular intervals, since the early 19th century (Thom 1986). Many of the records between 1950 and 1962 came from the Grampians and Cairngorms.

The earliest record of this species for the region is given by Sim (1903), who noted 'A specimen of this noble bird was picked up dead upon the Loch of Strathbeg about 1824'. Sim (1903) also lists a bird shot in Glennochty, in 1851 and another in 1864, shot at Rora, Longside. An adult female was shot on the Glenbervie estate, but Sim gave no date. The last listed by Sim, was of a sight record in November 1867, from the Hill of Cruden.

A bird is reported from Strichen in the winter of 1862 (*ASNH* Vol. 8), but this record was strangely not included in those given by Sim (1903).

Early this century there is a single record of a bird, thought to have been this species, seen at Port Errol, Cruden Bay, on 7th September 1918 (*Scot. Nat.* 1917–18).

Since the 1950s there have been irregular sightings of birds on the Cairngorm/Ben Macdhui Plateau (recorded in at least 14 years between 1963 and 1992). These birds wander around the whole area and probably enter several counties. It is uncertain how many individuals are involved. During 1975–88 at least one adult male, a young male and two females have been recorded in the Cairngorm mountains. Away from this area there have been two records from the Cairn O'Mount, Glen Dye area (1959 and 1960), two from the Glen Esk area on the Angus/Kincardine border (1958 and 1961), and single records from Bennachie (1988) and Corse Maol, between Huntly and Dufftown (1958).

In early May 1991, a female was located in a coastal field at St Fergus. The bird was feeding on rabbits shot by the local farmer.

In July 1992, a bird was taken into care from a Spanish trawler in Aberdeen Harbour. The bird had landed on the boat 200 miles off the Newfoundland coast. It was later released in upper Donside, and was still present in late November.

Snowy Owl
by M. Langman

Hawk Owl *Surnia ulula*

Breeds from Scandinavia eastwards to north west Siberia, Alaska and Canada. Dispersive and occasionally eruptive in winter.

There have been only five records of this species in Scotland (Evans 1994, Rogers *et al*. 1992, 1993, 1994, 1995). The fourth record for Scotland came from Gight in Aberdeenshire, where an adult female was shot on 21st November 1898.

ALL RECORDS
1898 21 Nov *Gight, Aberdeenshire* adult female shot

Little Owl *Athene noctua*

Widely distributed in Europe south of the Baltic, into north Africa and eastwards through southern Russia to central Asia. The British population was introduced during the 19th century, and is largely confined to England. Breeding in Scotland was first proven in Berwickshire, in 1958. There is now a very small breeding population in Scotland, although exact numbers are difficult to estimate.

The first record for the North East came in 1902, when a female was shot on 1st February at Blairs. The bird was said to be in excellent condition and had part of a Starling in its stomach (*ASNH* 1902). Sim (1903) thought that there was evidence that the bird was an escape, but gave no further details.

There were no further records until another female was picked up injured at Rothienorman on 2nd April 1986. The bird unfortunately died the following day. The post-mortem revealed that the bird had active ovaries. The farmer who found the bird reported that two had been in the area the previous year.

The last record was of a live bird which, obligingly, spent two days in the hedge at the Loch of Strathbeg reserve visitors' centre in May 1991.

ALL RECORDS
1902 1 Feb *Blairs College, Deeside*
1986 2 Apr *Rothienorman*
1991 4-5 May *Strathbeg*

Tengmalm's Owl *Aegolius funereus*

Breeds in central and south east Europe and from Scandinavia east to north east Siberia, Alaska and Canada. Dispersive with the northern populations, occasionally irruptive.

There has been only one record for the North East region of this very rare vagrant. A female was killed on 3rd February 1886 at Peterhead (*Scot. Nat.* Vol. 8).

ALL RECORDS
1886 3 Feb ***Peterhead*** female killed

Nightjar *Caprimulgus europaeus*

Breeds widely across Eurasia, from south east Norway and southern Sweden and Finland to north west Africa. The European population winters in Africa south of the Sahara.

The British population is estimated at 3,000 churring males, primarily in southern England and the English Midlands (Gibbons *et al.* 1993). There is a small number breeding regularly in south west Scotland, but away from there, breeding or suspected breeding is irregular.

At one time the Nightjar was widespread and fairly common in open woodlands throughout much of Scotland (Thom 1986). The earliest notes for the North East occur in the *New Statistical Account of Scotland* (1845) where there are records of 'goatsucker' for Banff (occasional), Banchory-Ternan, Methlick, Strathdon (occasional), Peterhead and Fyvie.

Several authors make reference to Nightjars during the mid to late 1800s. MacGillivray (1855) recorded them from the lower parts of Birse, arriving about 20th May. He did not know of them occurring above Ballater in Deeside. Thomas Edward noted them calling while out moth-hunting near the Loch of Strathbeg (*Naturalist* 1857). Gray (1871) called it a 'common bird in almost every Scottish county from Wigtown to the north of Caithness'. Sim (1903) thought them to be more common in 'Dee' than generally supposed, due to the nocturnal habits of the species.

The species was undoubtedly still breeding in the region at the end of the 19th century, but was described as uncommon by Holloway (1996). During the early part of this century a young bird was shot accidently at Durris, Kincardineshire on 22nd August, 1914, and it was further noted that 'the bird is fairly common in Dee' (*Scot. Nat.* 1914).

During the 1930s numbers had started to decline in regions such as Speyside, and by the 1960s it was described as scarce in the north and west Highlands (Thom 1986). It seems likely that the population in the North East was also declining during these periods as during the period 1968-72, there were no breeding records for the area, although there were still records for neighbouring Moray and Nairn (Thom 1986). The Nightjar has since become very rare indeed in the North East region.

During the 1970s there was only one record. This was in 1977 when there was a spring record of a bird near Insch. It was not until 1990 that another bird was recorded. Unfortunately this had been

brought ashore from the BP Forties Platform, and was released at New Deer. Subsequently a bird was heard churring in early summer, at an inland site in 1995, but breeding was not suspected. Amazingly another bird appeared near the Ythan in May 1996. This bird displayed in the finder's garden for at least two evenings before departing.

ALL RECENT RECORDS
1977 Spring *Auchleven, near Insch*
(**1990** 5 Jun *BP Forties Platform* female found exhausted. Taken into care and released next day at New Deer)
1995 12-23 Jun *Inland site* location withheld
1996 23-24 May *Waulkmill area, River Ythan*

Alpine Swift *Apus melba*

Breeds from Iberia and north west Africa east to India. Also found in eastern and southern Africa. The western Palearctic population winters in Africa south of the Sahara.

Since the first record for Scotland in 1951 there have been only 33 records. The first of the three records for the North East region came in April 1970, and was typically a short-staying individual. The second record concerned a bird in the Banchory-Devenick area of lower Deeside in June 1981. This bird was seen for over five days before it departed. Another bird appeared at Greg Ness in October 1984, again only a short-stayer.

ALL RECORDS
1970 19 Apr *Rattray* (N.Elkins, J.Elkins, M.R.Williams) (*BB* 64: RR)
1981 4-8 Jun *Banchory-Devenick* (L.Calle, B.J.Stewart, R. van Meurs) (*BB* 75: RR)
1984 19 Oct *Greg Ness* (R.Smith) (*BB* 78: RR)

Alpine Swift
by M. Langman

European Bee-eater *Merops apiaster*

Breeds from Iberia, southern France and north west Africa east to Kashmir and eastern Kazakhstan. Also occurs in South Africa. Winters in Africa south of the Sahara.

This species was recorded in Scotland in 13 years between 1950 and 1983 (Thom 1986) and this irregular occurrence has since continued.

The earliest note for the North East was of one shot near Peterhead in 1850. Sim (1903) noted that it had been shot from a party of three birds. In addition to this specimen he noted another killed on 4th June 1852 at Kinmundy.

Gray (1871) recorded that 'Mr Edward has informed me that a specimen was obtained some years ago in Banffshire'. Unfortunately he gave no specific details of this record, and this would probably account for Sim (1903) making no reference to it.

There have been four recent records, of which three were of single birds. In May 1993, two were seen together at Newburgh on the 22nd and early the following morning. In October 1995 there were two records, from Belhelvie and Durris. These probably relate to the same individual wandering around the area.

ALL RECENT RECORDS
1991 3 Jul *Crimond, Strathbeg*
1993 22-23 May *Newburgh* (2)
1995 5-7 Oct *Belhelvie, nr Balmedie*
1995 9-16 Oct *Durris* probably the above bird

Roller *Coracias garrulus*

Breeds from Iberia and north west Africa east to Kashmir and south west Siberia. Winters in Africa south of the Sahara.

There have been only 23 records of this species in Scotland since 1958 (Evans 1994, Rogers *et al.* 1992, 1993, 1994, 1995).

The majority of records for the North East region occurred in the last century. Several of these are poorly recorded. Gray (1871) makes reference to a letter from Thomas Edward who reported a bird killed at the Loch of Strathbeg, but no date is given. He also reports a bird shot in April 1847 at Seaton House, near Aberdeen. Baxter and Rantoul (1953) note a bird shot at St Cyrus in 1841, giving no further details. A female was shot at Boyndie, near Banff, on 25th September 1848 (*Zool.* Vol. 6), and Sim (1903) records a bird shot on the Parkhill Estate in either 1856 or 1857. Serle (1895) refers to the Strathbeg bird but adds no further information. He does, however, report 'one taken for a parrot shot at Cruden in June 1893'. The last record for the last century is of a bird shot 'five or six years ago' in Rubislaw, Aberdeen. The record appears to relate to around 1897 (*TAWMNHS* 1901-06).

In the early part of this century there is only one record, that of a female, shot at Auchmedden, New Aberdour, on 9th September 1905 (*Zool.* 1905 and *Brit. Birds* Vol. 1).

There has been only one accepted record for the last 30 years. A bird was seen at Peterhead between 28th June and 8th July 1969.

ALL RECENT RECORDS
1969 28 Jun-8 Jul ***Peterhead*** (Dr C.J.Feare, F.C.Feare, D.E.B.Lloyd *et al.*) (*BB* 63: RR)

Hoopoe *Upopa epops*

Breeds from Iberia and France east across Asia to China and south to south east Asia, Sri Lanka and South Africa. The western Palearctic population winters mainly in Africa south of the Sahara.

There have been many records of this species for North East Scotland going back into the last century. Gray (1871) gives several early records of which the first two were undated, and must predate the following 1826 record. The first dated record was shot in spring at Belhelvie, Blairton, in 1826, with another at Banchory in the spring of 1837 or 1838. Another was taken alive in 1841 on the banks of the Deveron, one was shot at Tillyhows in 1848, and one in the spring of 1852 near Kintore. Another was reportedly seen at Haddo House (no date). He knew of several other records but gave no details.

Sim (1903) in *The Vertebrate Fauna of Dee* noted most of those given by Gray (1871), but added a great many more:

Hoopoe
by M. Langman

1826 NA *Belhelvie Links* shot
1832 Sept *Duff House, nr Banff* (*Zool*. V6)
1848 NA *Tillyhows* shot
1852 NA *Kintore* (2) shot
1852 NA *Haddo House* 'seen'
1856 NA *Nether Banchory* shot
1868 23 April *Girdleness* shot
1868 25 April *Tillery* shot
1868 29 Sep *Muiresk, Turriff*
1886 16 Aug *Cruden Parish* shot
1887 NA *Fyvie Parish*
1888 11 Oct *Blairs* found dead
1891 26 Aug *Fyvie Parish* shot
1891 7 Sep *Skene House* 'seen'...it remained for
a week 'hopping about the shrubberies, and was
not shy'
1893 19 May *Gourdas, Fyvie* 'seen'
1893 13 Sep *Bonnykelly, New Pitsligo* killed
1894 12 Oct *Donmouth* immature shot.
1895 25 Sep *Newlands, Aberdeen*
immature shot
1896 22 Aug *Rhynie* another on 7 Sep
1898 Oct *Ardo, Banchory-Devenick* killed

These early records are from a
widespread number of locations with no
particular pattern to their occurrence.
Records were made in April–May and
August to October (although there are
several undated).

There are fewer records for the early part
of this century, with birds seen in
October at Clashnadarrock in 1921 and
another on Fraserburgh golf course in
1936 (month not given).

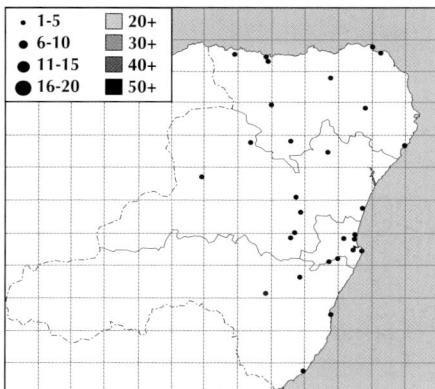

Legend:
• 1-5   ▨ 20+
● 6-10   ▦ 30+
● 11-15   ▩ 40+
⬤ 16-20   ■ 50+

Hoopoe sightings

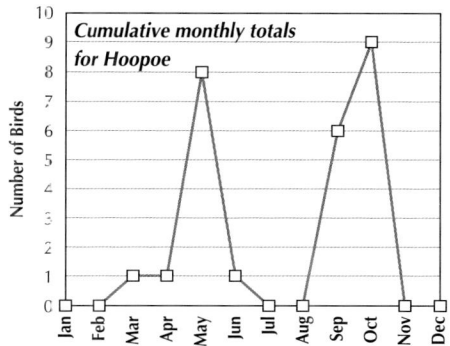

The occurrence of this species remains
erratic. Between 1966 and 1993 there
were a further 24 records of this species.
In most years there are only one or two
records, but in October 1993 at least six
birds were seen. As with the records in
the last century the recent reports come
from a widespread number of locations,
and birds are not restricted to the coast.
The best months are May (eight records),
September (seven records) and October
(nine records). All of the records relate to
single birds. Many are seen on one day
only, but several have stayed for
extended periods including a bird at
Inverurie in 1985 which was present
from September through to 26th
November.

ALL RECENT RECORDS

1966 18 May *Moss Side, Strachan*
1967 29 May *Inveray*
1967 26 Sept *Bridge of Don*
1968 12 Sep *Strachan*
1969 12-16 Sep *Johnshaven*
1969 4 May *Torry*
1969 13 May *Banff*
1971 7 May *Forter*
1975 9 May *Portsoy*
1976 29 Sep *Girdleness*
1981 21-25 May *Old Deer*
1983 5 May *Fetteresso*
1983 17 Sep *Portsoy*
1985 Sep-26 Nov *Inverurie* perished in early
snow
1986 18 Oct *Wells of Ythan*
1986 20-21 Oct *Johnshaven*

1987 12-14 Oct *Wells of Ythan*
1988 7 Jun *Dunecht*
1993 2 Oct *Dunnoter Castle* also seen in
Stonehaven
1993 3 Oct *north of Donmouth*
1993 8 Oct *Portsoy*
1993 9-17 Oct *nr New Pitsligo*

1993 18 Oct *Cairnbulg*
1993 30 Oct *Tornaveen*
1995 30 Mar *Downies, Portlethen*
1995 24 Apr-9 May *nr Longside*
1996 11-14 Sep *Newmachar*
1996 17 Sep *nr Banchory*

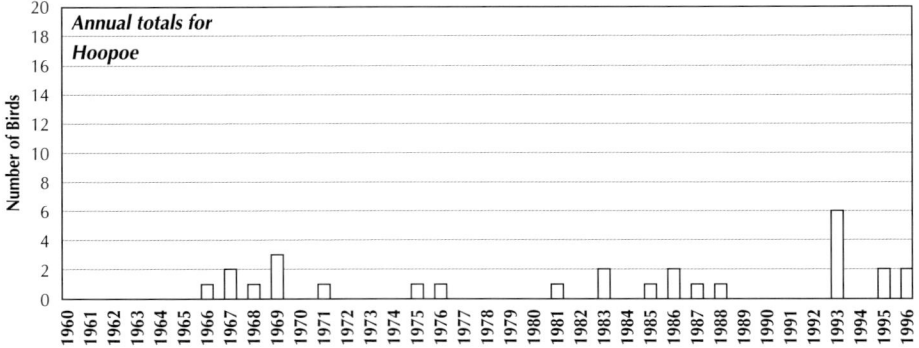

Annual totals for Hoopoe

Wryneck *Jynx torquilla*

Breeds from western Europe eastwards to eastern Asia. Birds from the northern Western Palearctic winter south of the Sahara.

Until recent times, the Wryneck was only known as an irregular passage migrant in Scotland. Breeding in Scotland was first proven in 1969 and possibly occurred in most subsequent years in small numbers, although not always confirmed (Thom, 1986).

In the North East region the species was very rare in the last century but Gray (1871) noted that the species had occurred in Aberdeenshire with one having been killed near Birse in July 1864. Sim (1903) noted that Wrynecks had 'been observed several seasons in succession at Aboyne....and at least once killed there' and birds had been seen at the Braes of Gight but gives no dates.

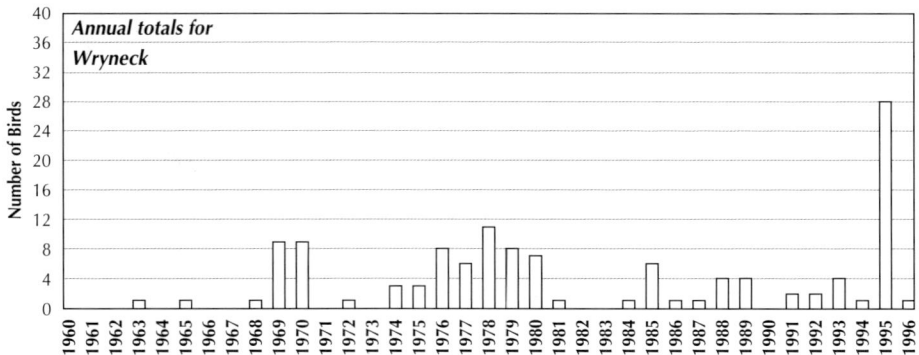

Annual totals for Wryneck

There are few records for the early part of this century. One was sent to the University of Aberdeen from Fraserburgh in the second week of May 1916. A note is made with the record that 'the species is seldom recorded from this area' (*Scot. Nat.* 1916).

Since 1963 the number of records has been increasing, but there is a large variation in the number of birds in any one year. In eight of the last 33 years there have been no records, yet in the large fall of migrants between 8th and 12th September 1995, there were 25 or more Wrynecks reported. This included the largest count at one coastal site of seven at Foveran bushes. Coastal migrants occur primarily in May, with a smaller spread from August to October. The large fall mentioned for September 1995 altered the general trend of more spring than autumn birds.

Records of migrants come from a large number of coastal locations, mainly in the east, with Cruden Bay, Girdleness and Foveran bushes regular sites.

Since 1979 small numbers of birds have been recorded inland in eight years, and breeding was first proven in 1980, when at least one pair raised young (*NESBR* 1980). In some years as few as one or two birds are heard singing, but up to six birds have been reported. In 1986 the remains of a bird were found inland at a Merlin plucking post.

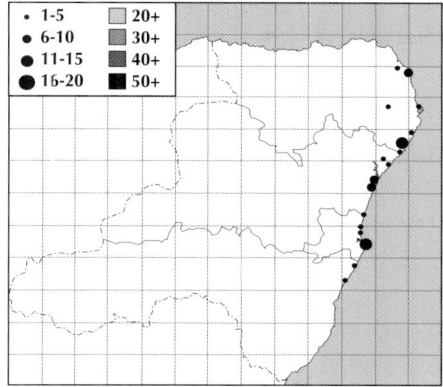

Wryneck sightings (migrants)

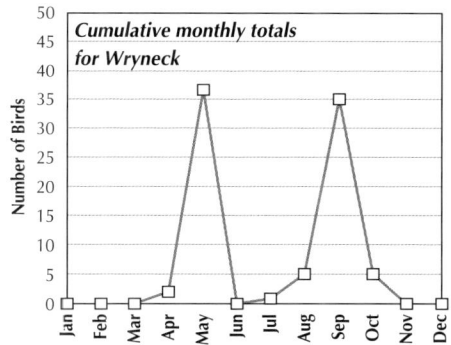

Cumulative monthly totals for Wryneck

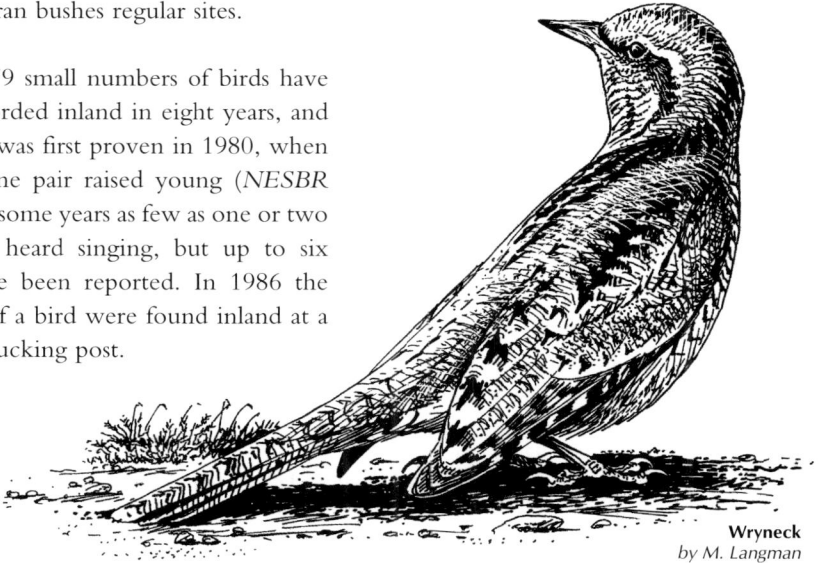

Wryneck
by M. Langman

Short-toed Lark Calandrella brachydactyla

Breeds from Iberia and north west Africa eastwards to Manchuria. Birds from the Western Palearctic winter in the south Sahara.

In Scotland there had been 163 birds recorded up to the end of 1990, with only one of these on the mainland (Evans 1994), with a further 34, all from islands, up to the end of 1993 (Rogers *et al.* 1992, 1993).

There has been only one record of this species in the North East region. A single bird was found in the sandy field at Rattray Head on 25th May 1995. This is only the second record for mainland Scotland.

ALL RECORDS
1995 25 May *Rattray Head* (T.W.Marshall)

Woodlark Lullula arborea

Breeds from southern England and southern Scandinavia southwards to north Africa and the Middle East. Winters in the southern part of the breeding range.

This species is very scarce in Scotland, with Fair Isle accounting for the majority of the early records (Baxter and Rintoul 1953).

There are few early references to this species occuring within the region. In a list of birds of north west Aberdeenshire, a Mr Forbes includes Woodlark, but does not give any dates or locations (*ASNH* Vol. 1, 1891). Smith (*Zool.* 1850) reports that Thomas Edward saw a bird at Duff House on 24th May 1850. The bird was described as '...seated on the top of a wall near to a field of grass, and in full song. From the markings on its breast and neck, its Lark-like manner, and its dumpy appearance, I had little difficulty in recognising it as a Woodlark....an entirely new visitor to this locality'.

Another, more curious, note of this species came from Fyvie, and reports that 'The song of the Woodlark was heard on Christmas Day amid the rigours of a snowstorm. This is the first time in this district we have heard the low sweet melodious voice of this gifted songster. Being captured for preservation, it proved to be a female, not withstanding its great musical faculties' (*Scot. Nat.* Vol. 6: 1897). The *Avi-Fauna of Buchan* (Serle 1895) notes one shot at Mill of Tifty in December 1880 and a few seen about Gourdas in March 1888, with one shot. Sim (1903) makes no reference to this species at all.

There is only one recent record.

ALL RECENT RECORDS
1993 2 Oct *Girdleness* (C.Barton, J.R.W.Gordon)

Shore Lark *Eremophila alpestris*

The nominate race breeds in Scandinavia and Russia, wintering from Britain eastwards to southern Scandinavia and the Baltic.

The earliest note of this species in North East Scotland is of one reported to have been shot on Boyndie Beach, Banffshire, about 1880. The same paper reports that a W. Brodie saw some strange birds on Boyndie Beach in the winter of 1915. 'They were six to seven inches long, had a brown back, white underparts, yellowish about the head and throat, with tufts of upright feathers on each side of the head'. He shot one , but unfortunately did not keep it. He said that the picture of Shore Lark resembled the birds in question (*Scot. Nat.* 1917-18).

Gray (1871) wrote that 'I have no doubt that this species is a frequent, if not an annual, visitant to the eastern shores of Scotland, ranging from Ythan to the Tweed', and Yarrell (1871-74) noted them '...seen at various localities, reaching from Aberdeen in the north to Weymouth....between the middle of November and the month of March'. The *BOU List* (1883) also noted them

from '...Aberdeen in the north to Tor Bay in the south'. As none of these gave any details of sites and dates, Sim (1903) was prompted to state '...we must wait till someone can show a Dee killed specimen before the Shore-Lark can with certainty be placed in the list, for suppositions cannot be accepted as facts, whoever may express them'.

There are few further records until the early 1960s when sporadic reports were published in *Scottish Birds*, typically subject to annual fluctuations. In many years there are no records, but in the winter of 1976-77 up to 33 birds were seen. Records came from four sites in that winter and some duplication of birds may have occurred.

The majority of records are of between one and three birds, but in 1976 a flock of 14 were at Rattray on 10th November, 11 were between Rosehearty and Sandhaven on 26th March 1977, seven

Shorelarks *by M. Langman*

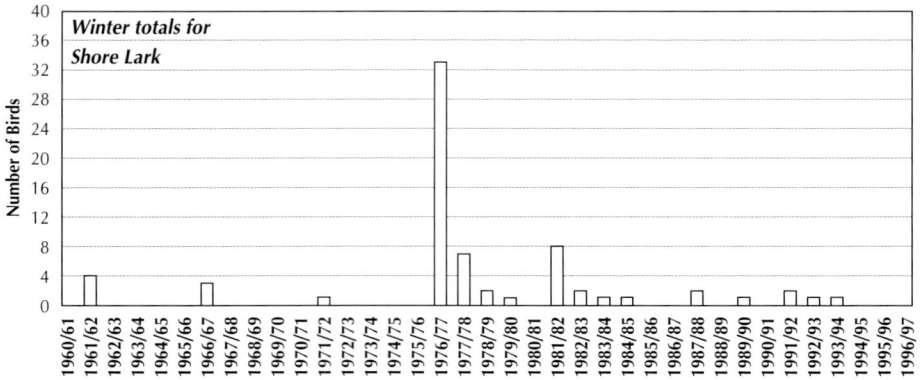

Winter totals for Shore Lark

were at Scotstown on 30th and 31st January 1977 and eight were at Rattray on 25th December 1981.

Short-staying birds are the norm for this region, but over-wintering birds have been recorded. In the winter of 1961-62, up to four birds were seen between 30th December and 5th March. Two birds were at Greg Ness between 14th January and 18th March 1978, and more recently a single bird was present in the Ythan area from 15th December 1991 until at least 27th January 1992, although often elusive.

The main arrival period of birds occurs in October and November, although birds can arrive in December and January. There is a smaller peak in March, suggesting return migration through the region. There have been two April records and two in May. The latest-ever record was of a bird at Cruden Bay on 22 May 1993.

Records have come from scattered sites along the east coast, and from the Sandhaven-Rosehearty stretch of the north coast. The Ythan area is probably the most favoured site, with Rattray well represented in the records.

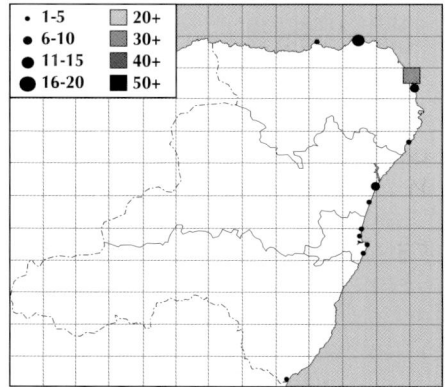

Shore Lark sightings

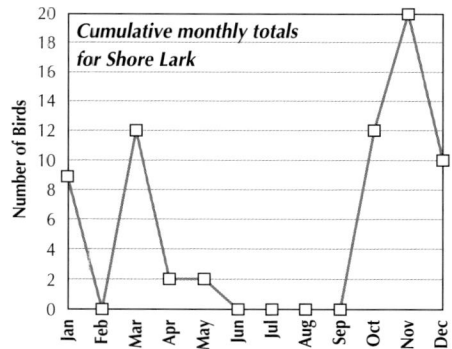

Cumulative monthly totals for Shore Lark

ALL RECENT RECORDS

1961/62 Winter *Ythan* 4 on 30 Dec, 4 on 6 Jan and 3 on 5 Mar
1966 Oct *Rattray* (3)
1966 23-30 Oct *Newburgh* (1-3)
1971 31 Dec *Kinnaber*
1976 30 Oct *Foveran*
1976 10 Nov *Rattray* (14)
1977 30-31 Jan *Scotstown* (7)
1977 26 Mar *Sandhaven-Rosehearty* (11)
1977 8 Oct *Donmouth*
1977 16 Oct *Rattray* (2)
1977 6-11 Nov *Girdleness* (2)

1978 14Jan-18 Mar *Greg Ness* (2)
1978 15 Oct *Balmedie-Ythan* (2)
1979 17-23 Nov *Aberdeen*
1981 25 Dec *Rattray* (8)
1982 13-21 Nov *Ythan*
1984 27-29 Apr *Girdleness*
1985 10 Mar *Troup Head*
1988 2 Nov *Rattray*
1990 15 Apr *Altens* male in summer plumage
1991 9 Nov *Rattray*
1991 15Dec-27Jan *Ythan*
1993 22 May *Cruden Bay*
1994 5 May *Rattray*

Red-rumped Swallow *Hirundo daurica*

Breeds in north west Africa, Iberia and southern France. Also Balkans east to Japan and south to Sri Lanka and also in central Africa. The Western Palearctic population winters in Africa south of the Sahara.

There had been only 26 birds recorded in Scotland up to the end of 1994 (Evans 1994, Rogers *et al.* 1992, 1993, 1994, 1995). Two of these records have occurred in the North East region, one in spring (1987) and the other in autumn (1988). Both were typical dates for this species' occurrence in Britain.

ALL RECORDS

1987 16 May *Nigg, Girdleness* (A.J.Leitch) (*BB* 82: RR)
1988 17 Nov *Kincorth, Aberdeen* (B.J.Stewart *et al.*) (*BB* 82: RR)

Red-rumped Swallow *by M. Langman*

Richard's Pipit *Anthus novaeseelandiae*

Breeds from western Siberia east to Mongolia and south east to New Zealand. Also in Africa. Northern populations winter in Pakistan and India east to south east Asia.

This species is annual in very small numbers in Scotland, particularly on Fair Isle and Shetland (Thom 1986). Since the first record for the North East in 1968, there have been 15 records of 16 birds. The majority of records refer to short-staying individuals, but two appeared together at Balmedie in 1990, and were present from 22nd October until at least 29th.

Most of the records have been in October, which is typical of British records. Single birds have been seen in September and November. There have been only two spring records, one at the Donmouth in May 1989 and another at Rattray in May 1995.

No one site is favoured by this species, and records have occurred at a variety of sites at or near the east coast from Rattray to Aberdeen.

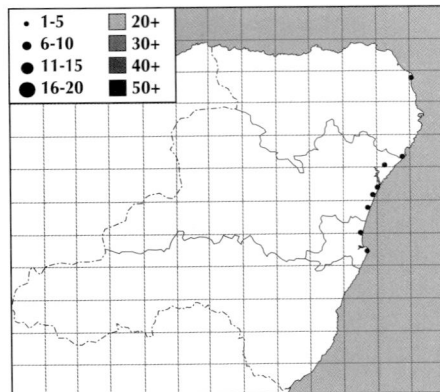

ALL RECORDS

1968 19 Oct *Girdleness* (A.Duncan, A.F.Leitch, M.A.Macdonald) (*BB* 62: RR)

1975 3 Oct *Drums* (P.M.Ellis, R.B.Hastings, M.Heubeck)

1977 30 Oct *Meikle* (R.W. & Mrs Byrne, C.J.Spray)

1979 13 Oct *Girdleness* (K.B.Shepherd *et al.*)

1987 21 Oct *Foveran* (R.D.Steele, J.A.Stephen, O.A.Hayward, J.Lee)

1987 21 Oct *Drums* (R.D.Steele *et al.*)

1989 6 May *Donmouth* (C.Barton, J.R.W.Gordon)

1990 3-10 Oct *Donmouth* (P.D.Bloor *et al.*)

1990 22-29 Oct *Balmedie* (2) (C.Barton, J.R.W.Gordon, F.Leckie *et al.*)

1991 27 Sept *Girdleness* (P.Cosgrove, S.A.Reeves)

1991 10 Oct *Rattray* (T.W.Marshall)

1994 11 Nov *Whinnyfold* (J.R.W.Gordon, I.A.Roberts)

1995 25 May *Rattray* (S.A.Ragnarsson)

1995 29 Oct *Rattray* (T.W.Marshall, J.R.W.Gordon, I.A.Roberts)

1995 12 Nov *Girdleness* (M.A.Sullivan, M.J.Sullivan)

Richard's Pipit
by M. Langman

• 1-5	▨ 20+
● 6-10	▥ 30+
⬤ 11-15	◼ 40+
⬤ 16-20	■ 50+

Richard's Pipit sightings

Tawny Pipit *Anthus campestris*

Breeds from north west Africa, Iberia, southern and eastern France and southern Sweden east to Mongolia. The Western Palearctic population winters in the Sahel zone of south Sahara and Saudi Arabia.

The Tawny Pipit is a very scarce and irregular visitor to Scotland, although the number of records have increased since 1970 (Thom 1986). There have been only two records of this large pipit in the North East region, one in May 1981 and a second in October 1987.

ALL RECORDS

1981 14 May **Newburgh** (K.B.Shepherd, C.R.McKay *et al.*)

1987 24-25 Oct **Foveran Bushes** (G.Anderson, O.A.Hayward, J.Lee, R.D.Steele)

Tawny Pipit
by J. P. Smith

Olive-backed Pipit *Anthus hodgsoni*

Breeds from north east Russia to central and east Asia and Japan. Winters in India, south east Asia and Phillipines.

Of the 90 or so records of this species in Scotland there have been only three records from the mainland (Evans 1994, Rogers *et al.* 1992, 1993, 1994, 1995). The single record for the North East region occurred on 20th October 1990, a typical date for this species in Britain.

ALL RECORDS

1990 20 Oct **Cruden Bay** (B.J.Best, L.T.A.Brain, A.L.Broom) (*BB* 85: RR)

Pechora Pipit *Anthus gustavi*

Breeds across Siberia to the Bering Strait, wintering in the Philippines, Borneo and Sulawesi.

Nearly all the accepted British records of this species have come from Fair Isle, Shetland and Orkney (Evans 1994). There has been only one record for the North East region and is the only record for mainland Scotland. The bird was seen by a single observer in October 1993.

ALL RECORDS
1993 11 Oct *St Fergus* (P.Doyle) (*BB* 87: RR)

Water Pipit *Anthus spinoletta*

Breeds in the mountains of central and southern Europe. Disperses to wetlands at lower altitudes in winter.

This species is still very rare in Scotland, although there has been an increase in records in recent years, particularly in winter. The difficulty in separating this species from the 'Scandinavian' Rock Pipit *Anthus petrosus littoralis* in spring prompted the local records committee to request a review of the North East records by the Scottish Birds Rarities Committee in 1995/96.

The result was that two records were accepted as Water Pipits and a third rejected because it was too poorly documented taking into account Scandinavian Rock Pipit.

ALL ACCEPTED RECORDS
1993 6-7 Apr *Loch of Strathbeg* (T.W.Marshall, W.Dunlop)
1994 8-12 Apr *Loch of Strathbeg* (K.Buchan et al.)

Water Pipit
by M. Langman

Thrush Nightingale *Luscinia luscinia*

Breeds from Denmark and southern Sweden east to south and central Siberia. Winters mainly in tropical east Africa.

Only 59 birds of this species had been recorded in Scotland up to the end of 1990, with the majority on Fair Isle, Shetland and the Isle of May (Evans 1994). The single record for the North East region was one of only four on the mainland during this period. Unfortunately the bird was discovered only after it had been killed by a cat.

ALL RECORDS
1981 12 May ***Newburgh*** (Dr C.H.Fry *per* Dr A.G.Knox) (*BB* 75: RR)

Nightingale *Luscinia megarhynchos*

Breeds in western Europe (including southern England) and north Africa. Most winter in Africa, south of the Sahara.

Between 1950 and 1983 there were 64 records of this species in Scotland, mainly on Fair Isle and the Isle of May (Thom 1986).

There have been only five records for the North East region, all of single birds in May, which is typical of overshooting spring migrants. The best site appears to be Girdleness which has had three records.

ALL RECORDS
1973 19-20 May ***Girdleness*** (A.D.K.Ramsay, R L.Swann, A.Duncan)
1977 23 May ***St Cyrus*** (M.Nicoll)
1989 12 May ***Bullers of Buchan*** (M.Innes, T.W.Marshall, R.A.Schofield)
1990 3 May ***Girdleness*** (S.A.Reeves *et al.*)
1993 12 May ***Girdleness*** (D.R.Landesman)
1996 20 May ***Balmedie*** (C.Barton)

Bluethroat *Luscinia svecica*

Breeds sporadically through Iberia, France, Norway and northern Sweden across Eurasia to north east Siberia and Mongolia. The Western Palearctic population winters mainly in the Sahel zone of south Sahara and Saudi Arabia

The Bluethroat is a regular migrant in North East Scotland, predominantly in spring. The first record for the region was of a bird which flew aboard a fisherman's boat, six miles off Aberdeen on 16th May 1872, with another shot at Aberdeen in May 1876. Serle (1895) recorded '...the Blue throated warbler has been observed at Fraserburgh, but whether white spotted or red spotted is not mentioned'. There are few subsequent records until recent times.

Indeed when Baxter and Rintoul (1953) wrote the *Birds of Scotland* they observed that there were 'not many records of the Red Spotted Bluethroat from the mainland...'

Since the late 1960s there have been regular records of this species, although the number observed in any one year varies greatly. Between 1969 and 1994 there were only five years when there were no records for this species. Generally there are less than five birds seen in any year, but there have been some exceptional years when between 11 and 30 birds have been seen. The best year was in 1985 when up to 30 birds were reported.

The majority of records occur in May, with most in the first half of the month. Autumn records are much rarer, with only two records for September and four for October. The east coast accounts for the great majority of records, as would be expected for a bird arriving from the south east in spring. Just under half of the records have come from Girdleness, with Rattray, Cruden Bay, the Collieston area and the Foveran-Ythanmouth area accounting for the majority of the remaining records.

All but one record has referred to the red-spotted form. The single record of the white-spotted race was of a single male at Balmedie on the 9th May 1969.

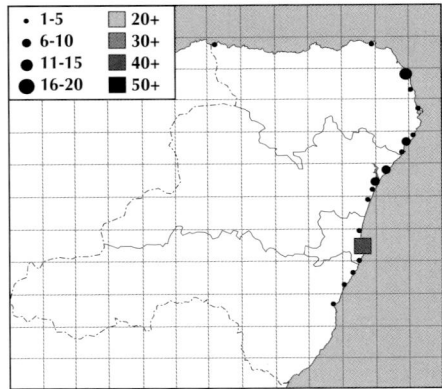

Bluethroat sightings

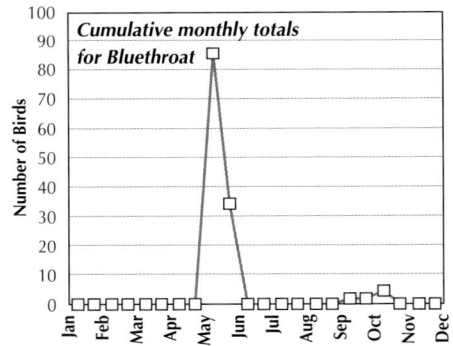

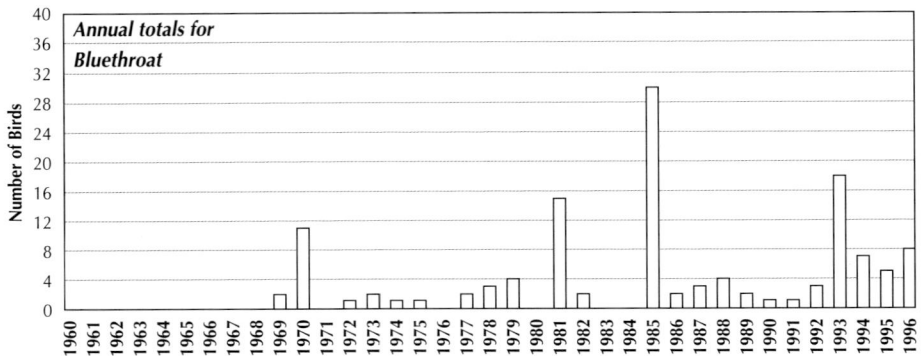

'Siberian' Stonechat *Saxicola torquata maura/stejnegeri*

Breeds from central Asia eastwards to Japan. Winters in the Middle East and Indochina.

There were only 56 birds identified as being 'eastern' Stonechats in Scotland up to the end of 1990 (Evans 1994). The majority of these have been from Fair Isle and Shetland. With increasing observer awareness there has been an increase in the number of records in recent years.

There have been only six accepted records of 'Siberian' Stonechat for the region. Two have occurred in October and two in November, which is typical of these races in Britain. An adult male held territory inland in the summer of 1993. The bird did not find a mate and departed after three weeks.

ALL RECORDS
1979 1-4 Nov *Foveran* (R.A.Schofield *et al.*)
1982 9-15 Oct *Rattray* (K.B.Shepherd *et al.*)
1990 24 Oct *Cruden Bay* (M.G.Pennington *et al.*)
1991 28 Sep *Rattray* (T.W.Marshall, S.A.Reeves)
1993 2 Jun-6 Jul *Forest of Birse area* adult male on territory inland (G.W.Rebecca, K.D.Shaw, A.W.Thorpe, A.Webb)
1994 8 Nov *Between Collieston and Whinnyfold* (J.R.W.Gordon, T.W.Marshall)

Isabelline Wheatear *Oenanthe isabellina*

Breeds in south west Russia, southern Greece and the Middle East eastwards to Mongolia. Winters in the Sahel zone of south Sahara, Arabia and Pakistan.

There had been only seven records of this species in Britain by the end of 1990 (Evans 1994), and only two subsequently to 1994 (Rogers *et al.* 1992, 1993, 1994, 1995). There has been only one record for the North East region, which was the third for Britain and the first for Scotland. The bird was an immature and appeared on the golf course at Girdleness on 17th October and stayed until 10th November. To date this has been the longest staying individual of this species in Britain.

ALL RECORDS
1979 17 Oct-10 Nov *Girdleness* immature trapped and ringed on 23rd, 3rd British Record (M.A.S.Beaman, Dr A.G.Knox, T.P.Milsom *et al.*) (BB: RR 1979)

Isabelline Wheatear *by M. Langman*

Pied Wheatear *Oenanthe pleschanka*

Breeds from Bulgaria and Romania eastwards across south Central Asia to Mongolia. Winters in East Africa.

There were only five records of this species for Scotland up to the end of 1990 (Evans 1994) with a further five up to the end of 1994 (Rogers *et al.* 1992, 1993, 1994, 1995). Of these, there have been two records in the North East region, both near the Donmouth. The first was in 1976, when a male was present from 26th September to 7th October. The bird was trapped and ringed on the 4th. At the time of its arrival it was the earliest ever. This was the third Scottish and fifth British record.

The second record was of an immature or female on the evening of 8th October 1993. Unlike the first record, this bird failed to stay, leaving many frustrated local birders the following morning.

ALL RECORDS
1976 26Sep-7Oct *Donmouth* male, trapped and ringed 4th Nov (Dr A.G.Knox *et al.*) (*BB* 70: RR)
1993 8 Oct *Donmouth* immature or female (S.L.Agnew, D.M.Pullen) (*BB* 87: RR)

White's Thrush *Zoothera dauma*

Breeds from central Siberia east to Japan and south to New Guinea. Winters in south east Asia.

There have been only 18 records of this large Siberian thrush in Scotland (Evans 1994, Rogers *et al.* 1992, 1993, 1994, 1995). There is only one record for the North East region, of a bird which flew into a window and killed itself on 6th October 1913.

ALL RECORDS
1913 6 Oct *Castlehill, Aberdeen*

Eye-browed Thrush *Turdus obscurus*

Breeds in Siberia, wintering in India, south east Asia and the Philippines.

There have been only seven records of this striking thrush in Scotland, with only three on the mainland (Evans 1994, Rogers *et al.* 1992, 1993, 1994, 1995, 1996). The only record for the North East region was unusually in May, 1981. This was the first spring record for Scotland, the first mainland record for Scotland and the fifth British record.

ALL RECORDS
1981 21 May *Newburgh* male (A.Anderson, M.V.Bell, Dr A.G.Knox) (*BB* 75: RR)

American Robin *Turdus migratorius*

Breeds in North America from as far north as Alaska and Quebec, south to southern Mexico. The northern birds are migratory, wintering in the United States and south to Guatamala.

There were only six records in Scotland up to the end of 1990 (Evans 1994). The only record for the North East region came over the Christmas period in 1988. The bird was a first-winter and was seen by many birders. There have been no live records to date in Britain since this bird.

ALL RECORDS
1988 24-29 Dec *Inverbervie* (Mrs J.Evans, R.McCurley *et al.*) (*BB* 82: RR)

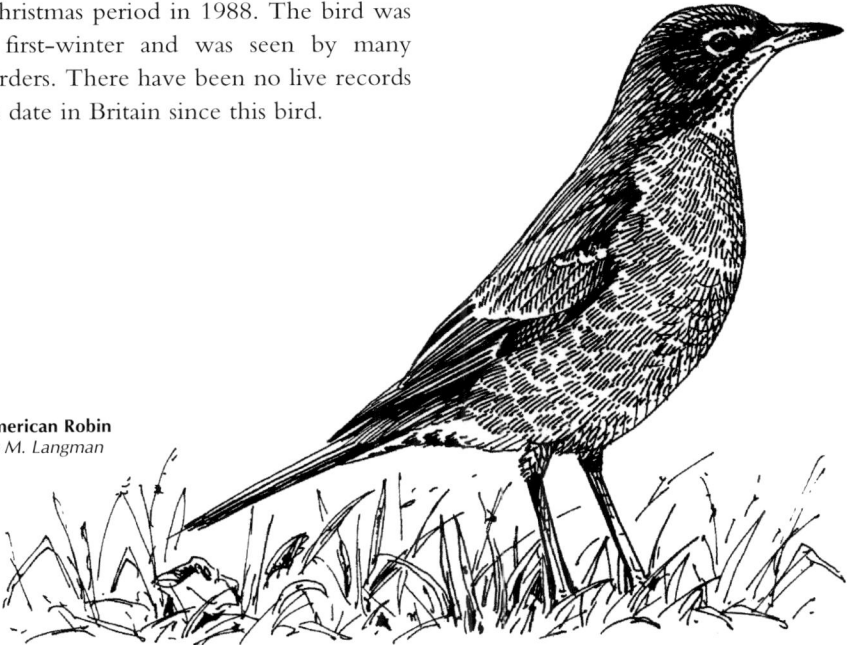

American Robin
by M. Langman

Marsh Warbler *Acrocephalus palustris*

Breeds in Europe as far north as southern Sweden and Finland, eastwards to the Urals. Winters in East Africa.

The Marsh Warbler is a scarce passage visitor to Scotland, mainly on the Northern Isles in June (Thom 1986). There has been only one record of this long awaited, and predicted, addition to the North East List. Fortunately it was trapped in spring, allowing full plumage details, biometrics and photographs to be taken.

ALL RECORDS
1993 31 May *Muchalls* (J.Swallow, A.Webb)

Reed Warbler *Acrocephalus scirpaceus*

The Reed Warbler is quite widely distributed as a breeding species in England as far north as Yorkshire. There are smaller populations in Cleveland, Northumberland and Cumbria (Gibbons et al. 1996). Since 1968 this species has occurred annually in Scotland, both in spring and autumn. Over 75% of the records were from the Northern Isles (Thom 1986).

There are few early references to this species occuring in the North East region. Serle (1895) in the *Avi-Fauna of Buchan* noted that 'Mr Sim, Gourdas, mentions having found a nest at Fetterletter'. This does seem unlikely, and there may have been some confusion with another species. Sim (1903) makes no reference to this species.

Since 1970, records have been more regular. The number reported in any one year can vary considerably, and there have been eight blank years since 1970, the most recent in 1991. This contrasts with 1993, when 19 birds were reported, and 1995, when at least 25 birds were seen. In most years, between one and seven birds are recorded.

Autumn records greatly outnumber those in spring. Autumn passage is noted

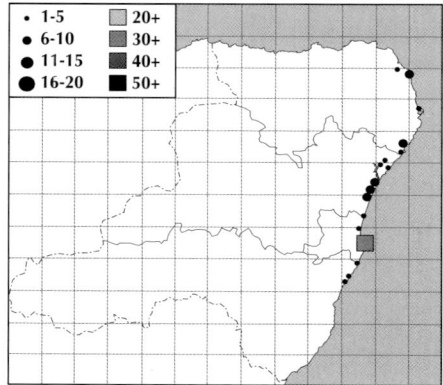

Reed Warbler sightings

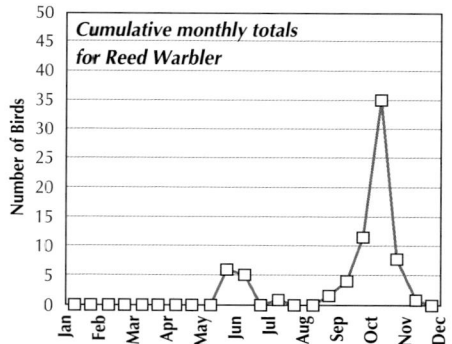

Cumulative monthly totals for Reed Warbler

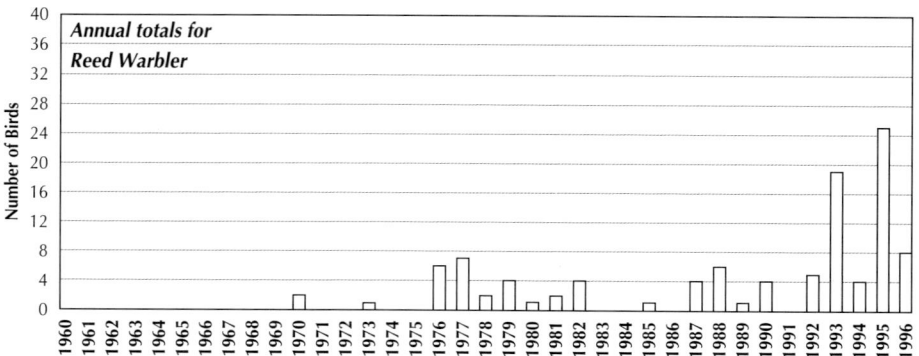

Annual totals for Reed Warbler

from the last half of August through to the first half of November. The peak is in the first half of October. In spring and summer there have been only 12 birds recorded, mainly in May or June, although there was a singing bird at the Loch of Strathbeg in July 1989. Breeding has not been proven.

Several early records were submitted only as 'unstreaked *Acrocephalus*' warblers. Confusion with the much rarer Marsh Warbler could not be ruled out. Claims of Marsh Warbler in autumn have resulted in nets being set to trap birds on several occasions: all to date have been identified as Reed Warblers.

Great Reed Warbler *Acrocephalus arundinaceus*

Breeds from north west Africa and most of continental Europe, north to southern Sweden and east to south west Asia. Winters in Africa south of the Sahara.

There were twenty-eight records in Scotland up to the end of 1994 (Evans 1994, Rogers *et al.* 1992, 1993, 1994, 1995) of which only six have been on the mainland. There has been only one record for the North East region, when a bird was found at Girdleness on 19th May 1985.

ALL RECORDS
1985 19 May **Girdleness** (D.C.Butcher, C.D.R.Heard, R.A.Schofield) (*BB* 79: RR)

Booted Warbler *Hippolais caligata*

Breeds from north west Russia east to westen Mongolia and south to southern Iran. Winters in India.

Evans (1994) gives 11 records for Scotland, of which ten were from the Northern Isles and the last from the Isle of May. In the subsequent four years there have been a further nine records for Scotland, again dominated by the islands. Surprisingly the only two records for mainland Scotland occurred in the North East region in successive years.

The first record for the region was found in Newtonhill on 23rd October 1993, and stayed until 19th November. It was,

at that time, the latest ever record of this species in Britain. This bird was seen by many observers during its prolonged stay. This record was followed by a second in November 1994, a much less confiding individual. Fortunately it was trapped, ringed and photographed.

ALL RECORDS
1993 23Oct-19 Nov **Newtonhill** (K.D.Shaw *et al.*) (*BB* 87: RR)
1994 11-13 Nov **Sand Loch, Collieston** (T.W.Marshall, S.A.Ragnarsson, A.W.Thorpe *et al.*) (*BB* 88: RR)

Icterine Warbler *Hippolais icterina*

Breeds from north east France north to Norway and Sweden and east to western Siberia. Also in northern Iran. Winters in Africa south of the Sahara.

Thom (1986) described the Icterine Warbler as an uncommon visitor to Scotland, occuring in both spring and autumn in most years.

The first record for the region was in 1965, when a single bird was seen at Rattray. In the following 30 years there have been only a further 24 birds reported. Fourteen of these records have been in the last four years, with four birds seen in 1994 and nine in 1995, of which eight occurred in a huge fall over a six-day period in September.

The majority of records are of birds arriving from August through to October, peaking in September. There have been only five records in spring or early summer, with one of these a singing bird away from the coast in June 1992. The east coast has, not surprisingly, accounted for all but one of the records. Girdleness is the most favoured site for this species, with few other sites having had more than two records.

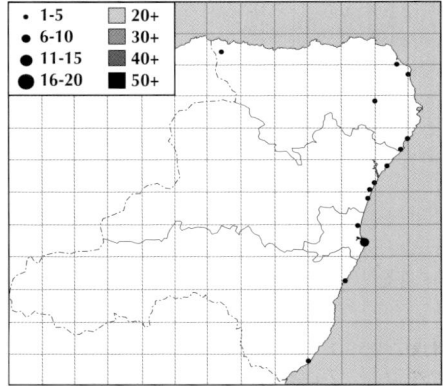

Icterine Warbler sightings

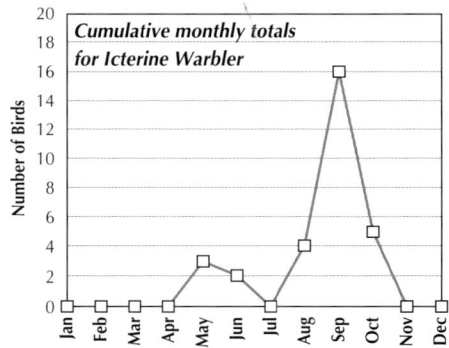

Legend:
- 1-5
- 6-10
- 11-15
- 16-20
- 20+
- 30+
- 40+
- 50+

Cumulative monthly totals for Icterine Warbler

Icterine Warbler
by M. Langman

ALL RECORDS

1965 27 Sep *Rattray*
1973 13 Sep *Cruden Bay*
1974 3 Sep *Girdleness*
1978 7 Sep *Drums* trapped
1979 17-20 Aug *Girdleness* trapped
1980 15 Aug *Girdleness*
1980 27 Sep *Drums*
1982 25-29 Sep *Foveran*
1984 5-6 Jun *Strathbeg*
1986 3 Aug *Strathbeg*
1992 29 May *Whinnyfold*
1992 17-22 Jun *Fordyce* singing male, inland
1992 16-19 Sep *Girdleness*
1993 2 Oct *Girdleness*

1993 24 Oct-10 Nov *Newtonhill*
1993 10 Oct *Donmouth*
1994 24 May *Collieston*
1994 31 Aug *Girdleness*
1994 6 Oct *Mintlaw* inland
1994 23 Oct *Johnshaven*
1995 8-9 Sept *Girdleness* (2)
1995 8-9 Sept *Newtonhill*
1995 8 Sept *Balmedie*
1995 10 Sept *Girdleness* new bird
1995 10 Sept *Balmedie*
1995 10-12 Sept *Collieston* possibly 2 individuals
1995 11-13 Sept *Girdleness* new bird
1996 20 May *Collieston*

Melodious Warbler *Hippolais polyglotta*

Breeds in north west Africa, Iberia, France, Switzerland and Italy. Winters in Africa south of the Sahara.

Unlike the similar Icterine Warbler, this species is less than annual in Scotland, with most records referring to trapped birds (Thom 1986).

There has been only one record of this species in the North East, an elusive bird found in heavy rain and only seen for a few hours on 1st October 1993.

ALL RECORDS

1993 1 Oct *Girdleness* (I.D.Ball, S.A.Reeves, R.A.Schofield)

Subalpine Warbler *Sylvia cantillans*

Breeds in southern Europe, west Turkey and north west Africa. Winters in the Sahel zone of south Sahara.

Evans (1994) records 92 birds from Scotland up to the end of 1990. The majority of these come from Fair Isle, Shetland, Orkney and the Isle of May.

There have been only two records of this delicate warbler in the North East, both in spring and both from Rattray.

ALL RECORDS

1987 28 May *Rattray* female or first-summer male (G.M.Cresswell) (*BB* 81: RR)
1993 17 Apr *Rattray* first-summer male (T.W.Marshall *et al.*) (*BB* 87: RR)

Orphean Warbler _Sylvia hortensis_

Breeds from north west Africa and Iberia east to north west India. Winters in the Sahel zone of south Sahara and in India.

There have been only five records of this species in Britain (Evans 1994). The only Scottish record came from Seaton Park in Aberdeen on 10th October 1982. The bird was trapped and ringed.

ALL RECORDS
1982 10 Oct **Seaton Park, Aberdeen** (R.Duncan) (_BB_ 77: RR)

Barred Warbler _Sylvia nisoria_

Breeds from northern Italy, Germany and southern Sweden east to Mongolia. Winters in southern Arabia and north east Africa south to Kenya.

Thom (1986) described this Warbler as a scarce passage migrant to Scotland. The majority of records come from the Northern Isles and the Isle of May.

The first record of this species in the North East region was as recently as 1970, when an adult was seen at Cruden Bay on 10th May. To date this is the only spring record for the area.

Barred Warbler _by M. Langman_

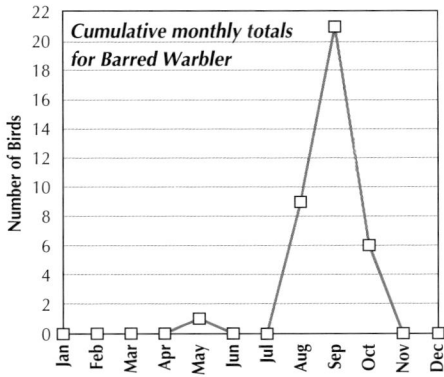

Cumulative monthly totals for Barred Warbler

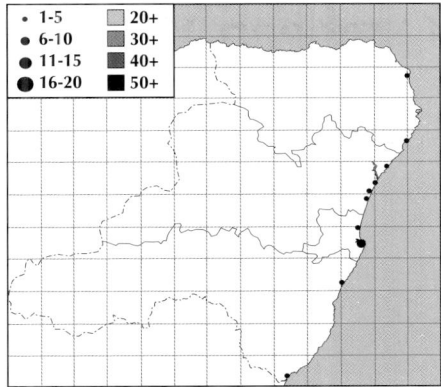

Barred Warbler sightings

Autumn records are noted from August through to October, with a peak in September. All of the 31 records have come from the east coast, with Girdleness (eight), the Newburgh-Foveran area (six) and Drums (five) the most favoured sites. This species is notoriously difficult to see and it is no surprise that the majority of records refer to short-staying individuals. A bird ringed at Foveran on 3rd September 1988 was subsequently seen at Hatterseat between 15th and 23rd October, a stay in the region of 50 days.

The number of birds seen in any one year can vary. A single record is most common, but in 1988 and 1996 at least four individuals were recorded and in 1976 five birds were reported.

ALL RECORDS

1970 10 May *Cruden Bay* adult
1970 22 Aug *Collieston*
1972 7 Oct *Newburgh*
1973 30 Aug *Newburgh*
1973 3 Sep *Rattray*
1975 2-3 Sep *Donmouth*
1976 18 Sep *Drums* a bird present also on 21 Sep
1976 18-27 Sep *Foveran*
1976 21 Sep *Girdleness*
1976 22 Sep *Balmedie*
1976 2 Oct *Ythan*
1977 25 Aug *Rattray*
1977 24 Sep *Girdleness*
1978 4-9 Aug *Girdleness*
1978 7 Sep *Drums* (2)
1979 18 Aug *Rattray*
1980 26 Aug *Girdleness*
1981 4 Oct *Drums*
1986 15 Aug *Rattray*
1988 3 Sep *Foveran* ringed
1988 3 Oct *Foveran* ringed
1988 4 Oct *Foveran* ringed
1988 12 Oct *Girdleness* first-winter
1988 13 Oct *Foveran* a ringed bird, possibly one from Foveran
1988 15-23 Oct *Hatterseat* re-trapped bird, ringed at Foveran on 3rd Sept
1989 15-21 Sep *Newtonhill* first-winter
1991 3-6 Sep *Girdleness* first-winter
1992 30 Aug *Girdleness* first-winter
1993 15 Sep *St Cyrus* first-winter
1994 31 Aug *Girdleness* first-winter
1995 6 Sep *Ordiquhill*
1995 8 Sep *Collieston* first-winter
1995 9 Sep *Balmedie*
1995 10 Sep *Port Errol, Cruden Bay*
1996 15 Sep *Strathbeg*
1996 18 Sep *Girdleness*
1996 21 Sep *Drums*
1996 21-22 Sep *Rattray*

Greenish Warbler _Phylloscopus trochiloides_

**Breeding: North east Germany and Finland east to Sea of Japan.
Also occurs in the Himalayas. Winters in India and south east Asia.**

There had been 63 birds seen in Scotland up to the end of 1990 (Evans 1994), and a further 21 in the following four years (Rogers _et al._ 1992, 1993, 1994, 1995).

The first record for the North East came as recently as 1991, after several years of expectant discussion. It was quickly followed in 1992 by the first spring record for the area, and then in 1994 by the first multiple record, when two were present in a garden at Collieston. All but one of the records have referred to first-winter birds arriving in the last week of August and the first week of September. This pattern is typical of British records of this species (Dymond _et al._ 1989).

ALL RECORDS

1991 1-2 Sep **Collieston Churchyard** first-winter (I.M.Phillips, S.A.Reeves) (_BB_ 85: RR)

1992 31 May **Rattray** singing (L.T.A.Brain, T.W.Marshall, A.Webb _et al._) (_BB_ 86: RR)

1992 23-25Aug **Girdleness** (S.A.Reeves, R.A.Schofield, K.D.Shaw _et al._) (_BB_ 86: RR)

1994 24 Aug **Collieston** (2) first-winter, until 25th, with one present until 29th at least (P.Cosgrove, P.Doyle, T.W.Marshall _et al._) (_BB_ 88: RR)

1996 24 Aug **Rattray** (T.W.Marshall)

Greenish Warbler
by J. P. Smith

Arctic Warbler _Phylloscopus borealis_

**Breeds from northern Scandinavia east through northern Siberia to
Alaska. Winters in southern south east Asia.**

There had been 96 Arctic Warblers seen in Scotland up to the end of 1990 (Evans 1994), with a further 25 in the following four years (Rogers _et al._ 1992, 1993, 1994, 1995). As with the preceeding species, most are recorded on the Northern Isles.

There have been only two records for the North East region, the first in 1958 from Forvie was initially rejected, but was reconsidered and accepted the following year. It was the first record for

mainland Scotland. There was then a considerable gap until the second record in 1979. Both birds occurred in autumn, with one in mid–August and one in early September.

ALL RECORDS

1958 2 Sep **Sands of Forvie** (A.J.M.Smith) (_BB_ 53: RR)

1979 19 Aug **Foveran Links** (T.P.Milsom) (_BB_ 73: RR)

Pallas's Warbler *Phylloscopus proregulus*

Breeds from the Sea of Okhotsk west to south central Siberia, also occurs in the Himalayas. Winters in southern China and northern south east Asia, also in the Himalayan foothills.

This striking warbler has been almost annual in small numbers in Scotland since 1975 (Thom 1986). The first record for the North East region was in 1968 and was only the second Scottish record (first for the mainland). Subsequently there have been 38 more records of this species in the region.

The number seen in any one year varies considerably. After the first record in 1968, there was a gap of 11 years until the second. There were two more blank years, but in 1982 there was an influx of birds with six individuals recorded. There were no further records until 1988. There have been only three blank years since: 1991, 1995 and 1996. An unprecedented influx occurred in 1994, when 24 individuals were recorded from 29th October to 10th November. Unusually there were two birds at Drums, two at Strathbeg, two at Hatterseat and five birds at Foveran.

The majority of records are of single birds at east coast localities during October. The exceptional fall of 24 birds in November 1994 obviously disrupts this trend. The most favoured site for this species is Cruden Bay (seven records), along with Drums (four), Foveran bushes (five), Girdleness (three) and Strathbeg (three).

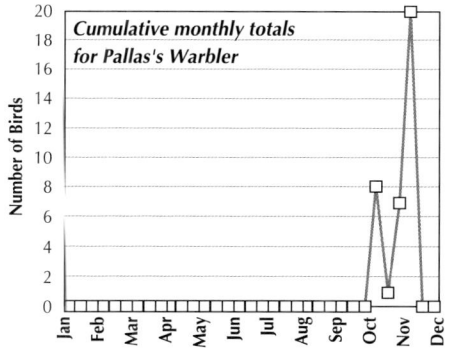

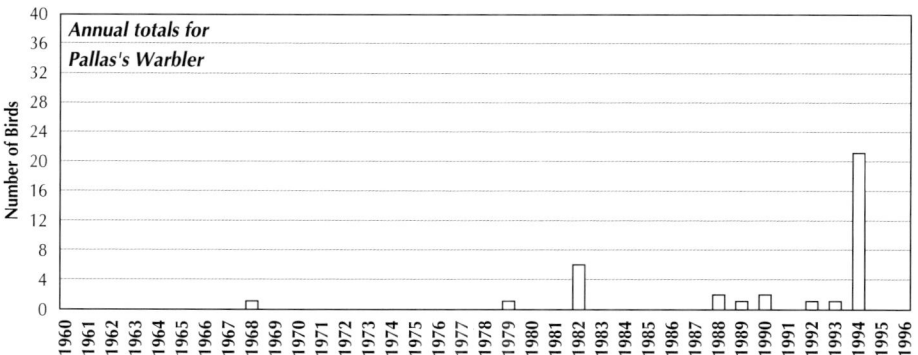

Cumulative monthly totals for Pallas's Warbler

Annual totals for Pallas's Warbler

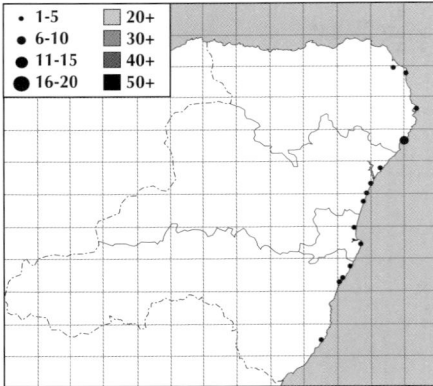

Pallas's Warbler sightings

ALL RECORDS

1968 22-24 Oct *Collieston*
1979 16 Oct *Girdleness*
1982 9-10Oct *Rattray*
1982 11-12Oct *Girdleness*
1982 12 Oct *Strathbeg*
1982 13-15Oct *Cruden Bay*
1982 13-14Oct *Newburgh*
1982 15-17Oct *Drums*
1988 19-22 Oct *Cruden Bay*
1988 22 Oct *Drums*
1989 28-29 Oct *Cruden Bay*
1990 21 Oct *Muchalls*
1990 22 Oct *Cruden Bay*
1992 3-4 Oct *Cruden Bay*
1993 8 Oct *Peterhead*
1994 29Oct-1Nov *Girdleness*
1994 3-4 Nov *Cruden Bay* (1) probably 2
1994 3 Nov *Donmouth*
1994 4 Nov *Collieston*
1994 4-7 Nov *Foveran* (5)
1994 4 Nov *Drums* (2)
1994 4-7 Nov *Hatterseat* (2)
1994 4-6 Nov *Newtonhill*
1994 5 Nov *Drums Farm*
1994 5 Nov *South Hatterseat*
1994 5 Nov *Easter Muchalls*
1994 5 Nov *Kineff Old Church*
1994 5 Nov *Findon*
1994 5 Nov *Balmedie*
1994 6 Nov *Strathbeg* (2)
1994 10 Nov *Hatterseat*

Pallas's Warbler *by M. Langman*

Yellow-browed Warbler *Phylloscopus inornatus*

Breeds from northern Siberia south to Afghanistan, into north western India and as far east as the Sea of Japan. Winters in south east Asia and India.

This species has been recorded almost annually in Scotland in variable numbers since 1968 (Thom 1986).

Since the first record for the region in 1976 there have been 81 records of this small *Phylloscopus* warbler. All records have been of autumn birds, generally in September and October, with two records in November and a single record in December. The peak occurrence is from mid–September to mid–October. The number of records varies from year to year. In the 29 years since the first record there have been 12 blank years. This contrasts with 1988 when a possible 16 birds were recorded. Ten birds were seen in 1985, eight in both 1990 and 1992, and six in 1994.

All records have been from east coast locations, with the exception of single birds inland at Longside in 1992 and again in 1994. The Girdleness area has produced the most records to date (20),

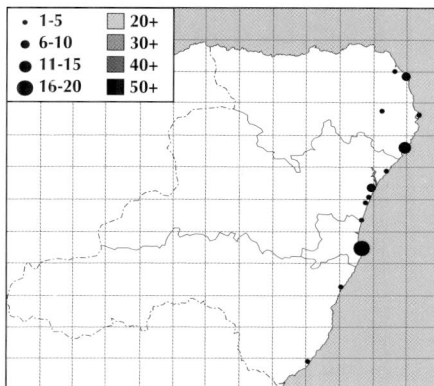

Legend:
- 1-5
- 6-10
- 11-15
- 16-20
- 20+
- 30+
- 40+
- 50+

Yellow-browed Warbler sightings

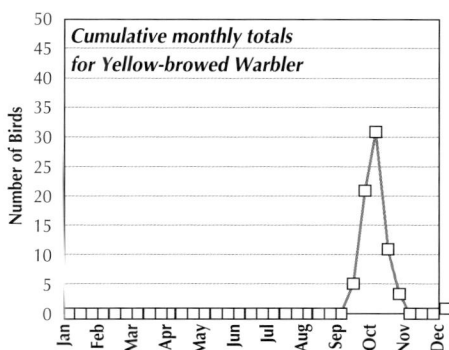

Cumulative monthly totals for Yellow-browed Warbler

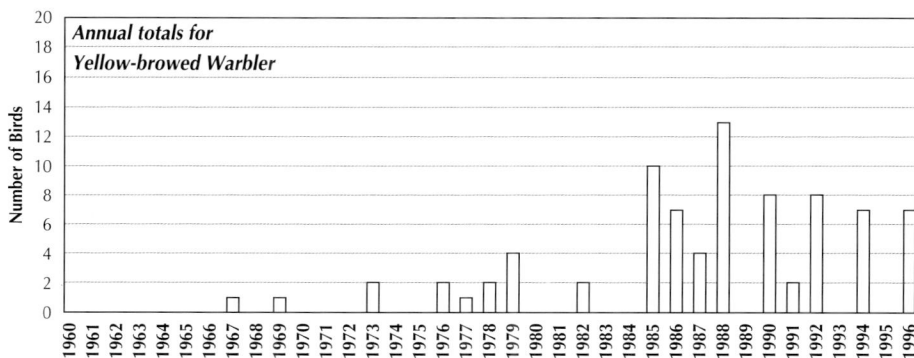

Annual totals for Yellow-browed Warbler

with good numbers from Cruden Bay (13), Rattray (12) and the Foveran-Newburgh area (eight). Smaller numbers of birds have been recorded from a further 11 sites.

The pattern of occurrence in North East Scotland conforms to the general pattern of this species throughout the rest of Britain (Dymond *et al.* 1989).

Yellow-browed Warbler
by M. Langman

Hume's Warbler *Phylloscopus humei*

Breeds in Afghanistan, Pamirs, Tian Shan, the Altai, Sayans, western Mongolia and the western Himalayas. Winters in India and south east Asia (Evans 1994).

Until recently this species was considered to be a sub-species of Yellow-browed Warbler. The BOURC recently announced recommendations to accept the 'split' and the species becomes *Phylloscopus humei* (*Birding World* Vol. 9: 248).

The situation of this species in Britain is not clear, and BBRC will probably undertake a review to clarify its status. Evans (1994) reports only two probable records for North East Scotland.

The first accepted record of this species came in November 1994, a bird showing well and calling occasionally. A bird which occurred in late October 1990, at Cruden Bay, is now being considered by BBRC, although it was not identified as *humei* at the time.

ALL RECORDS
1994 10 Nov **Bullers of Buchan** (T.W.Marshall et al.)

Radde's Warbler *Phylloscopus schwarzi*

Breeds from south-central Siberia east to Sakhalin. Winters in south east Asia.

With only 18 records of this species in Scotland to the end of 1990, this species remains very rare (Evans 1994). The majority of Scottish records occur in the Northern Isles and the Isle of May.

There have been only two records of this species in North East Scotland. The first was at Cruden Bay in 1979, the second from Girdleness in 1991. The latter record was enjoyed by many local birders. Typically both records have been in early October on the east coast.

ALL RECORDS

1979 7 Oct *Cruden Bay* (W.R.Brackenridge) (*BB* 73: RR)

1991 11 Oct *Girdleness* (N.Picozzi, B.J.Stewart, M.A.Sullivan) (*BB* 86: RR)

Dusky Warbler *Phylloscopus fuscatus*

Breeds from west-central Siberia east to north east Siberia. Winters in north east India and south east Asia.

Evans (1994) recorded 18 birds in Scotland up to the end of 1990, with the Northern Isles dominating the records.

There has been only one record of this extremely rare species in North East Scotland. A bird was seen and heard at Rattray on 13th October 1988.

ALL RECORDS

1988 13 Oct *Rattray* (M.Marquiss) (*BB* 82: RR)

Radde's/Dusky Warbler

A bird seen at Cruden Bay was accepted by BBRC only as Radde's/Dusky.

1989 12 Nov *Cruden Bay* (A.Webb)

Bonelli's Warbler *Phylloscopus bonelli*

Breeds from Iberia and France east to Germany and Austria. Also occurs in Balkans, southern Turkey, Lebanon and north west Africa. Winters in the Sahel zone of south Sahara.

There had been only ten records of this species in Scotland up to the end of 1990 (Evans 1994) and only five subsequent records (Rogers *et al.* 1992, 1993, 1994, 1995). The bulk of the records come from the Northern Isles.

There has been only one record for the North East region: a bird spent three days at Drums in late September 1980.

ALL RECORDS
1980 22-24 Sep ***Drums*** (Dr A.G.Knox *et al.*)
(*BB* 74: RR)

Firecrest *Regulus ignicapillus*

Breeds from the Mediterranean to the Netherlands, Denmark and Germany. Small numbers breed in southern England. Winters in the southern part of the breeding range.

Since 1979, Firecrests have been recorded annually in Scotland in very small numbers (Thom 1986).

There have been only 16 records of this species in North East Scotland, since the first in 1974. Between 1974 and 1981 there were records in all but two years. There followed seven blank years, before records in 1989, 1990, 1993 and 1994. Most records have been in autumn, with birds arriving from September to November and a small peak in October. There have been four records in spring: a single bird in March and three in May.

Firecrest
by M. Langman

East coast sites have accounted for all the records, with Foveran–Newburgh the most favoured area.

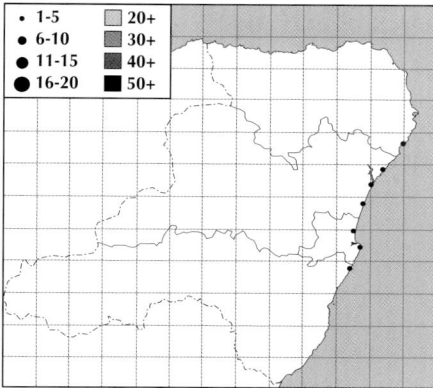

Firecrest sightings

ALL RECORDS
1974 11 May *Cruden Bay*
1975 11 May *Foveran*
1975 7 Sep *Newburgh*
1976 2 Oct *Foveran*
1977 8 May *Donmouth*
1977 26 Sep *Forvie*
1980 3 Nov *Newburgh*
1980 4 Nov *Cruden Bay*
1981 4 Oct *Foveran*
1989 27 Mar *Girdleness*
1989 29 Oct *Findon*
1990 14 Oct *Drums* male trapped and ringed
1993 4 Oct *nr Collieston*
1994 21-23 Oct *Balmedie* trapped and ringed
1994 5 Nov *Balmedie*
1996 14-16 Oct *Girdleness*

Red-breasted Flycatcher *Ficedula parva*

Breeds from southern Sweden south to Austria and Bulgaria and east across Siberia. Winters in Pakistan, India and south east Asia.

In Scotland the Red-breasted Flycatcher is an annual visitor in autumn and less so in spring (Thom 1986). Since the first record for the area in 1959, the species has been less than annual in the North East with only 48 birds reported. The number of birds seen in any one year can vary considerably. In the 37 years since the first record, there have been no records in 15 of these. In contrast four birds were seen in 1987 and 1991, with five in 1973 and 1981.

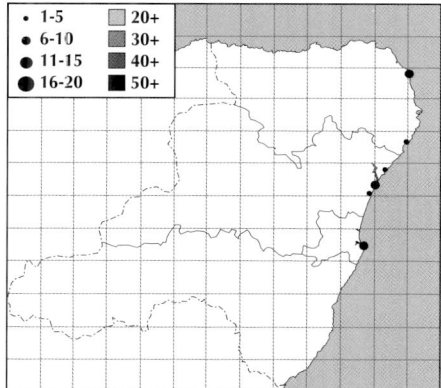

Red-breasted Flycatcher sightings

The majority of records occur in the last half of September and the first half of October. Spring birds are much rarer and there have been only four records, all in May. Typically for scarce migrants, all of the records have been from the east coast. Most records refer to single birds

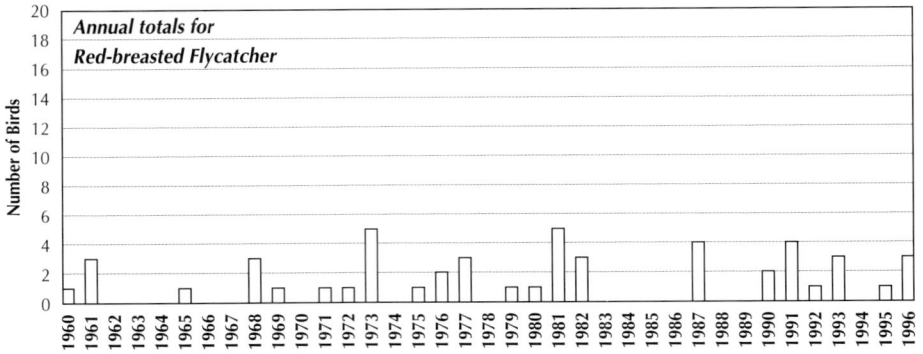

Annual totals for Red-breasted Flycatcher

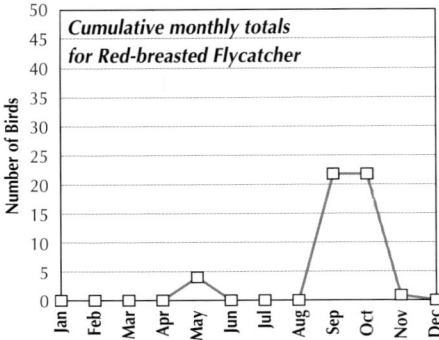

Cumulative monthly totals for Red-breasted Flycatcher

but two were seen together at Muchalls on 4th October 1987, and two were trapped and ringed at Foveran bushes on 10th October 1991. The favoured sites for this species are Rattray (eight records), Girdleness (nine), Foveran bushes (seven) and the Collieston area (four). Several other sites have had up to three records.

Red-breasted Flycatcher *by M. Langman*

Bearded Tit *Panurus biarmicus*

Breeds patchily in the Western Palearctic and eastwards across central Asia to eastern China. Largely dispersive and eruptive outside the breeding season. The small British population is largely confined to the south of a line from Humberside in the east to Leighton Moss in the west.

There are two records of this species from the last century. One was reported to have been shot in Aberdeenshire by Thomas Edward, but Sim (1903) placed square brackets around the note indicating his mistrust of the record. He gave more credit to a bird shot by a gamekeeper at Rothienorman in 1865 (*ASNH* Vol. 8: 358). There is no mention of these records by either Baxter and Rintoul (1956) or by Thom (1986).

Thom (1986) reports the first record for Scotland as being from the Loch of Strathbeg in 1972, when a male and two females appeared in November and at least two remained until March the following year. This was part of a larger influx: 17 were reported subsequently in Scotland in 1972. There have been only two further records for the region; a single bird was again at the Loch of Strathbeg in April 1976, and four birds (three males, one female) at the same site in March 1997.

ALL RECORDS
1972 5 Nov **Strathbeg** 2 males and a female, 2 remained until 11 March 1973
1976 12 Apr **Strathbeg**
1997 3 Mar **Strathbeg** 3 males and a female

Bearded Tit
by M. Langman

Willow Tit *Parus montanus*

**A widely distributed species breeding across northern Europe.
The British population is widespread in England extending up the
east coast through Northumberland into south east Scotland. There is
also a resident population in south west Scotland.**

The status of this species in the North East is somewhat confused. There are several references to 'Marsh Tit' from the last century, with notes for Banchory-Ternan and Fyvie in the *New Statistical Account of Scotland* (1845).

Witherby and Ticehurst (1907-08) reported one or two Marsh Tits seen near Alford on 21st August 1907. They further noted that specimens of 'Marsh Tit' from Forth and Moray had been ascribed to Willow Tit by Dr Hartert in his, *Fauna of Tay Basin* and thought that the Alford birds may have also been Willow Tits.

On 17th September 1919, birds identified as Willow Tits were seen feeding and calling in heather by the Braemar to Aviemore Road (by Seton Gordon in *Brit. Birds* Vol. 13).

Baxter and Rintoul (1953) again pointed out the possibility of confusion between Marsh and Willow Tits, and assumed that most old records of Marsh Tit actually referred to Willow Tit. Thom (1986) pointed out that with the recent spread of the Marsh Tit it is no longer safe to do so. Holloway (1996), however, still felt that it was likely that the majority of 19th century records were of Willow Tit.

Crested Tit *Parus cristatus*

**Breeds in much of continental Europe from Spain and Portugal
north to Scandinavia and east to western Asia. There is an
isolated population in Scotland, centered around the native
pinewoods of Speyside.**

There are few references to this species from the last century. A note on *Banffshire Birds* by A. Mahood (*Scot. Nat.* 1917-18), which revised notes by Harvie-Brown's *Deveron Valley Bird Life* of 1897, mentioned a Crested Tit seen east of the Deveron at Montcoffer Wood. The species had also been seen near Cullen. In January 1897, a W. Stewart reported seeing Crested Tits at Aboyne (*ASNH* 1925-26).

There were no further records until Dr Eagle Clarke wrote that the Crested Tit was breeding eastward in Banff to the frontier of Aberdeen and in 1939 Colonel J. P. Grant of Rothiemurchus informed Baxter and Rintoul that the Crested Tit had arrived in the Forest of Mar, having apparently travelled by way of the Larig Ghrue (Baxter and Rintoul 1953).

On 21st September 1946, several Crested Tits were seen in a wood at the foot of Knock Hill, seven miles south of Portsoy (*Brit. Birds* Vol. 40: 1947) and birds were also seen at the Linn of Dee in the autumn of 1950 (*Scot. Birds* 1983).

Crested Tit
by M. Langman

During the 1970s there were regular records of this species from Deeside and associated glens. Records generally referred to between one and four birds, but 13 were seen in Glen Quoich in September 1973 (Knox 1983). The last record of this species came in 1987, when a bird was present at a bird table on several dates between 14th February and 23rd May.

ALL RECENT RECORDS
1973 18 Sep *Glen Quoich* (13)
1973 22 Sep-2 Oct *Aboyne* (4)
1973 28 Sep *Birse Burn* (4)
1973 2 Nov *Forest of Birse* (1)
1974 4 Jan *Fungle, Aboyne* (3)
1974 5 Jan *Aboyne* (1)
1974 30 Jan *Drumochty Forest* (1-5)
1974 17 Mar *Glen Quoich*
1974 5 May *Glen Tanar* (2-3 heard)
1975 17 Mar *Deeside-Glen Quoich*
1977 8 May *Deeside* site withheld
1977 11-12 May *Glen Dye*
1987 14 Feb-23May *Kemnay*

Golden Oriole *Oriolus oriolus*

Breeds from north west Africa and continental Europe east to Mongolia and India. A few pairs breed in East Anglia. Winters in Africa south of the Sahara and in the Indian region.

The Golden Oriole reaches Scotland annually in very small numbers, with the majority of records from the Northern Isles (Thom 1986).

There are three records of this species from the last century. A bird was seen near Pitsligo in 1886 (Serle 1895) and another was shot at Aberdeen in the same year (Sim 1903). Sim (1903) also recorded a bird shot at Glack, but gave no date.

There have been only five records of six birds since 1968. Typically most of these have been single birds in late spring or summer. In 1985 a pair was seen in Deeside, but breeding was not proven. In 1968 a bird was seen in Seaton Park, Aberdeen in October.

ALL RECENT RECORDS
1968 6 Oct *Seaton Park*
1981 24 May *Strathbeg*
1985 Jun/Jul *Deeside* a pair
1987 27 Apr *Forglen*
1996 20 Jun *Strathbeg*

Red-backed Shrike *Lanius collurio*

Breeds throughout continental Europe and eastwards to Siberia. Winters in southern and eastern Africa.

In the last century there are references in the *New Statistical Account of Scotland* (1845) to this species having been obtained around Peterhead. Both Horn (1880) and Gray (1871) report this bird as having been a male shot about 1833. Sim (1903) noted that a pair were shot near Peterhead in May 1891, and that in 1892 he was informed that this species had been seen 'for six or seven years, and always about the same place, the south east shoulder of Bennachie, and always about the nesting season.' Sim was shown an egg from the nest and confirmed it to be of a Red-backed Shrike. Sim (1903) further reported another pair of birds in the garden of Midmar Castle in both 1895 and 1896. One was shot at Rattray on 7th September 1896 (*Buchan Field Club* Vol. 5).

Subsequently there are few records until the 1960s, when, with the production of *Scottish Birds,* references become more frequent. During the 1960s and early 1970s the species was apparently less than annual. From 1974 onwards there has been only one blank year (1982). The number of birds seen in any one year varies greatly with between one and five seen in most years but in 1976 there were 12 birds, in 1978 there were 16, and in 1992 there were 15.

The majority of records are of single birds at east coast locations peaking in May, but with a significant number in June. Autumn passage is less marked with birds appearing from August through to early November. Numbers peak in September, with good numbers in

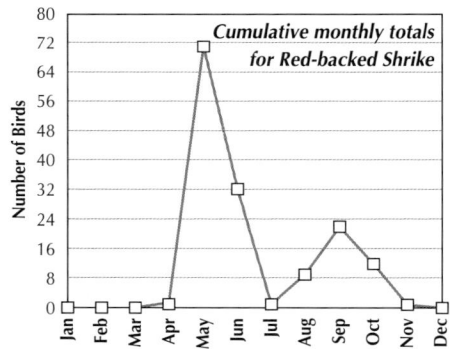

Cumulative monthly totals for Red-backed Shrike

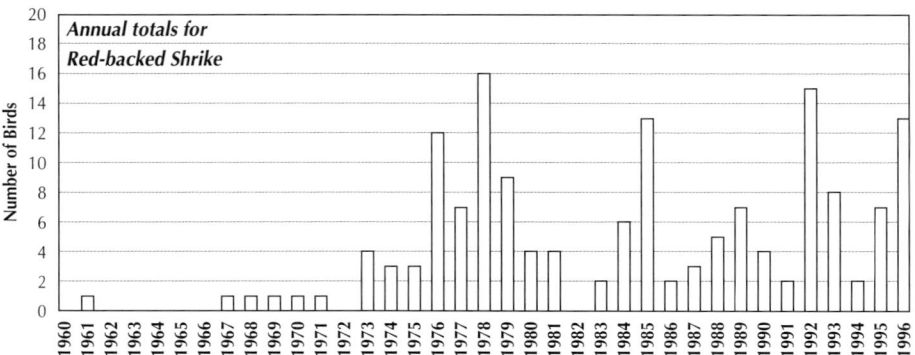

Annual totals for Red-backed Shrike

October. Records come from a number of sites along the east coast, with Rattray, Girdleness, Whinnyfold and Cruden Bay among the most regular.

Records of birds at inland locations during the breeding season have been received in four years (1977, 1979, 1987 and 1992). Breeding was confirmed in 1977 and subsequently in 1979.

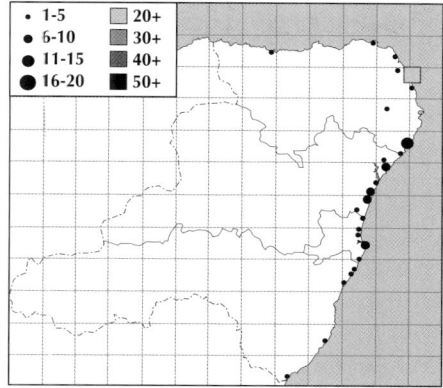

• 1-5	☐ 20+
• 6-10	▨ 30+
● 11-15	▩ 40+
● 16-20	■ 50+

Red-backed Shrike sightings

Lesser Grey Shrike *Lanius minor*

Breeds from France and Germany east to Turkestan and Afghanistan. Winters in Africa south of the Sahara.

Evans (1994) gives 47 records of this species in Scotland up to the end of 1990. There have been only four records since (Rogers *et al.* 1992, 1993, 1994, 1995). The majority of records come from the Northern Isles.

The single record for the North East region came in 1958 and was the first for mainland Scotland. The circumstances surrounding the find are exceptional. The bird was found just alive down a chimney in Aberdeen on 15th October, after the fire had been lit. Unfortunately, but not surprisingly, the singed bird died later. The bird had been ringed (and photographed) at the Monks House Observatory, Northumberland, on 13th September that year.

ALL RECORDS
1952 15 Oct *Aberdeen* dead (*BB* 46: plate 31b)

Lesser Grey Shrike
by M. Langman

Great Grey Shrike *Lanius excubitor*

Breeds across much of the Palearctic and Africa and also in North America. The northern populations move south and west in winter.

Small numbers pass through Scotland in autumn and a few overwinter (Thom 1986). This pattern is mirrored in the North East region.

The earliest record of this species is given by Adams, who reports a bird shot at Durris in 1844, another near Banchory in 1845 and one in 1859 (Sim 1903). One reported shot on the banks of the Dee in autumn 1846 may be one of these birds (*Naturalist* 1853).

Sim (1903) noted the species as a frequent though irregular visitor to 'Dee'. He gave instances of birds shot at Ballogie in 1865, Parkhill in 1866 and Lumphanan in 1889. Another note refers to a bird obtained at Old Aberdeen, giving no date. A bird wintered at Skene House in 1889–90 and in February 1890 a bird was shot at Aden and another on the Newton Estate. There was a third bird for that year, but he again gave no details other than it was a female. In March 1890, a female was shot at Aden,

and in May a bird flew aboard a fishing boat at sea off Aberdeen. The winter of 1889–90 was obviously an exceptional period for this species.

Sim (1903) also referred to a pair which apparently built a nest in a Spruce tree in the garden at Fyvie Castle. The nest contained one egg, but the female was later found dead at the foot of the tree. He gave no dates or no indication as to where the records had come from. A bird was seen in the same garden from November 1889 to February 1890, frequently catching Tits and Goldcrests, and another at Pitfour around 1891 (Serle 1895).

A female killed at Mintlaw in November 1895 (*Buchan Field Club* Vol. 5) is not mentioned by Sim (1903).

In the early part of this century there are even fewer notes. One was obtained near Littlewood, Alford, in January 1904 and another at Broomend, Inverurie on 21st

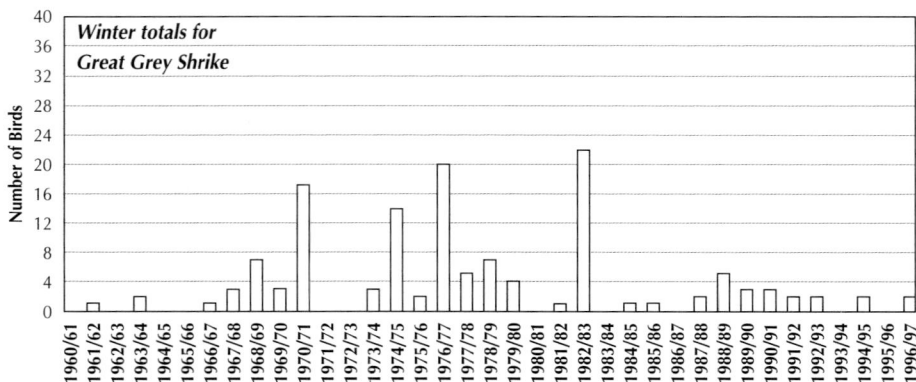

Winter totals for Great Grey Shrike

February 1904 (*TAWMNH Soc.* 1901-06). Mahood (1917-18) mentions one shot near Cullen in February 1908.

Since 1960 records have become more regular, and almost annual, but the number of birds reported in any one year varies considerably. In most years between one and three birds are seen. In other years notable influxes are recorded, with up to 17 birds in the winter of 1970-71, up to 20 in 1976-77 and up to 22 in the winter of 1982-83.

Coastal birds are reported during both spring and autumn migration periods. Autumn birds generally arrive between September and November, with a marked peak in October. The spring passage is less marked and birds have been reported between March and early May. These records of migrants are generally of single birds seen for short periods of time (one or two days) at east coast sites. No one site is considered to be more favoured than any other for migrant Great Grey Shrikes.

Records of inland birds are not uncommon, and small numbers of birds overwinter. The areas chosen by these over-wintering birds are often remote. This combined with poor observer coverage and a tendency for the birds to range over a wide area makes it often difficult to assess how many birds are over-wintering. Favoured areas appear to be Glen Tanar, the Forest of Birse area and the Davan and Kinnord region. A bird that had possibly over-wintered in 1974 in Glen Dye was heard in song on 5th April.

Woodchat Shrike *Lanius senator*

Breeds from north west Africa north to France and east to the Ukraine and southern Iran. Winters in Africa south of the Sahara.

This species is less than annual in Scotland, with the majority of records from the Northern Isles (Thom, 1986).

There have been two records of this species in the North East region, both in spring, which is typical of this species' occurrence in Scotland.

ALL RECORDS
1981 13-14 May **Rattray** (R.A.Schofield *et al.*)
1996 6 June **Girdleness** (S.A.Reeves)

Woodchat Shrike *by J. P. Smith*

Nutcracker *Nucifraga caryocatactes*

Breeds in the mountains of central and south eastern Europe and southern Fenno-Scandia east to Kamchatka. Mainly resident, though sometimes eruptive.

This species is extremely rare in Scotland, with only six birds seen this century and only three according to Thom (1986) for the last century.

There is only one record for the North East region. A bird is reported in the *New Statistical Account of Scotland* (1845) from the parish of Alford. Sim (1903) also noted this record in *The Vertebrate Fauna of Dee* reporting that a specimen '...had been found in the parish of Alford...', but he gave no further details. Baxter and Rintoul (1953) however, thought the record to be doubtful, but gave no reasons for arriving at this conclusion.

Rose-coloured Starling *Sturnus roseus*

Breeds from Hungary and the Balkans east to Kazakhstan and southern Iran. May erupt west in large numbers in summer. Winters in the Indian subcontinent.

The Rose-coloured Starling has been recorded almost annually in Scotland since 1968 (Thom 1986). The numbers reaching Scotland are small and most records come from the Northern Isles.

There is a note in the *New Statistical Account of Scotland* (1845) of this species being recorded from St Cyrus. Gray (1871) noted one shot near Aberdeen in June 1867, and another shot around the same time also near Aberdeen. He also noted a breeding attempt around Methlick in the summer of 1840. The birds were nesting in a sand bank before it was destroyed by small boys. Sim (1903) notes this also, but adds that the originator of the record made no reference to boys having destroyed the bank, nor that the bird had nested, only that the bird 'was there a considerable time, and might have been long enough to bring out a young brood.' Sim (1903) notes three records of this species. One was shot at Micras, Crathie, in 1867, and in the same year one shot near Aberdeen (obviously the birds mentioned by Gray, 1871). Another was shot at Manar, Donside, in 1879.

Rose-coloured Starling *by M. Langman*

In the early part of this century a report appeared in the *Courier*, of a bird shot in Deeside on 12th August 1922 (*Scot. Nat.* 1923-24) and another was reported from Luthermuir in August 1938. Baxter and Rintoul (1953) stated that the species 'has been authentically recorded in....Kincardine, Aberdeen, Banff...', but gave no details.

In more recent times there have been only five records of this species, all but one have referred to adults. One record came in June, two records have been in July and two in October. This species is often found/reported by non-birdwatchers well away from regular sites and we are grateful for these records: an interesting example of how non-birdwatchers can contribute to ornithological records.

ALL RECENT RECORDS
1974 17-29 Jun *Methlick* adult (T.Hodd, Mrs P.Hodd) (*BB* 68: RR)
1976 23 Oct-5Nov *Braemar* (Mrs J.Beech *et al.*) (*BB* 71: RR)
1993 24-27 Oct *Newburgh* juv (A.Anderson, P.Doyle, F.White) (*BB* 87: RR)
1994 15 Jul *Fraserburgh* adult (G.Noble, Mrs L.Noble) (*BB* 88: RR)
1995 6-9 Jul *New Deer* adult (L.T.A.Brain *et al.*) (*BB* 89: RR)

Arctic Redpoll *Cardulis hornemanni*

Breeds in circumpolar Arctic. Limited southward movement in winter.

This species is regularly reported in Scotland from the Northern Isles, with fewer from mainland Scotland (Evans 1994).

The first record of this species for the North East was of a single bird at Rattray on 20th January 1985. There was then a gap until 1994, when the second bird was seen at Girdleness in October, and the third at Cruden Bay in November.

There was an unprecedented influx of 'mealy' and Arctic Redpolls in the winter of 1995-96, with in excess of 200 Arctic Redpolls being reported from around Britain. This was mirrored in the North East region. Single birds were noted with small numbers of 'mealy' Redpolls along the coast in the early part of the winter. Individuals were seen at Fraserburgh and Rattray. Two different individuals were at Cruden Bay in November and December. Perhaps not surprisingly, birds were also being reported away from the coast. The first accepted record of this species inland was of a bird with a large flock of 'mealies' at the Loch of Davan, some 40 miles inland, on 28th December.

The turn of the year brought even more records. Two birds were together among a flock of 300 'mealies' at Aboyne on 8th January, the first multiple record of this species for the region. On the same day another bird was seen at Arnhall Moss, Westhill. Further searching of the Arnhall Moss flock produced at least five additional birds. All of the records to date that winter were then eclipsed by the discovery of a flock of Lesser, 'mealy' and Arctic Redpolls at Garlogie. This flock was present intermittently between

12th January and mid-March, and contained over 1,000 birds at its height. The number of Arctic Redpolls present in this flock was difficult to assess, with between 25 and 48 birds being reported. Photographic evidence along with detailed descriptions meant that up to 48 birds were accepted by BBRC.

ALL RECORDS

1985 20 Jan *Rattray* (G.Cresswell, D.Dickson et al.) (*BB* 79: RR)

1994 17 Oct *Girdleness* (J.R.W.Gordon, S.A.Reeves) (*BB* 89: RR)

1994 13 Nov *Cruden Bay* (J.Oates, I.M.Phillips, K.D.Shaw) (*BB* 88: RR)

1995 11 Nov *Rattray Head* (T.W.Marshall)

1995 12 Nov *Cruden Bay* (C.Barton, J.R.W.Gordon, I.Roberts) (*BB* 89: RR)

1995 10 Dec *Cruden Bay* (P.Bloor, C.Cronin, I.M.Phillips) (*BB* 89: RR)

1995 28 Dec *Kinnord* (I.M.Phillips, K.D.Shaw) (*BB* 89: RR)

1995 30-31 Dec *Fraserburgh* (I.Francis, I.M.Phillips, A.Webb) (*BB* 89: RR)

1996 8 Jan *Aboyne* (2) (I.M.Phillips, K.D.Shaw) (*BB* 90: RR)

1996 8-14 Jan *Arnhall Moss, Westhill* at least 5 (J.Oates, I.M.Phillips et al.)

1996 13-14 Jan *Garlogie* at least 10 (J.Oates, I.M.Phillips, M.Scott et al.)

1996 21-23 Mar *Garlogie* at least 48, all accepted by BBRC (I.M.Phillips, M.Scott, A.Webb et al.)

1996 26 Mar *nr Kintore* (2) (I.M.Phillips) (*BB* 90: RR)

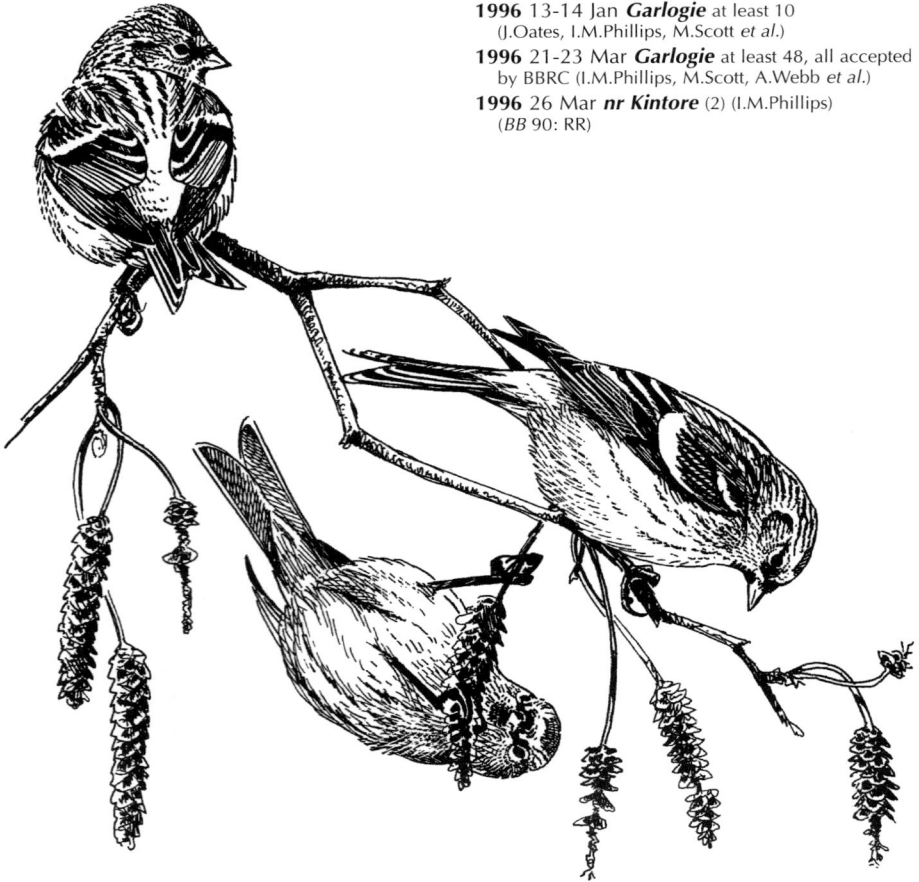

Arctic Redpolls with a Lesser Redpoll by M. Langman

Common Rosefinch *Carpodacus erythrinus*

Breeds from Germany and southern Sweden east to Kamchatka. Also from Georgia east to central China. This species is expanding its range in Europe and colonisation of Britain has been expected for some years. Winters in India, south east Asia and southern China.

The Common Rosefinch occurs annually in Scotland in small numbers and has bred (Thom 1986).

There have been 16 records of Common Rosefinch in the North East, since the first in 1979. Most records have been in Autumn (September and early October). Twelve records have occurred in the last five years, with eight of these in 1993. With this species' range expansion in Europe, the increase in records (both spring and autumn) is expected to continue.

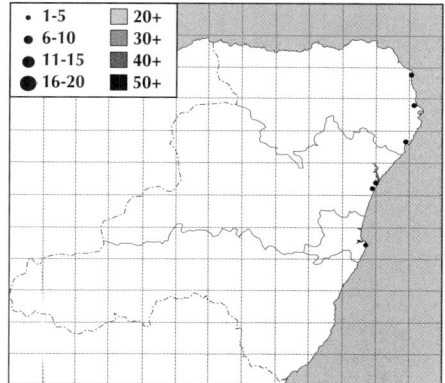

• 1-5	☐ 20+
• 6-10	▨ 30+
● 11-15	▦ 40+
⬤ 16-20	■ 50+

Common Rosefinch sightings

ALL RECORDS
1979 6 Oct *Drums*
1982 5 Oct *Newburgh*
1986 25 Oct *Rattray*
1987 3-4 Sep *Rattray* imm/female
1990 9-20 Sep *Cruden Bay* imm/female
1991 23 Aug *Girdleness* adult male
1992 11 Jun *Banff* singing first-summer male
1992 22 Sep *Rattray* imm/female
1993 1-4 June *Bridge of Don* male
1993 11 Jun *Donmouth* female
1993 12 Sep *Balmedie* imm/female
1993 20-22 Sep *Girdleness* imm/female
1993 30 Sep *Collieston* imm/female
1993 2 Oct *Cruden Bay* imm/female
1994 20 May *Cruden Bay* first-summer male trapped and ringed.
1994 30 May *Inverugie*
1995 27 May *Girdleness*

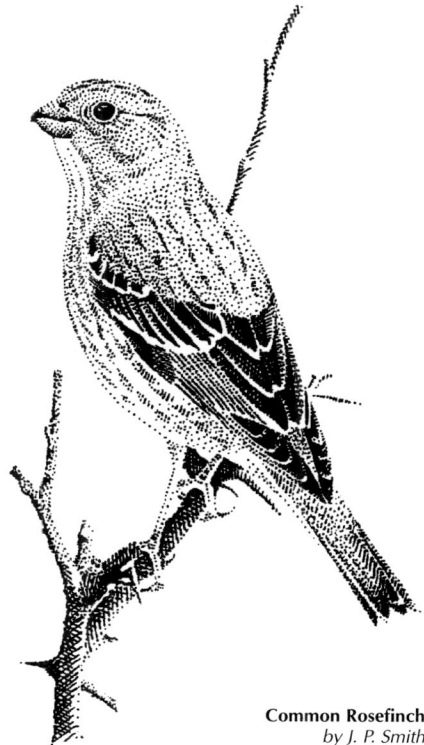

Common Rosefinch
by J. P. Smith

Hawfinch *Coccothraustes coccothraustes*

Breeds in the Palearctic from Spain and North Africa to Japan. Largely sedentary though some birds in the north of the breeding range move south in winter.

In Britain the Hawfinch is widely distributed in the south east of England, with local pockets through central and northern England. In Scotland there are only a scattering of records, mainly in the south east but extending as far north as Perthshire and Fife (Gibbons *et al.* 1993).

The oldest note of this species in the North East region is given by Gray (1871) who noted its occurrence in Aberdeenshire and Banffshire but gave no details. Sim (1903) placed the species in square brackets, quoting Gray's comments but adding that he knew of no specimen found in Dee.

The first definite record came on the 19th July 1904, when an immature male was shot near Peterhead. The condition of its plumage indicated that it may have been bred in the district (*TAWMNH Soc.* 1901-06). This was followed in July 1920, by the finding of the first nest at Methlick (*Scot. Nat.* 1920, *Brit. Birds* Vol. 15).

Since this time there have been sporadic records of this elusive finch. Many of these records have come from inland locations and may relate to small, localised breeding populations. Several coastal records at various times of the year may relate to migrants, or wandering birds. The majority of recent records have come from the Banchory area of Deeside. These are generally from the early part of the year, with birds appearing in gardens to feed. Breeding has been proven (adults feeding juveniles) in this area in recent years. There are scattered records from other parts of Deeside, the Ythan valley and as far north as Aden Country Park.

ALL RECENT RECORDS
1958 5 Oct *Allervale Cemetry, Aberdeen* (2)
1966 20 Apr *Aboyne* (2)
1967 14 Sep *Ellon* rescued from a cat
1975 22 Jan *Aberdeen* (2)
1980 18 Jan *Blackhall, Banchory*
1980 5 Jun *Gairn Bridge, Ballater*
1982 4 Jan *Aberdeen* ringed
1982 11 Jan-18 Feb *Banchory* (1-3)
1982 14 Oct *Newburgh* (2)
1984 26 Mar *Fyvie*
1984 29 Mar *Peterhead* (2)
1984 6-8 Apr *Oldmeldrum*
1985 28 Jul *Bieldside*
1986 31 May-1 Jun *Aboyne*
1988 22 May *Peterhead*
1988 23-30 Oct *Memsie* (1-3)
1990 11 Jun *Crathes Castle*
1992 3 Apr *Portlethen*
1992 13-23 May *Banchory (Blackhall)* (2)
1992 26 Oct *Aden Country Park*
1993 Jan-Mar *Banchory* several dates
1993 Jul *Banchory* 2 adults feeding 1 juv
1994 5 Jan *Banchory* (3)
1994 16 Jan *Banchory* (2)
1994 5 Mar *Banchory* (4)
1994 26 Nov *Banchory*
1995 18 Mar *Westhill Golf Course*
1996 31 Jul *Aberdeen* 2 adults feeding juv

Lapland Bunting *Calcarius lapponicus*

Breeds in the Arctic Circle. Small numbers have bred in Scotland. Northern Eurasian birds move south in winter.

Thom (1986) described Lapland Buntings as regular but scarce passage visitors, occasionally wintering. Birds are fairly regular on the east coast from Aberdeen to East Lothian.

The first record for the North East region came in January 1953 when a single bird was seen on the Tarty Burn, near Newburgh. In 1956, three were seen at Forvie on 30th September and were incorrectly thought to be the first for the region. From 1962 onwards there have been reports of this species in most years. The number of birds present in any one year can vary greatly, and the number at any site also varies. The records generally refer to small numbers of birds with between one and eight regular. In exceptional years flocks can build up over time to contain high numbers of birds. In the winter of 1977-78 a large flock wintered on the Ythan. It reached 34 birds on 17th December

1977, with 30 still present on 14th January the following year. Even this flock was surpassed in the winter of 1993-94, when a flock of nine birds appeared in a stubble field between Fraserburgh and Sandend on the 18th December and quickly built up to 50 birds by early February. This flock soon dispersed, with only small numbers recorded during March.

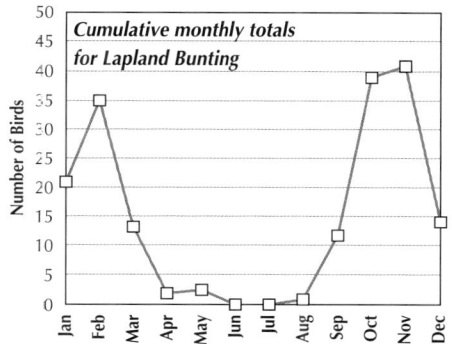

Cumulative monthly totals for Lapland Bunting

Lapland Bunting *by M. Langman*

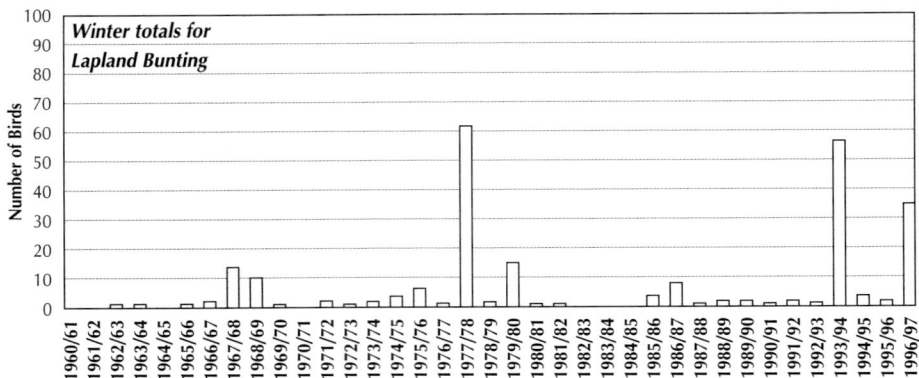

The majority of birds arrive in the region during October and November. A smaller number appear in February and March, indicating a return migration through the region. The east coast accounts for the majority of records, with the Ythan-Forvie area and Girdleness favoured sites. Despite this, coastal stubble fields in winter anywhere along the coastal strip are worth checking for this species.

There was a record of a single male inland in June 1995.

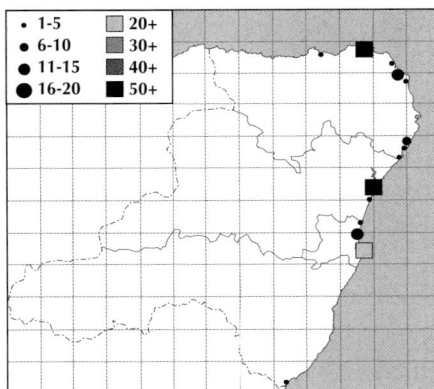

Lapland Bunting sightings

Ortolan Bunting *Emberiza hortulana*

Breeds from continental Europe and Fenno-Scandia east to northern Iran and Mongolia. Winters in south Arabia and the Sahel zone of the south Sahara.

This species was described as a scarce and decreasing migrant to Scotland, mainly in spring (Thom 1986). This situation remains true today.

The first note of this species for the North East region is given by Gray (1871), who refers to a letter from a Mr Angus who wrote that he had found a pair of Ortolan Buntings amongst a large quantity of Larks for sale at Castle Street, Aberdeen. They had been captured in a turnip field the previous day (last week of November 1863). Sim (1903) square-bracketed this reference, making no comment on it (This record is also noted in *ASNH* Vol. 4: 330, and *ASNH* Vol. 8: 362).

There have been only three recent records of this species from North East region. The recent records have all been of single birds, one in spring and two in autumn.

ALL RECENT RECORDS
1969 3 May *Torry*
1979 31 Aug *Girdleness* (A.Douglas)
1990 9 Sep *Cruden Bay* immature male or
  female (R.J.Aspinall, S.J.Aspinall)

Ortolan Bunting *by M. Langman*

Rustic Bunting *Emberiza rustica*

Breeds from Fenno-Scandia east to Kamchatka. Winters from Turkestan to Manchuria and eastern China.

This species is annual in Scotland in very small numbers. The majority of records have come from the Northern Isles and the Isle of May (Evans 1994).

There have been only three records (of four birds) in the North East region. Unusually this includes a pair 'obtained' in March 1905 (*ASNH* 1907). The date is very early for the occurrence of this species. The male at Rattray in June 1993 was well watched and appreciated by local birders.

ALL RECORDS
1905 Mar *Torphins* (2)
1986 5 Oct *Drums* (G.M.Cresswell, W.N.Hughes)
  (*EB* 80: RR)
1993 1 Jun *Rattray Head* male (T.W.Marshall)
  (*BB* 87: RR)

Little Bunting *Emberiza pusilla*

Breeds from Fenno-Scandia east to Sea of Okhotsk. Winters from Turkestan to south east Asia and China.

This species is annual in very small numbers in Scotland, particularly on the Northern Isles (Thom 1986).

The first record for the North East region was as recently as 1988. Unusually, this bird was seen on 2-4th May, the only spring record for the area and the only one to stay for more than a few hours. There have been only two further records, both of single birds on the east coast. One was at Balmedie in October 1992 and another at Girdleness in October 1993.

ALL RECORDS
1988 2-4 May *Rattray* (T.W.Marshall, A.Webb
  et al.) (*BB* 82: RR)
1992 1 Oct *Balmedie* (H.Gregory, I.M.Phillips)
  (*BB* 86: RR)
1993 9 Oct *Girdleness* (S.A.Reeves, B.J.Stewart)
  (*BB* 87: RR)

Recorded species
not on the regional list

Greater Flamingo *Phoenicopterus ruber*

The sub-species P.r.roseus breeds very locally in southern France, southern Spain, north west Africa, from the eastern states of the former USSR and Iraq eastwards to western India, also in Kenya and South Africa. The sub-species P.r.ruber breeds in the Caribbean and South America.

The British Ornithologists' Union Records Committee (BOURC) currently places all records of this species in Category D of the British list, as although vagrancy is possible, there is a liklihood of captive origin. The status of this species in Britain is currently under review by the BOURC, particularly as the population in France is increasing (Tucker and Heath 1994).

There is only one record for the area, that of an adult bird on the Ythan estuary from 31st May until 28th June 1994. The identification has been accepted by BBRC.

ALL RECORDS
1994 31 May-28 Jun *Ythan, nr Newburgh*

Ross's Goose *Anser rossi*

Breeds in the Canadian Arctic and on the shores of the Hudson Bay and the Beaufort Sea. The wintering areas were once exclusively restricted to the Sacremento valley in California but small numbers now reach northern Mexico and the Gulf Coasts of Louisiana and Texas.

This species is regularly kept in wildfowl collections. The escape potential is considered to be very high and as such the species is not on the British List. Several records from Scotland have definitely been escapes. During the 1960s a ringed pair regularly wintered in Central Scotland until 1972 when the last bird was found dead at Loch Leven (Evans 1994).

Other Scottish records may, however, have been genuine vagrants. A bird was present among Pink-footed Geese at Meikle Loch on 17th March 1985, and another (or the same) was in the Slains area in March 1988 (Scott 1992).

ALL RECORDS
1985 17 Mar *Meikle Loch*
1988 19 Mar *Slains area*

Ruddy Shelduck *Tadorna ferruginea*

Breeds in north west Africa, and from the Balkans eastward across southern Siberia to Mongolia. Mainly resident in north west Africa. The small Western Palearctic population winters mainly in Turkey and Egypt; also Iran and Iraq.

Small numbers occur annually in Britain, but most, if not all, are considered to be escapes or wanderers from recently established feral populations in the Netherlands (Dymond *et al*. 1989).

There are reports of two birds shot at Haddo House in 1893 (Sim 1903) with no comment on the suspected origin.

The species is irregular in its occurrence in the North East region, with single birds most often reported. In 1988 between four and eight birds were reported.

ALL RECENT RECORDS
1981 28 Jun *Ythan*
1981 4 Jul *Strathbeg* poss same as above
1984 1 May *Ythan*
1988 7 Aug *Balmedie* (4)
1988 16 Aug *Starthbeg* (2)
1988 27-28 Sept *Rashierieve* (4)
1988 27 Sept *Middlemuir* (4)
1988 18 Dec *Middlemuir*
1989 12 Feb *Meikle-Collieston area*
1989 3 Apr *Potterton* poss same as above
1995 14 May-17 Jun *Strathbeg*
1996 6 Oct *Strathbeg*

Yellow-legged Gull *Larus cachinnans*

Breeds from Iberia through the Mediterranean to the Black Sea and Caspian Sea. Winters throughout the breeding range and as far south as the Persian Gulf. There has been a recent and rapid range expansion to the Atlantic coast of France.

The Yellow-legged Gull was formerly considered to be a race of Herring Gull *L.argentatus*, but has recently been given full specific status by many authorities (except the BOU, which does not as yet recognise it as a full species).

The status of Yellow-legged Gull in Scotland is complicated by the fact that a proportion of Herring Gulls of the race *L. argentatus* breeding around the eastern Baltic have yellow legs, these being generally referred to as L. a. *omissus*. The status of *omissus* birds is poorly understood. Some authorities consider them to be a separate race of Herring Gull (Forrester 1995).

On 19 January 1969 a gull with yellow legs was seen at the Bridge of Don. The characters given by the finder were 'pure white, unstreaked head. Identical to nearby Herring Gulls in size, build and general behaviour. Bill appeared slightly brighter yellow with more noticeable red spot. Its back and wings were slightly darker than those of other Herring Gulls. The legs and feet were dull yellow, not as bright as those of a Lesser Black-backed Gull *L. fuscus*, but distinctly yellow and not merely pale flesh or ivory as in many Herring Gulls' (*Scot. Birds* Vol. 5). The author considered the bird to show characteristics of Scandinavian Herring Gull *L.a.omissus*. Forrester (1995) in a review of Scottish records of Yellow-legged Gull thought that the bird showed some characteristics of Yellow-legged Gull.

An adult Yellow-legged Gull thought to be of the race *L. c. michahellis* was present in the gull roost at the Donmouth on 5th June 1991. The identification of this bird was accepted by the local records committee, but is now regarded as inconclusive by SBRC.

ALL RECORDS
1969 19 Jan **Donmouth** possibly *omissus*
1991 5 Jun **Donmouth** (P.D.Bloor)

White-throated Sparrow *Zonotrichia albicollis*

Breeds mainly in Canada, wintering in the USA as far south as northern Mexico.

There is a record of a bird shot on Aberdeen Links on 17th August 1867. There was a comment with the record that 'the bird bore no traces of having been in confinement, the wings, tail and all the lower plumage, being quite clean.' (*Trans. Nat. Hist. Soc. of Glasgow* 1858-69, Vol. 1). This species was relegated to their Appendix of birds 'considered to be escapes' by Baxter and Rintoul (1953) and this included the bird now accepted as the first British record on the Flannan Isles in 1909 (Dymond *et al.* 1989).

Red-headed Bunting *Emberiza bruniceps*

Breeds from south east Russia eastwards into China and south to Iran. Winters in northern India.

The Red-headed Bunting is widely kept as a cagebird, Although the possibility of true vagrancy cannot be ruled out, most - if not all - occurrences in Britain are currently regarded as escapes from captivity.

There have been several records of this species in the North East region. A bird was trapped near Stonehaven on 29th May 1951 and another on 25th May 1969. A male was at Old Aberdeen on 25th May 1974 and another at St Cyrus on 27th July 1974.

Long-tailed Rosefinch *Uragus sibiricus*

Breeds in the foothills of southern Siberia and eastern Asia. Winters in the southern part of its range and in China, Korea and Japan.

Long-tailed Rosefinches have become an abundant cagebird since 1989, with large numbers now being offered for sale (Evans 1994).

There has been only one record of this species in the region: an adult male was present at Drums on the 4th May 1995.

North East Scotland birder's calendar

The birder's calendar

The calendar has been included to illustrate at a glance which of the rarer species were present on any day in the year. Brief summaries for each month indicate which of the scarce species may be likely during that month. This is not meant to be a comprehensive review, but a suggestion of what may (*or may not*) occur.

JANUARY

A month for hard work looking through winter geese and swans for Bean Goose and Bewick's Swans. Well worth checking gulls for Glaucous and Iceland Gulls with the chance of one of the rarer winter gulls. Offshore at favoured sights there may be wintering grebes, none of which are very common. Stubble fields, particulalry along the north coast, are worth checking for Lapland Bunting and Shore Lark.

JANUARY 1

Bittern	1973	Loch of Pitfour
Grey Phalarope	1978	Whitehills
Ivory Gull	1977	Westhill

JANUARY 2

Bittern	1973	Loch of Pitfour
Grey Phalarope	1978	Whitehills
Ivory Gull	1977	Westhill

JANUARY 3

Bittern	1973	Loch of Pitfour
Bewick's Swan (9)	1987	Ythan
Grey Phalarope	1978	Whitehills
Ivory Gull	1977	Westhill

JANUARY 4

Bittern	1973	Loch of Pitfour
Grey Phalarope	1978	Whitehills

JANUARY 5

Bittern	1973	Loch of Pitfour
Bittern	1992	Strathbeg
Grey Phalarope	1978	Whitehills

JANUARY 6

Bittern	1973	Loch of Pitfour
Bewick's Swan (4)	1991	Loirston
Grey Phalarope	1978	Whitehills

JANUARY 7

Bittern	1973	Loch of Pitfour
Grey Phalarope	1978	Whitehills

JANUARY 8

Bittern	1973	Loch of Pitfour
Bewick's Swan (3)	1992	Longside
Ring-billed Gull	1992	Donmouth

JANUARY 9

Pied-billed Grebe	1977	Strathbeg
Bittern	1973	Loch of Pitfour
Bewick's Swan	1977	Strathbeg

JANUARY 10

Pied-billed Grebe	1977	Strathbeg
Bittern	1973	Loch of Pitfour

JANUARY 11

Pied-billed Grebe	1977	Strathbeg
Bittern	1973	Loch of Pitfour
Sabine's Gull	1979	Fraserburgh

JANUARY 12

Pied-billed Grebe	1977	Strathbeg
Bittern	1973	Loch of Pitfour
Bewick's Swan (5)	1975	Skene
Grey Phalarope	1996	Fraserburgh

JANUARY 13

Pied-billed Grebe	1977	Strathbeg
Bittern	1973	Loch of Pitfour
Grey Phalarope	1996	Fraserburgh

JANUARY 14

Pied-billed Grebe	1977	Strathbeg
Bittern	1973	Loch of Pitfour
Grey Phalarope	1996	Fraserburgh

JANUARY 15

Pied-billed Grebe	1977	Strathbeg
Bittern	1973	Loch of Pitfour
Grey Phalarope	1996	Fraserburgh

JANUARY 16

Pied-billed Grebe	1977	Strathbeg
Bittern	1973	Loch of Pitfour
Grey Phalarope	1996	Fraserburgh

JANUARY 17

Pied-billed Grebe	1977	Strathbeg
Bittern	1973	Loch of Pitfour
Bewick's Swan (6)	1971	Strathbeg
Lesser Yellowlegs	1980	Cairnbulg
Grey Phalarope	1996	Fraserburgh

JANUARY 18
Pied-billed Grebe	1977	Strathbeg
Bittern	1973	Loch of Pitfour
Lesser Yellowlegs	1980	Cairnbulg
Grey Phalarope	1993	Fraserburgh
Grey Phalarope	1996	Fraserburgh
Ross's Gull (1-3)	1993	Fraserburgh

JANUARY 19
Pied-billed Grebe	1977	Strathbeg
Bittern	1973	Loch of Pitfour
Avocet	1986	Strathbeg
Lesser Yellowlegs	1980	Cairnbulg
Grey Phalarope	1993	Fraserburgh
Grey Phalarope	1996	Fraserburgh
Ross's Gull (1-3)	1993	Fraserburgh

JANUARY 20
Pied-billed Grebe	1977	Strathbeg
Bittern	1973	Loch of Pitfour
Avocet	1986	Strathbeg
Lesser Yellowlegs	1980	Cairnbulg
Grey Phalarope	1993	Fraserburgh
Grey Phalarope	1996	Fraserburgh
Ross's Gull (1-3)	1993	Fraserburgh

JANUARY 21
Pied-billed Grebe	1977	Strathbeg
Bittern	1973	Loch of Pitfour
Bewick's Swan	1996	North of Mintlaw
Avocet	1986	Strathbeg
Lesser Yellowlegs	1980	Cairnbulg
Grey Phalarope	1993	Fraserburgh
Grey Phalarope	1996	Fraserburgh
Ross's Gull (1-3)	1993	Fraserburgh

JANUARY 22
Pied-billed Grebe	1977	Strathbeg
Bittern	1973	Loch of Pitfour
Avocet	1986	Strathbeg
Lesser Yellowlegs	1980	Cairnbulg
Grey Phalarope	1993	Fraserburgh
Grey Phalarope	1995	Stonehaven
Ross's Gull (1-3)	1993	Fraserburgh

JANUARY 23
Pied-billed Grebe	1977	Strathbeg
Bittern	1973	Loch of Pitfour
Bittern	1977	River Deveron
Lesser Yellowlegs	1980	Cairnbulg
Grey Phalarope	1993	Fraserburgh
Ross's Gull (1-3)	1993	Fraserburgh

JANUARY 24
Pied-billed Grebe	1977	Strathbeg
Bittern	1973	Loch of Pitfour
Lesser Yellowlegs	1980	Cairnbulg
Ross's Gull (1-3)	1993	Fraserburgh

JANUARY 25
Pied-billed Grebe	1977	Strathbeg
Bittern	1973	Loch of Pitfour
Bittern	1980	Newburgh
Lesser Yellowlegs	1980	Cairnbulg
Ross's Gull (1-3)	1987	Fraserburgh

JANUARY 26
Pied-billed Grebe	1977	Strathbeg
Bittern	1973	Loch of Pitfour
Lesser Yellowlegs	1980	Cairnbulg
Ross's Gull (1-3)	1993	Fraserburgh

JANUARY 27
Pied-billed Grebe	1977	Strathbeg
Bittern	1973	Loch of Pitfour
Lesser Yellowlegs	1980	Cairnbulg
Ross's Gull (1-3)	1993	Fraserburgh

JANUARY 28
Pied-billed Grebe	1977	Strathbeg
Bittern	1973	Loch of Pitfour
Lesser Yellowlegs	1980	Cairnbulg
Ross's Gull (1-3)	1993	Fraserburgh

JANUARY 29
Pied-billed Grebe	1977	Strathbeg
Bittern	1973	Loch of Pitfour
Bittern	1987	Ythan
Bewick's Swan (6)	1992	St Fergus
Lesser Yellowlegs	1980	Cairnbulg
Ross's Gull (1-3)	1993	Fraserburgh

JANUARY 30
Pied-billed Grebe	1977	Strathbeg
Bittern	1973	Loch of Pitfour
Bittern	1991	Strathbeg
Lesser Yellowlegs	1980	Cairnbulg
Ross's Gull (1-3)	1993	Fraserburgh

JANUARY 31
Pied-billed Grebe	1977	Strathbeg
Bittern	1973	Loch of Pitfour
Lesser Yellowlegs	1980	Cairnbulg
Ross's Gull	1997	Fraserburgh

FEBRUARY

Another month for wildfowl and gulls. Sightings of Red-necked Grebes peak in this month. Coastal finch/bunting flocks may still hold variable numbers of Lapland Buntings and even Shore Lark. Inland overwintering Great Grey Shrikes may still be located.

FEBRUARY 1
Pied-billed Grebe	1977	Strathbeg
Bittern	1973	Loch of Pitfour
Lesser Yellowlegs	1980	Cairnbulg
Ross's Gull	1997	Fraserburgh

FEBRUARY 2
Pied-billed Grebe	1977	Strathbeg
Bittern	1973	Loch of Pitfour
Lesser Yellowlegs	1980	Cairnbulg

FEBRUARY 3
Pied-billed Grebe	1977	Strathbeg
Bittern	1973	Loch of Pitfour
Lesser Yellowlegs	1980	Cairnbulg

FEBRUARY 4
Pied-billed Grebe	1977	Strathbeg
Lesser Yellowlegs	1980	Cairnbulg
Grey Phalarope	1995	Fraserburgh

FEBRUARY 5
| Pied-billed Grebe | 1977 | Strathbeg |
| Lesser Yellowlegs | 1980 | Cairnbulg |

FEBRUARY 6
Pied-billed Grebe	1977	Strathbeg
Lesser Yellowlegs	1980	Cairnbulg
Ring-billed Gull	1993	Murcar

FEBRUARY 7
Pied-billed Grebe	1977	Strathbeg
Bewick's Swan	1965	Pittenheath
Lesser Yellowlegs	1980	Cairnbulg

FEBRUARY 8
| Pied-billed Grebe | 1977 | Strathbeg |
| Lesser Yellowlegs | 1980 | Cairnbulg |

FEBRUARY 9
| Pied-billed Grebe | 1977 | Strathbeg |
| Lesser Yellowlegs | 1980 | Cairnbulg |

FEBRUARY 10
Pied-billed Grebe	1977	Strathbeg
Bittern	1991	Strathbeg
Lesser Yellowlegs	1980	Cairnbulg

FEBRUARY 11
| Pied-billed Grebe | 1977 | Strathbeg |
| Lesser Yellowlegs | 1980 | Cairnbulg |

FEBRUARY 12
| Pied-billed Grebe | 1977 | Strathbeg |
| Lesser Yellowlegs | 1980 | Cairnbulg |

FEBRUARY 13
Pied-billed Grebe	1977	Strathbeg
Bewick's Swan (3)	1976	New Aberdour
Lesser Yellowlegs	1980	Cairnbulg

FEBRUARY 14
Pied-billed Grebe	1977	Strathbeg
Great Shearwater	1981	Fraserburgh
Lesser Yellowlegs	1980	Cairnbulg
Ring-billed Gull	1976	Ythan

FEBRUARY 15
Pied-billed Grebe	1977	Strathbeg
Bewick's Swan (3)	1964	Skene
Lesser Yellowlegs	1980	Cairnbulg

FEBRUARY 16
Pied-billed Grebe	1977	Strathbeg
Ring-necked Duck	1969	Donmouth
Lesser Yellowlegs	1980	Cairnbulg

FEBRUARY 17
Pied-billed Grebe	1977	Strathbeg
Avocet	1980	Ythan
Lesser Yellowlegs	1980	Cairnbulg
Grey Phalarope	1979	Collieston

FEBRUARY 18
Pied-billed Grebe	1977	Strathbeg
Lesser Yellowlegs	1980	Cairnbulg
Grey Phalarope	1979	Collieston

FEBRUARY 19
Pied-billed Grebe	1977	Strathbeg
Bewick's Swan (6)	1964	Strathbeg
Lesser Yellowlegs	1980	Cairnbulg
Grey Phalarope	1979	Collieston

FEBRUARY 20
Pied-billed Grebe	1977	Strathbeg
Lesser Yellowlegs	1980	Cairnbulg
Grey Phalarope	1979	Collieston

FEBRUARY 21
Pied-billed Grebe	1977	Strathbeg
Bewick's Swan	1974	Birsemore
Lesser Yellowlegs	1980	Cairnbulg

FEBRUARY 22
| Pied-billed Grebe | 1977 | Strathbeg |
| Lesser Yellowlegs | 1980 | Cairnbulg |

FEBRUARY 23
White-billed Diver	1979	Banff Bay
Pied-billed Grebe	1977	Strathbeg
Lesser Yellowlegs	1980	Cairnbulg

FEBRUARY 24
| Pied-billed Grebe | 1977 | Strathbeg |
| Lesser Yellowlegs | 1980 | Cairnbulg |

FEBRUARY 25
| Pied-billed Grebe | 1977 | Strathbeg |
| Lesser Yellowlegs | 1980 | Cairnbulg |

FEBRUARY 26
| Pied-billed Grebe | 1977 | Strathbeg |
| Lesser Yellowlegs | 1980 | Cairnbulg |

FEBRUARY 27
Pied-billed Grebe	1977	Strathbeg
White Stork	1977	Monymusk
Lesser Yellowlegs	1980	Cairnbulg

FEBRUARY 28
| Pied-billed Grebe | 1977 | Strathbeg |
| Lesser Yellowlegs | 1980 | Cairnbulg |

MARCH

March sees the start of a turnover in birds as wildfowl start to move north. This may result in short staying Bean Geese moving north from the wintering grounds in England and south west Scotland. As Wigeon numbers change it is worth checking for American

Wigeon, particularly at the Loch of Strathbeg. This is also probably the best month for Rough-legged Buzzard as wintering birds start their move north for the summer.

MARCH 1
Pied-billed Grebe	1977	Strathbeg
Bewick's Swan (6)	1992	St Fergus
Lesser Yellowlegs	1980	Cairnbulg

MARCH 2
Pied-billed Grebe	1977	Strathbeg
Bewick's Swan (6)	1992	St Fergus
Lesser Yellowlegs	1980	Cairnbulg

MARCH 3
| Pied-billed Grebe | 1977 | Strathbeg |
| Lesser Yellowlegs | 1980 | Cairnbulg |

MARCH 4
| Pied-billed Grebe | 1977 | Strathbeg |
| Lesser Yellowlegs | 1980 | Cairnbulg |

MARCH 5
Pied-billed Grebe	1977	Strathbeg
Bewick's Swan (3)	1972	Strathbeg
Lesser Yellowlegs	1980	Cairnbulg

MARCH 6
| Pied-billed Grebe | 1977 | Strathbeg |
| Lesser Yellowlegs | 1980 | Cairnbulg |

MARCH 7
| Pied-billed Grebe | 1977 | Strathbeg |
| Lesser Yellowlegs | 1980 | Cairnbulg |

MARCH 8
| Pied-billed Grebe | 1977 | Strathbeg |
| Lesser Yellowlegs | 1980 | Cairnbulg |

MARCH 9
| Pied-billed Grebe | 1977 | Strathbeg |
| Lesser Yellowlegs | 1980 | Cairnbulg |

MARCH 10
| Pied-billed Grebe | 1977 | Strathbeg |
| Lesser Yellowlegs | 1980 | Cairnbulg |

MARCH 11
| Pied-billed Grebe | 1977 | Strathbeg |
| Lesser Yellowlegs | 1980 | Cairnbulg |

MARCH 12
Pied-billed Grebe	1977	Strathbeg
Ferruginous Duck	1977	Strathbeg
Lesser Yellowlegs	1980	Cairnbulg

MARCH 13
Pied-billed Grebe	1977	Strathbeg
Ferruginous Duck	1977	Strathbeg
Lesser Yellowlegs	1980	Cairnbulg

MARCH 14
Pied-billed Grebe	1977	Strathbeg
Ferruginous Duck	1977	Strathbeg
Lesser Yellowlegs	1980	Cairnbulg

MARCH 15
Pied-billed Grebe	1977	Strathbeg
Ferruginous Duck	1977	Strathbeg
Lesser Yellowlegs	1980	Cairnbulg

MARCH 16
Pied-billed Grebe	1977	Strathbeg
Ferruginous Duck	1977	Strathbeg
Lesser Yellowlegs	1980	Cairnbulg

MARCH 17
Pied-billed Grebe	1977	Strathbeg
Bewick's Swan	1979	Monymusk
Ferruginous Duck	1977	Strathbeg
Lesser Yellowlegs	1980	Cairnbulg

MARCH 18
Pied-billed Grebe	1977	Strathbeg
Bewick's Swan	1979	Monymusk
Ferruginous Duck	1977	Strathbeg
Lesser Yellowlegs	1980	Cairnbulg

MARCH 19
Pied-billed Grebe	1977	Strathbeg
Bewick's Swan	1979	Monymusk
Ferruginous Duck	1977	Strathbeg
Lesser Yellowlegs	1980	Cairnbulg

MARCH 20
Pied-billed Grebe	1977	Strathbeg
Bewick's Swan	1979	Monymusk
Ferruginous Duck	1977	Strathbeg
Lesser Yellowlegs	1980	Cairnbulg

MARCH 21
Pied-billed Grebe	1977	Strathbeg
American Wigeon	1974	near Strathbeg
Ferruginous Duck	1977	Strathbeg
Lesser Yellowlegs	1980	Cairnbulg

MARCH 22
Pied-billed Grebe	1977	Strathbeg
American Wigeon	1974	near Strathbeg
Ferruginous Duck	1977	Strathbeg
Lesser Yellowlegs	1980	Cairnbulg

MARCH 23
Pied-billed Grebe	1977	Strathbeg
Ferruginous Duck	1977	Strathbeg
Avocet	1969	Ythan
Lesser Yellowlegs	1980	Cairnbulg

MARCH 24
White-billed Diver	1969	Rattray
White-billed Diver	1996	Peterhead
Pied-billed Grebe	1977	Strathbeg
Ferruginous Duck	1977	Strathbeg
Avocet	1969	Ythan
Lesser Yellowlegs	1980	Cairnbulg

MARCH 25
White-billed Diver	1996	Peterhead
Pied-billed Grebe	1977	Strathbeg
Ferruginous Duck	1977	Strathbeg
Avocet	1969	Ythan
Lesser Yellowlegs	1980	Cairnbulg

MARCH 26
| White-billed Diver | 1996 | Peterhead |
| Pied-billed Grebe | 1977 | Strathbeg |

Ferruginous Duck	1977	Strathbeg
Avocet	1969	Ythan
Lesser Yellowlegs	1980	Cairnbulg

MARCH 27
Pied-billed Grebe	1977	Strathbeg
Bewick's Swan (2)	1989	Logie Buchan
Ferruginous Duck	1977	Strathbeg
Avocet (2)	1984	Ythan
Lesser Yellowlegs	1980	Cairnbulg
Firecrest	1989	Girdleness

MARCH 28
Lesser Yellowlegs	1980	Cairnbulg

MARCH 29
Lesser Yellowlegs	1980	Cairnbulg

MARCH 30
Lesser Yellowlegs	1980	Cairnbulg
Hoopoe	1995	Downies

MARCH 31
Lesser Yellowlegs	1980	Cairnbulg

APRIL

As a feel for spring arrives in April the opportunities for rare and scarce migrants improve. The number of records of Slavonian Grebe increases in April as birds move into their Scottish breeding areas in neighbouring districts. Towards the end of the month migrant Honey Buzzards could be seen or even the elusive Gyr Falcon. At least one King Eider usually arrives on the Ythan by the months end.

APRIL 1
Lesser Yellowlegs	1980	Cairnbulg

APRIL 2
Lesser Yellowlegs	1980	Cairnbulg
Little Owl	1986	Rothienorman

APRIL 3
Lesser Yellowlegs	1980	Cairnbulg

APRIL 4
Lesser Yellowlegs	1980	Cairnbulg

APRIL 5
Lesser Yellowlegs	1980	Cairnbulg

APRIL 6
Lesser Yellowlegs	1980	Cairnbulg
Water Pipit	1993	Strathbeg

APRIL 7
Lesser Yellowlegs	1980	Cairnbulg
Water Pipit	1993	Strathbeg

APRIL 8
Lesser Yellowlegs	1980	Cairnbulg
Water Pipit	1994	Strathbeg

APRIL 9
Lesser Yellowlegs	1980	Cairnbulg
Water Pipit	1994	Strathbeg

APRIL 10
Lesser Yellowlegs	1980	Cairnbulg
Water Pipit	1994	Strathbeg

APRIL 11
Lesser Yellowlegs	1980	Cairnbulg
Water Pipit	1994	Strathbeg

APRIL 12
Lesser Yellowlegs	1980	Cairnbulg
Water Pipit	1994	Strathbeg

APRIL 13
Killdeer	1995	Strathbeg
Lesser Yellowlegs	1980	Cairnbulg

APRIL 14
Gyr Falcon	1993	Ben Macdhui
Lesser Yellowlegs	1980	Cairnbulg

APRIL 15
White Stork	1969	Milltimber/Balmedie
American Wigeon	1972	Auchlossan
American Wigeon	1996	Strathbeg
Lesser Yellowlegs	1980	Cairnbulg

APRIL 16
White Stork	1969	Milltimber/Balmedie
White Stork	1982	Rora
American Wigeon	1972	Auchlossan
Lesser Yellowlegs	1980	Cairnbulg

APRIL 17
White Stork	1969	Milltimber/Balmedie
American Wigeon	1972	Auchlossan
Avocet	1979	Ythan
Lesser Yellowlegs	1980	Cairnbulg
Subalpine Warbler	1993	Rattray

APRIL 18
White Stork	1969	Milltimber/Balmedie
American Wigeon	1972	Auchlossan
Lesser Yellowlegs	1980	Cairnbulg

APRIL 19
White Stork	1969	Milltimber/Balmedie
American Wigeon	1972	Auchlossan
Gyr Falcon	1973	Glen Tanar
Avocet	1990	Ythan
Lesser Yellowlegs	1980	Cairnbulg
Alpine Swift	1970	Rattray

APRIL 20
White Stork	1969	Milltimber/Balmedie
American Wigeon	1972	Auchlossan
Avocet	1990	Ythan
Lesser Yellowlegs	1980	Cairnbulg

APRIL 21
Great White Egret	1989	Loirston

American Wigeon	1972	Auchlossan
Gyr Falcon	1990	Strathdon
Avocet	1990	Ythan
Lesser Yellowlegs	1980	Cairnbulg

APRIL 22

Great White Egret	1978	Loirston
American Wigeon	1972	Auchlossan
Lesser Yellowlegs	1980	Cairnbulg

APRIL 23

Spoonbill	1978	Strathbeg
American Wigeon	1972	Auchlossan
Lesser Yellowlegs	1980	Cairnbulg

APRIL 24

Spoonbill	1978	Strathbeg
Gyr Falcon	1995	Glen Quoich
Hoopoe	1995	near Longside

APRIL 25

White Stork	1979	Banchory/Maryculter
Spoonbill	1978	Strathbeg
Red-necked Phalarope	1979	Fraserburgh
Hoopoe	1995	near Longside

APRIL 26

White Stork	1979	Banchory/Maryculter
Spoonbill	1978	Strathbeg
Hoopoe	1995	near Longside

APRIL 27

White Stork	1979	Banchory/Maryculter
Spoonbill	1978	Strathbeg
Hoopoe	1995	near Longside
Golden Oriole	1987	Forglen

APRIL 28

White Stork	1979	Banchory/Maryculter
Spoonbill	1978	Strathbeg
Hoopoe	1995	near Longside

APRIL 29

White Stork	1979	Banchory/Maryculter
Spoonbill	1978	Strathbeg
Hoopoe	1995	near Longside

APRIL 30

White Stork	1979	Banchory/Maryculter
Spoonbill	1978	Strathbeg
Kentish Plover	1984	Rattray
Hoopoe	1995	near Longside

MAY

This is the month when hopes of rare migrants is at its spring peak. Bluethroats, Red-backed Shrikes, Hoopoes and Wrynecks all occur in variable numbers throughout the month. Rarities have included Greenish Warbler, Richard's Pipit, Nightingale, Little

Bunting, Kentish Plover, Broad-billed sandpiper and Lesser Yellowlegs. Spring passage of Common Rosefinch occurs but numbers are still small. The number of Marsh Harriers passing through the region, particularly the Loch of Strathbeg, peaks during the month. The majority of records of Red-footed Falcon occur in May. The end of the month often sees a light passage of Temminck's Stints. Variable numbers of Black Terns pass through the area during May.

MAY 1

White Stork	1979	Banchory/Maryculter
Spoonbill	1978	Strathbeg
Hoopoe	1995	near Longside

MAY 2

White Stork	1979	Banchory/Maryculter
Spoonbill	1978	Strathbeg
Hoopoe	1995	near Longside
Little Bunting	1988	Rattray

MAY 3

Night Heron	1975	Newburgh
White Stork	1979	Banchory/Maryculter
Spoonbill	1978	Strathbeg
Black Kite	1996	Girdleness
Kentish Plover	1962	Ythan
Forster's Tern	1995	Ythan
Hoopoe	1995	near Longside
Nightingale	1990	Girdleness
Ortolan Bunting	1969	Torry
Little Bunting	1988	Rattray

MAY 4

Night Heron	1975	Newburgh
White Stork	1979	Banchory/Maryculter
Spoonbill	1978	Strathbeg
American Wigeon	1957	Meikle Loch
Kentish Plover	1962	Ythan
Forster's Tern	1995	Ythan
Little Owl	1991	Strathbeg
Hoopoe	1969	Torry
Hoopoe	1995	near Longside

MAY 5

Night Heron	1975	Newburgh
White Stork	1979	Banchory/Maryculter
Spoonbill	1978	Strathbeg
American Wigeon	1957	Meikle Loch
Black Kite	1996	Meikle Loch
Forster's Tern	1995	Ythan
Little Owl	1991	Strathbeg

Hoopoe	1983	Fetteresso
Hoopoe	1995	near Longside

MAY 6

Night Heron	1975	Newburgh
Little Egret	1993	Cults Pool
Little Egret	1995	North Esk
White Stork	1979	Banchory/Maryculter
Spoonbill	1978	Strathbeg
Bewick's Swan	1976	Strathbeg
Forster's Tern	1995	Ythan
Hoopoe	1995	near Longside
Richard's Pipit	1989	Donmouth

MAY 7

Bittern	1970	Laurencekirk
Night Heron	1975	Newburgh
White Stork	1979	Banchory/Maryculter
Spoonbill	1978	Strathbeg
Spoonbill	1988	Strathbeg
Avocet (2)	1993	Strathbeg
Forster's Tern	1995	Ythan
Hoopoe	1971	Forter
Hoopoe	1995	near Longside

MAY 8

Night Heron	1975	Newburgh
White Stork	1979	Banchory/Maryculter
Spoonbill	1978	Strathbeg
Spoonbill	1988	Strathbeg
Forster's Tern	1995	Ythan
Hoopoe	1995	near Longside
Firecrest	1977	Donmouth

MAY 9

White Stork	1979	Banchory/Maryculter
Spoonbill	1978	Strathbeg
Spoonbill	1988	Strathbeg
Honey Buzzard	1981	Deeside
Forster's Tern	1995	Ythan
Hoopoe	1975	Portsoy
Hoopoe	1995	near Longside

MAY 10

Purple Heron	1992	Corby Loch
White Stork	1979	Banchory/Maryculter
Spoonbill	1978	Strathbeg
Spoonbill	1988	Strathbeg
Ring-necked Duck	1992	Strathbeg
Kentish Plover	1981	Ythan
Forster's Tern	1995	Ythan

MAY 11

White Stork	1971	Bridge of Alvah
White Stork	1975	Fintray
White Stork	1979	Banchory/Maryculter
Spoonbill	1978	Strathbeg
Spoonbill	1988	Strathbeg
Ring-necked Duck	1992	Strathbeg
Kentish Plover	1981	Ythan
Temminck's Stint	1993	Strathbeg
Long-billed Dowitcher	1980	Meikle
Forster's Tern	1995	Ythan
Firecrest	1974	Cruden Bay
Firecrest	1975	Foveran

MAY 12

White Stork	1975	Fintray

White Stork	1979	Banchory/Maryculter
Spoonbill	1978	Strathbeg
Spoonbill	1988	Strathbeg
Ring-necked Duck	1992	Strathbeg
Kentish Plover	1981	Ythan
Long-billed Dowitcher	1980	Meikle
Forster's Tern	1995	Ythan
Thrush Nightingale	1981	Newburgh
Nightingale	1989	Bullers of Buchan
Nightingale	1993	Girdleness

MAY 13

White Stork	1975	Fintray
White Stork	1979	Banchory/Maryculter
Spoonbill	1978	Strathbeg
Spoonbill	1988	Strathbeg
Ring-necked Duck	1992	Strathbeg
Kentish Plover	1981	Ythan
Temminck's Stint	1975	Auchmacoy
Temminck's Stint	1989	Donmouth
Forster's Tern	1995	Ythan
Hoopoe	1969	Banff
Woodchat Shrike	1981	Rattray

MAY 14

White Stork	1975	Fintray
White Stork	1979	Banchory/Maryculter
Spoonbill	1978	Strathbeg
Spoonbill	1988	Strathbeg
Ring-necked Duck	1992	Strathbeg
Kentish Plover	1981	Ythan
Temminck's Stint	1989	Donmouth
Forster's Tern	1995	Ythan
Tawny Pipit	1981	Newburgh
Woodchat Shrike	1981	Rattray

MAY 15

White Stork	1975	Fintray
White Stork	1979	Banchory/Maryculter
Spoonbill	1974	Strathbeg
Spoonbill	1975	Strathbeg
Spoonbill	1978	Strathbeg
Spoonbill	1988	Strathbeg
Marsh Sandpiper	1990	Cotehill
Forster's Tern	1995	Ythan

MAY 16

White Stork	1975	Fintray
White Stork	1979	Banchory/Maryculter
Spoonbill	1974	Strathbeg
Spoonbill	1975	Strathbeg
Spoonbill	1978	Strathbeg
Spoonbill	1988	Strathbeg
Forster's Tern	1995	Ythan
Red-rumped Swallow	1987	Nigg, Girdleness

MAY 17

White Stork	1975	Fintray
White Stork	1979	Banchory/Maryculter
Spoonbill	1974	Strathbeg
Spoonbill	1975	Strathbeg
Spoonbill	1975	Strathbeg
Spoonbill	1978	Strathbeg
Spoonbill	1988	Strathbeg
Forster's Tern	1995	Ythan
Hoopoe	1966	Strachan

The following entries appear at the top of the right column before MAY 13:

White Stork	1979	Banchory/Maryculter
Spoonbill	1978	Strathbeg
Spoonbill	1988	Strathbeg
Ring-necked Duck	1992	Strathbeg
Kentish Plover	1981	Ythan

MAY 18

White Stork	1975	Fintray
White Stork	1979	Banchory/Maryculter
Spoonbill	1974	Strathbeg
Spoonbill	1975	Strathbeg
Spoonbill	1975	Strathbeg
Spoonbill	1978	Strathbeg
Spoonbill	1988	Strathbeg
Lesser Yellowlegs	1992	Cults Pool
Forster's Tern	1995	Ythan

MAY 19

White Stork	1975	Fintray
Spoonbill	1974	Strathbeg
Spoonbill	1975	Strathbeg
Spoonbill	1975	Strathbeg
Spoonbill	1978	Strathbeg
Spoonbill	1988	Strathbeg
Temminck's Stint	1989	Rigifa
Lesser Yellowlegs	1992	Cults Pool
Grey Phalarope	1975	North Esk
Forster's Tern	1995	Ythan
Nightingale	1973	Girdleness
Great Reed Warbler	1985	Girdleness

MAY 20

White Stork	1975	Fintray
Spoonbill	1974	Strathbeg
Spoonbill	1975	Strathbeg
Spoonbill	1978	Strathbeg
Spoonbill	1988	Strathbeg
Temminck's Stint	1989	Strathbeg
Forster's Tern	1995	Ythan
Nightingale	1973	Girdleness
Common Rosefinch	1994	Cruden Bay

MAY 21

White Stork	1975	Fintray
Spoonbill	1975	Strathbeg
Spoonbill	1978	Strathbeg
Spoonbill	1988	Strathbeg
Forster's Tern	1995	Ythan
Hoopoe	1981	New Deer
Eye-browed Thrush	1981	Newburgh

MAY 22

Little Egret	1974	Strathbeg
White Stork	1975	Fintray
Spoonbill	1975	Strathbeg
Spoonbill	1978	Strathbeg
Spoonbill	1988	Strathbeg
Forster's Tern	1995	Ythan
Bee-eater (2)	1993	Newburgh
Hoopoe	1981	New Deer

MAY 23

Little Egret	1974	Strathbeg
White Stork	1975	Fintray
Spoonbill	1975	Strathbeg
Spoonbill	1978	Strathbeg
Forster's Tern	1995	Ythan
White-winged Black Tern	1987	Meikle
White-winged Black Tern	1992	Strathbeg
Bee-eater (2)	1993	Newburgh
Hoopoe	1981	New Deer
Nightingale	1977	St Cyrus

MAY 24

Little Egret	1974	Strathbeg
White Stork	1975	Fintray
Spoonbill	1975	Strathbeg
Spoonbill	1978	Strathbeg
Montague's Harrier	1993	Boddam
Forster's Tern	1995	Ythan
White-winged Black Tern	1987	Meikle
Hoopoe	1981	New Deer
Icterine Warbler	1994	Collieston
Golden Oriole	1981	Strathbeg

MAY 25

Little Egret	1974	Strathbeg
White Stork	1975	Fintray
Spoonbill	1975	Strathbeg
Spoonbill	1978	Strathbeg
Broad-billed Sandpiper	1974	North Esk
Forster's Tern	1995	Ythan
White-winged Black Tern	1975	Meikle
White-winged Black Tern	1987	Meikle
Hoopoe	1981	New Deer
Short-toed Lark	1995	Rattray
Richard's Pipit	1995	Rattray

MAY 26

Little Egret	1974	Strathbeg
White Stork	1975	Fintray
Spoonbill	1975	Strathbeg
Spoonbill	1978	Strathbeg
Spoonbill	1992	Strathbeg
Montague's Harrier	1963	Ythan
Temminck's Stint	1975	Strathbeg
Forster's Tern	1995	Ythan
White-winged Black Tern	1987	Meikle

MAY 27

Little Egret	1974	Strathbeg
White Stork	1975	Fintray
Spoonbill	1975	Strathbeg
Spoonbill	1978	Strathbeg
Spoonbill	1992	Strathbeg
Forster's Tern	1995	Ythan
Common Rosefinch	1995	Girdleness

MAY 28

Little Egret	1974	Strathbeg
White Stork	1975	Fintray
Spoonbill	1975	Strathbeg
Spoonbill	1978	Strathbeg
Spoonbill	1992	Strathbeg
Forster's Tern	1995	Ythan
Suba pine Warbler	1987	Rattray

MAY 29

Little Egret	1974	Strathbeg
White Stork	1975	Fintray
Spoonbill	1975	Strathbeg
Spoonbill	1978	Strathbeg
Spoonbill	1992	Strathbeg
Spoonbill	1992	Ythan
Red-footed Falcon	1985	Auchmacoy
Temminck's Stint	1975	Meikle
Temminck's Stint	1978	St Fergus
Forster's Tern	1995	Ythan
Hoopoe	1967	Inveray
Icterine Warbler	1992	Whinnyfold

MAY 30

White Stork	1975	Fintray
Spoonbill	1975	Strathbeg
Spoonbill	1978	Strathbeg
Spoonbill	1992	Strathbeg
Black Kite	1979	Strathbeg
Red-footed Falcon	1985	Auchmacoy
Temminck's Stint	1978	Strathbeg
Temminck's Stint	1985	Donmouth
Temminck's Stint	1992	Strathbeg
Broad-billed Sandpiper	1988	Ythan
Forster's Tern	1995	Ythan
Common Rosefinch	1994	Inverugie

MAY 31

White Stork	1975	Fintray
Spoonbill	1975	Strathbeg
Spoonbill	1975	Strathbeg
Spoonbill	1978	Strathbeg
Spoonbill	1992	Strathbeg
Honey Buzzard	1976	St Cyrus
Red-footed Falcon	1992	Kirkton
Temminck's Stint	1975	St Cyrus
Temminck's Stint	1985	Donmouth
Temminck's Stint	1991	Strathbeg
Temminck's Stint	1992	Strathbeg
Broad-billed Sandpiper	1988	Ythan
Forster's Tern	1995	Ythan
Marsh Warbler	1993	Muchalls
Greenish Warbler	1992	Rattray

JUNE

Migration often continues into June with Red-backed Shrikes and Bluethroats still possible. Most Surf Scoters are reported from this period, generally from the Murcar-Blackdog area. Hobbies are frequently seen during June and Little Egrets have started to wander around the region in recent years. Temminck's Stints still pass through at this time and early (or late?) Pectoral Sandpipers have also been reported during June.

JUNE 1

Little Egret	1993	Strathbeg
White Stork	1975	Fintray
Spoonbill	1975	Strathbeg
Spoonbill	1978	Strathbeg

Spoonbill	1992	Strathbeg
Red-footed Falcon	1992	Kirkton
Temminck's Stint	1992	Strathbeg
Broad-billed Sandpiper	1988	Ythan
Forster's Tern	1995	Ythan
Rustic Bunting	1993	Rattray

JUNE 2

Little Egret	1993	Strathbeg
White Stork	1967	Inverurie
White Stork	1975	Fintray
Spoonbill	1975	Strathbeg
Spoonbill	1978	Strathbeg
Spoonbill	1992	Strathbeg
Blue-winged Teal	1980	Rattray
Red-footed Falcon	1992	Kirkton
Temminck's Stint	1977	Meikle
Temminck's Stint	1992	Strathbeg
Broad-billed Sandpiper	1988	Ythan
Forster's Tern	1995	Ythan
Siberian Stonechat	1993	Forest of Birse

JUNE 3

Little Egret	1993	Strathbeg
White Stork	1975	Fintray
Spoonbill	1975	Strathbeg
Spoonbill	1978	Strathbeg
Spoonbill	1992	Strathbeg
Montague's Harrier	1991	Ythan
Red-footed Falcon	1992	Kirkton
Temminck's Stint	1976	Strathbeg
Broad-billed Sandpiper	1988	Ythan
Forster's Tern	1995	Ythan
Siberian Stonechat	1993	Forest of Birse
Common Rosefinch	1993	Bridge of Don

JUNE 4

Little Egret	1993	Strathbeg
White Stork	1975	Fintray
Spoonbill	1975	Strathbeg
Spoonbill	1978	Strathbeg
Spoonbill	1992	Strathbeg
Honey Buzzard	1981	Strathbeg
Montague's Harrier	1991	Ythan
Red-footed Falcon	1992	Kirkton
Forster's Tern	1995	Ythan
Alpine Swift	1981	Banchory-Devenick
Siberian Stonechat	1993	Forest of Birse
Common Rosefinch	1993	Bridge of Don

JUNE 5

Little Egret	1993	Strathbeg
White Stork	1975	Fintray
Spoonbill	1975	Strathbeg
Spoonbill	1978	Strathbeg
Spoonbill	1992	Strathbeg
Red-footed Falcon	1992	Kirkton
Forster's Tern	1995	Ythan
Alpine Swift	1981	Banchory-Devenick
Siberian Stonechat	1993	Forest of Birse
Icterine Warbler	1984	Strathbeg

JUNE 6

Little Egret	1993	Strathbeg
Little Egret	1996	Strathbeg
White Stork	1975	Fintray
Spoonbill	1975	Strathbeg

Spoonbill	1978	Strathbeg
Spoonbill	1992	Strathbeg
American Wigeon	1992	Strathbeg
Red-footed Falcon	1992	Kirkton
Pectoral Sandpiper	1990	Strathbeg
Forster's Tern	1995	Ythan
Alpine Swift	1981	Banchory-Devenick
Siberian Stonechat	1993	Forest of Birse
Icterine Warbler	1984	Strathbeg
Woodchat Shrike	1996	Girdleness

JUNE 7

Little Egret	1993	Strathbeg
White Stork	1967	Ellon
White Stork	1975	Fintray
Spoonbill (2)	1972	Ythan
Spoonbill	1975	Strathbeg
Spoonbill	1978	Strathbeg
Spoonbill	1992	Strathbeg
American Wigeon	1992	Strathbeg
Red-footed Falcon	1992	Kirkton
Pectoral Sandpiper	1990	Strathbeg
Forster's Tern	1995	Ythan
Alpine Swift	1981	Banchory-Devenick
Hoopoe	1988	Dunecht
Siberian Stonechat	1993	Forest of Birse

JUNE 8

Little Egret	1996	Ythan
White Stork	1967	Ellon
White Stork	1975	Fintray
Spoonbill (2)	1972	Ythan
Spoonbill	1975	Strathbeg
Spoonbill	1978	Strathbeg
Spoonbill	1992	Strathbeg
American Wigeon	1992	Strathbeg
Honey Buzzard	1984	Gight
Red-footed Falcon	1992	Kirkton
Temminck's Stint	1976	Strathbeg
Temminck's Stint	1977	Strathbeg
Pectoral Sandpiper	1990	Strathbeg
Forster's Tern	1995	Ythan
Alpine Swift	1981	Banchory-Devenick
Siberian Stonechat	1993	Forest of Birse

JUNE 9

Little Egret	1996	Ythan
White Stork	1967	Ellon
White Stork	1975	Fintray
Spoonbill	1970	Strathbeg
Spoonbill (2)	1972	Ythan
Spoonbill	1975	Strathbeg
Spoonbill	1978	Strathbeg
Spoonbill	1992	Strathbeg
Red-footed Falcon	1992	Kirkton
Pectoral Sandpiper	1990	Strathbeg
Sabine's Gull	1995	Girdleness
Forster's Tern	1995	Ythan
Siberian Stonechat	1993	Forest of Birse

JUNE 10

Little Egret	1996	Ythan
Great White Egret	1992	Ythan
Purple Heron	1996	Strathbeg
White Stork	1975	Fintray
Spoonbill	1970	Strathbeg

Spoonbill (2)	1972	Ythan
Spoonbill	1975	Strathbeg
Spoonbill	1978	Strathbeg
Spoonbill	1981	Strathbeg
Spoonbill	1992	Strathbeg
Red-footed Falcon	1992	Kirkton
Temminck's Stint	1976	Strathbeg
Pectoral Sandpiper	1990	Strathbeg
Sabine's Gull	1995	Girdleness
Forster's Tern	1995	Ythan
Siberian Stonechat	1993	Forest of Birse

JUNE 11

Little Egret	1996	Ythan
Great White Egret	1992	Ythan
Purple Heron	1996	Strathbeg
White Stork	1975	Fintray
Spoonbill	1970	Strathbeg
Spoonbill (2)	1972	Ythan
Spoonbill	1975	Strathbeg
Spoonbill	1978	Strathbeg
Spoonbill	1992	Strathbeg
Red-footed Falcon	1992	Kirkton
Pectoral Sandpiper	1992	Strathbeg
Sabine's Gull	1995	Girdleness
Forster's Tern	1995	Ythan
Siberian Stonechat	1993	Forest of Birse
Common Rosefinch	1992	Banff
Common Rosefinch	1993	Donmouth

JUNE 12

Little Egret	1996	Ythan
Great White Egret	1992	Ythan
Purple Heron	1996	Strathbeg
White Stork	1975	Fintray
Spoonbill	1970	Strathbeg
Spoonbill (2)	1972	Ythan
Spoonbill	1975	Strathbeg
Spoonbill	1978	Strathbeg
Spoonbill	1992	Strathbeg
Honey Buzzard	1976	New Deer
Red-footed Falcon	1992	Kirkton
Red-necked Phalarope	1978	Strathbeg
Sabine's Gull	1995	Girdleness
Forster's Tern	1995	Ythan
Siberian Stonechat	1993	Forest of Birse

JUNE 13

Little Egret	1996	Ythan
Great White Egret	1992	Ythan
Purple Heron	1996	Strathbeg
White Stork	1975	Fintray
Spoonbill	1970	Strathbeg
Spoonbill (2)	1972	Ythan
Spoonbill	1975	Strathbeg
Spoonbill	1978	Strathbeg
Spoonbill	1992	Strathbeg
Honey Buzzard	1974	Deeside
Red-footed Falcon	1992	Kirkton
Forster's Tern	1995	Ythan
Siberian Stonechat	1993	Forest of Birse

JUNE 14

Little Egret	1983	Haddo House
Little Egret	1996	Ythan
Great White Egret	1992	Ythan

White Stork	1975	Fintray
Spoonbill (2)	1972	Ythan
Spoonbill	1975	Strathbeg
Spoonbill	1978	Strathbeg
Spoonbill	1992	Strathbeg
Forster's Tern	1995	Ythan
Siberian Stonechat	1993	Forest of Birse

JUNE 15

Little Egret	1996	Ythan
Great White Egret	1992	Ythan
White Stork	1975	Fintray
Spoonbill (2)	1972	Ythan
Spoonbill	1978	Strathbeg
Spoonbill	1992	Strathbeg
Forster's Tern	1995	Ythan
Siberian Stonechat	1993	Forest of Birse

JUNE 16

Great Shearwater	1971	Rattray
Little Egret	1996	Ythan
White Stork	1975	Fintray
Spoonbill	1972	Ythan
Spoonbill	1978	Strathbeg
Spoonbill	1992	Strathbeg
Forster's Tern	1995	Ythan
Siberian Stonechat	1993	Forest of Birse

JUNE 17

Little Egret	1996	Ythan
White Stork	1975	Fintray
Spoonbill	1972	Ythan
Spoonbill	1978	Strathbeg
Spoonbill	1992	Strathbeg
Forster's Tern	1995	Ythan
Siberian Stonechat	1993	Forest of Birse
Icterine Warbler	1992	Fordyce
Rose-coloured Starling	1974	Methlick

JUNE 18

Bittern	1991	Strathbeg
Little Egret	1996	Ythan
White Stork	1975	Fintray
Spoonbill	1972	Ythan
Spoonbill	1978	Strathbeg
Spoonbill	1992	Strathbeg
Forster's Tern	1995	Ythan
Siberian Stonechat	1993	Forest of Birse
Icterine Warbler	1992	Fordyce
Rose-coloured Starling	1974	Methlick

JUNE 19

Bittern	1991	Strathbeg
Little Egret	1996	Ythan
White Stork	1975	Fintray
Spoonbill	1972	Ythan
Spoonbill	1978	Strathbeg
Spoonbill	1992	Strathbeg
Forster's Tern	1995	Ythan
Siberian Stonechat	1993	Forest of Birse
Icterine Warbler	1992	Fordyce
Rose-coloured Starling	1974	Methlick

JUNE 20

Bittern	1991	Strathbeg
Little Egret	1996	Ythan
White Stork	1975	Fintray

Spoonbill	1972	Ythan
Spoonbill	1978	Strathbeg
Spoonbill	1992	Strathbeg
Honey Buzzard	1988	Glen Dye
Red-footed Falcon	1975	Crimmond
Forster's Tern	1995	Ythan
Siberian Stonechat	1993	Forest of Birse
Icterine Warbler	1992	Fordyce
Rose-coloured Starling	1974	Methlick

JUNE 21

Bittern	1991	Strathbeg
Little Egret	1996	Ythan
Spoonbill	1972	Ythan
Spoonbill	1978	Strathbeg
Spoonbill	1992	Strathbeg
Forster's Tern	1995	Ythan
White-winged Black Tern	1967	Meikle
Siberian Stonechat	1993	Forest of Birse
Icterine Warbler	1992	Fordyce
Rose-coloured Starling	1974	Methlick

JUNE 22

Bittern	1991	Strathbeg
Little Egret	1996	Ythan
Spoonbill	1972	Ythan
Spoonbill	1978	Strathbeg
Spoonbill	1992	Strathbeg
Forster's Tern	1995	Ythan
Siberian Stonechat	1993	Forest of Birse
Icterine Warbler	1992	Fordyce
Rose-coloured Starling	1974	Methlick

JUNE 23

Bittern	1991	Strathbeg
Little Egret	1996	Ythan
Great White Egret	1978	Strathbeg
Spoonbill	1972	Ythan
Spoonbill	1978	Strathbeg
Spoonbill	1992	Strathbeg
Forster's Tern	1995	Ythan
Siberian Stonechat	1993	Forest of Birse
Rose-coloured Starling	1974	Methlick

JUNE 24

Little Egret	1996	Ythan
Great White Egret	1978	Strathbeg
Spoonbill	1970	Ythan
Spoonbill	1972	Ythan
Spoonbill	1978	Strathbeg
Spoonbill	1992	Strathbeg
Forster's Tern	1995	Ythan
Siberian Stonechat	1993	Forest of Birse
Rose-coloured Starling	1974	Methlick

JUNE 25

Little Egret	1996	Ythan
Great White Egret	1978	Strathbeg
Spoonbill	1970	Ythan
Spoonbill	1972	Ythan
Spoonbill	1978	Strathbeg
Spoonbill	1992	Strathbeg
Honey Buzzard	1994	Peterhead
Caspian Tern	1975	Ythan
Forster's Tern	1995	Ythan
White-winged Black Tern	1989	Meikle

| Siberian Stonechat | 1993 | Forest of Birse |
| Rose-coloured Starling | 1974 | Methlick |

JUNE 26

Little Egret	1996	Ythan
Great White Egret	1978	Strathbeg
Spoonbill	1970	Ythan
Spoonbill	1972	Ythan
Spoonbill	1992	Strathbeg
Pectoral Sandpiper	1989	Strathbeg
Forster's Tern	1995	Ythan
White-winged Black Tern	1989	Meikle
Siberian Stonechat	1993	Forest of Birse
Rose-coloured Starling	1974	Methlick

JUNE 27

Little Egret	1996	Ythan
Great White Egret	1978	Strathbeg
Spoonbill	1970	Ythan
Spoonbill	1972	Ythan
Spoonbill	1991	Strathbeg
Spoonbill	1992	Strathbeg
Pectoral Sandpiper	1989	Strathbeg
Forster's Tern	1995	Ythan
Siberian Stonechat	1993	Forest of Birse
Rose-coloured Starling	1974	Methlick

JUNE 28

Little Egret	1996	Ythan
Great White Egret	1978	Strathbeg
Spoonbill	1970	Ythan
Spoonbill	1972	Ythan
Spoonbill	1991	Strathbeg
Spoonbill	1992	Strathbeg
Temminck's Stint	1977	Rattray
Pectoral Sandpiper	1989	Strathbeg
Forster's Tern	1995	Ythan
Roller	1969	Peterhead
Siberian Stonechat	1993	Forest of Birse
Rose-coloured Starling	1974	Methlick

JUNE 29

Little Egret	1996	Ythan
Spoonbill	1970	Ythan
Spoonbill	1972	Ythan
Spoonbill	1991	Strathbeg
Spoonbill	1992	Strathbeg
Forster's Tern	1995	Ythan
Roller	1969	Peterhead
Siberian Stonechat	1993	Forest of Birse
Rose-coloured Starling	1974	Methlick

JUNE 30

Little Egret	1996	Ythan
Spoonbill	1970	Ythan
Spoonbill	1972	Ythan
Spoonbill	1991	Strathbeg
Spoonbill	1992	Strathbeg
Red-necked Phalarope	1979	Meikle
Red-necked Phalarope	1984	Meikle
Forster's Tern	1995	Ythan
Roller	1969	Peterhead
Siberian Stonechat	1993	Forest of Birse

JULY

Temminck's Stints are often recorded, possibly as non-breeders return south. Two adult White-rumped Sandpipers, the only American Golden Plover and the only Least Sandpiper have been recorded during July illustrating the months potential for rare waders.

JULY 1

Little Egret	1996	Ythan
Spoonbill	1970	Ythan
Spoonbill	1972	Ythan
Spoonbill	1978	Ythan
Spoonbill	1991	Strathbeg
Spoonbill	1992	Strathbeg
Forster's Tern	1995	Ythan
Roller	1969	Peterhead
Siberian Stonechat	1993	Forest of Birse

JULY 2

Little Egret	1996	Ythan
Spoonbill	1970	Ythan
Spoonbill	1972	Ythan
Spoonbill	1977	Strathbeg
Spoonbill	1978	Ythan
Spoonbill	1991	Strathbeg
Spoonbill	1992	Strathbeg
Forster's Tern	1995	Ythan
Roller	1969	Peterhead
Siberian Stonechat	1993	Forest of Birse

JULY 3

Little Egret	1996	Ythan
Spoonbill	1970	Ythan
Spoonbill	1972	Ythan
Spoonbill	1977	Strathbeg
Spoonbill	1991	Strathbeg
Spoonbill	1992	Strathbeg
Honey Buzzard	1988	Ben Macdhui
Temminck's Stint	1977	Meikle
Forster's Tern	1995	Ythan
Bee-eater	1991	Crimmond
Roller	1969	Peterhead
Siberian Stonechat	1993	Forest of Birse

JULY 4

Little Egret	1996	Ythan
Spoonbill	1970	Ythan
Spoonbill	1972	Ythan
Spoonbill	1977	Strathbeg
Spoonbill	1991	Strathbeg
Spoonbill	1992	Strathbeg
White-rumped Sandpiper	1993	Strathbeg
Forster's Tern	1995	Ythan

Roller	1969	Peterhead
Siberian Stonechat	1993	Forest of Birse

JULY 5

Little Egret	1996	Ythan
Spoonbill	1970	Ythan
Spoonbill	1972	Ythan
Spoonbill	1991	Strathbeg
Spoonbill	1992	Strathbeg
Forster's Tern	1995	Ythan
Roller	1969	Peterhead
Siberian Stonechat	1993	Forest of Birse

JULY 6

Little Egret	1996	Ythan
Spoonbill	1970	Ythan
Spoonbill	1972	Ythan
Spoonbill	1986	Ythan
Spoonbill	1991	Strathbeg
Spoonbill	1992	Strathbeg
Avocet	1986	Ythan
Sabine's Gull	1995	Girdleness
Forster's Tern	1995	Ythan
Roller	1969	Peterhead
Siberian Stonechat	1993	Forest of Birse
Rose-coloured Starling	1995	New Deer

JULY 7

Little Egret	1996	Ythan
Spoonbill	1970	Ythan
Spoonbill	1972	Ythan
Spoonbill	1991	Strathbeg
Spoonbill	1992	Strathbeg
Avocet	1986	Ythan
Forster's Tern	1995	Ythan
Roller	1969	Peterhead
Rose-coloured Starling	1995	New Deer

JULY 8

Little Egret	1996	Ythan
Spoonbill	1970	Ythan
Spoonbill	1971	Ythan
Spoonbill	1972	Ythan
Spoonbill	1991	Strathbeg
Spoonbill	1992	Strathbeg
Avocet	1986	Ythan
Forster's Tern	1995	Ythan
Roller	1969	Peterhead
Rose-coloured Starling	1995	New Deer

JULY 9

Little Egret	1996	Ythan
Spoonbill	1970	Ythan
Spoonbill	1972	Ythan
Spoonbill	1977	Ythan
Spoonbill	1991	Strathbeg
Spoonbill	1992	Strathbeg
American Golden Plover	1995	Ythan
Forster's Tern	1995	Ythan
Rose-coloured Starling	1995	New Deer

JULY 10

Little Egret	1996	Ythan
Spoonbill	1970	Ythan
Spoonbill	1972	Ythan
Spoonbill	1991	Strathbeg
Spoonbill	1992	Strathbeg
Forster's Tern	1995	Ythan

JULY 11

Little Egret	1996	Ythan
Spoonbill	1970	Ythan
Spoonbill	1972	Ythan
Spoonbill	1991	Strathbeg
Spoonbill	1992	Strathbeg
Forster's Tern	1995	Ythan

JULY 12

Little Egret	1996	Ythan
Spoonbill	1970	Ythan
Spoonbill	1972	Ythan
Spoonbill	1991	Strathbeg
Spoonbill	1992	Strathbeg
Honey Buzzard	1980	Deeside
Forster's Tern	1995	Ythan

JULY 13

Little Egret	1996	Ythan
Spoonbill	1970	Ythan
Spoonbill	1972	Ythan
Spoonbill	1991	Strathbeg
Spoonbill	1992	Strathbeg
Forster's Tern	1995	Ythan

JULY 14

Little Egret	1996	Ythan
Spoonbill	1970	Ythan
Spoonbill	1972	Ythan
Spoonbill	1991	Strathbeg
Spoonbill	1992	Strathbeg
Forster's Tern	1995	Ythan
White-winged Black Tern	1991	Annachie

JULY 15

Little Egret	1996	Ythan
Spoonbill	1970	Ythan
Spoonbill	1972	Ythan
Spoonbill	1991	Strathbeg
Spoonbill	1992	Strathbeg
Temminck's Stint	1977	Meikle
Forster's Tern	1995	Ythan
White-winged Black Tern	1991	Annachie
Rose-coloured Starling	1994	Fraserburgh

JULY 16

Little Egret	1996	Ythan
Spoonbill	1970	Ythan
Spoonbill	1972	Ythan
Spoonbill	1991	Strathbeg
Spoonbill	1992	Strathbeg
American Wigeon	1989	Cotehill Loch
Forster's Tern	1995	Ythan
White-winged Black Tern	1991	Annachie

JULY 17

Little Egret	1996	Ythan
Spoonbill	1970	Ythan
Spoonbill	1972	Ythan
Spoonbill	1991	Strathbeg
Spoonbill	1992	Strathbeg
American Wigeon	1989	Cotehill Loch
Forster's Tern	1995	Ythan
White-winged Black Tern	1991	Annachie

JULY 18

Little Egret	1996	Ythan
Spoonbill	1970	Ythan

Spoonbill	1972	Ythan
Spoonbill	1991	Strathbeg
Spoonbill	1992	Strathbeg
Spoonbill	1993	Strathbeg
Temminck's Stint	1975	Meikle
Forster's Tern	1995	Ythan
White-winged Black Tern	1991	Annachie

JULY 19

Leach's Petrel	1988	Collieston
Little Egret	1996	Ythan
Spoonbill	1970	Ythan
Spoonbill	1972	Ythan
Spoonbill	1991	Strathbeg
Spoonbill	1992	Strathbeg
Spoonbill	1993	Strathbeg
Temminck's Stint	1975	Meikle
Forster's Tern	1995	Ythan
White-winged Black Tern	1991	Annachie

JULY 20

Little Egret	1996	Ythan
Spoonbill	1970	Ythan
Spoonbill	1972	Ythan
Spoonbill	1991	Strathbeg
Spoonbill	1992	Strathbeg
Spoonbill	1993	Strathbeg
Red-footed Falcon	1978	Balmedie
Temminck's Stint	1975	Meikle
Forster's Tern	1995	Ythan
White-winged Black Tern	1991	Annachie

JULY 21

Little Egret	1996	Ythan
Spoonbill	1970	Ythan
Spoonbill	1972	Ythan
Spoonbill	1991	Strathbeg
Spoonbill	1992	Strathbeg
Spoonbill	1993	Strathbeg
Red-footed Falcon	1978	Balmedie
Temminck's Stint	1975	Meikle
Temminck's Stint	1977	Ythan
Pectoral Sandpiper	1993	Strathbeg
Forster's Tern	1995	Ythan
White-winged Black Tern	1991	Annachie

JULY 22

Little Egret	1996	Ythan
Spoonbill	1970	Ythan
Spoonbill	1972	Ythan
Spoonbill	1984	Strathbeg
Spoonbill	1991	Strathbeg
Spoonbill	1992	Strathbeg
Spoonbill	1993	Strathbeg
Temminck's Stint	1975	Meikle
Pectoral Sandpiper	1993	Strathbeg
Forster's Tern	1995	Ythan
White-winged Black Tern	1991	Annachie

JULY 23

Little Egret	1996	Ythan
Spoonbill	1970	Ythan
Spoonbill	1972	Ythan
Spoonbill	1984	Strathbeg
Spoonbill	1991	Strathbeg
Spoonbill	1992	Strathbeg
Spoonbill	1993	Strathbeg

Temminck's Stint	1975	Meikle
Forster's Tern	1995	Ythan

JULY 24

Cory's Shearwater	1990	Girdleness
Little Egret	1996	Ythan
Spoonbill	1970	Ythan
Spoonbill	1972	Ythan
Spoonbill	1984	Strathbeg
Spoonbill	1991	Strathbeg
Spoonbill	1992	Strathbeg
Spoonbill	1993	Strathbeg
Temminck's Stint	1975	Meikle
Forster's Tern	1995	Ythan

JULY 25

Little Egret	1996	Ythan
Spoonbill	1970	Ythan
Spoonbill	1972	Ythan
Spoonbill	1984	Strathbeg
Spoonbill	1991	Strathbeg
Spoonbill	1992	Strathbeg
Spoonbill	1993	Strathbeg
Temminck's Stint	1975	Meikle
Caspian Tern	1976	Ythan
Forster's Tern	1995	Ythan

JULY 26

Little Egret	1996	Ythan
Spoonbill	1970	Ythan
Spoonbill	1972	Ythan
Spoonbill	1991	Strathbeg
Spoonbill	1992	Strathbeg
Spoonbill	1993	Strathbeg
American Wigeon	1989	North Esk
Temminck's Stint	1976	Meikle
Forster's Tern	1995	Ythan

JULY 27

Leach's Petrel	1987	Peterhead
Little Egret	1996	Ythan
Spoonbill	1970	Ythan
Spoonbill	1972	Ythan
Spoonbill	1991	Strathbeg
Spoonbill	1992	Strathbeg
Spoonbill	1993	Strathbeg
American Wigeon	1989	North Esk
Temminck's Stint	1976	Meikle
Forster's Tern	1995	Ythan

JULY 28

Little Egret	1996	Ythan
Spoonbill	1970	Ythan
Spoonbill	1972	Ythan
Spoonbill	1991	Strathbeg
Spoonbill	1992	Strathbeg
Spoonbill	1993	Strathbeg
American Wigeon	1989	North Esk
Forster's Tern	1995	Ythan

JULY 29

Little Egret	1996	Ythan
Spoonbill	1970	Ythan
Spoonbill	1972	Ythan
Spoonbill	1991	Strathbeg
Spoonbill	1992	Strathbeg
American Wigeon	1989	North Esk

<table>
Ring-billed Gull	1995	Donmouth
Forster's Tern	1995	Ythan
</table>

JULY 30

Little Egret	1996	Ythan
Spoonbill	1970	Ythan
Spoonbill	1972	Ythan
Spoonbill	1991	Strathbeg
Spoonbill	1992	Strathbeg
American Wigeon	1989	North Esk
White-rumped Sandpiper	1995	Annachie
Forster's Tern	1995	Ythan

JULY 31

Leach's Petrel	1985	Greg Ness
Little Egret	1996	Ythan
Spoonbill	1970	Ythan
Spoonbill	1972	Ythan
Spoonbill	1991	Strathbeg
Spoonbill	1992	Strathbeg
American Wigeon	1989	North Esk
Least Sandpiper	1988	Rigifa
White-rumped Sandpiper	1995	Annachie
Grey Phalarope	1977	Strathbeg
Forster's Tern	1995	Ythan

AUGUST

Autumn migration starts often in August. Passage of Black Terns is often noticeable around the region and a number of Pectoral Sandpiper records are from this month. Greenish Warblers and Barred Warblers have both been recorded this early in the autumn. Seawatching at this time has produced the majority of records of Mediterranean Shearwater, Cory's Shearwater and Great Shearwater.

AUGUST 1

Little Egret	1996	Ythan
Spoonbill	1970	Ythan
Spoonbill	1972	Ythan
Spoonbill	1991	Strathbeg
Spoonbill	1992	Strathbeg
American Wigeon	1989	North Esk
Honey Buzzard	1976	Deeside
Forster's Tern	1995	Ythan

AUGUST 2

Great Shearwater	1989	Girdleness
Little Egret	1996	Ythan
Spoonbill	1970	Ythan
Spoonbill	1972	Ythan
Spoonbill	1991	Strathbeg
Spoonbill	1992	Strathbeg
American Wigeon	1989	North Esk
Bridled Tern	1988	Ythan

AUGUST 3

Great Shearwater (8)	1969	Rattray
Leach's Petrel	1987	Collieston
Little Egret	1996	Ythan
Spoonbill	1970	Ythan
Spoonbill	1972	Ythan
Spoonbill	1991	Strathbeg
Spoonbill	1992	Strathbeg
American Wigeon	1989	North Esk
Icterine Warbler	1986	Strathbeg

AUGUST 4

Little Egret	1996	Ythan
Spoonbill	1970	Ythan
Spoonbill	1972	Ythan
Spoonbill	1991	Strathbeg
Spoonbill	1992	Strathbeg
American Wigeon	1989	North Esk
Pectoral Sandpiper	1990	Strathbeg

AUGUST 5

Great Shearwater (2)	1969	Rattray
Great Shearwater	1973	Collieston
Leach's Petrel	1978	Drums
Little Egret	1996	Ythan
Spoonbill	1970	Ythan
Spoonbill	1972	Ythan
Spoonbill	1991	Strathbeg
Spoonbill	1992	Strathbeg
American Wigeon	1989	North Esk

AUGUST 6

Little Egret	1996	Ythan
Spoonbill	1970	Ythan
Spoonbill	1972	Ythan
Spoonbill	1991	Strathbeg
Spoonbill	1992	Strathbeg
American Wigeon	1989	North Esk
Lesser Yellowlegs	1980	Ythan

AUGUST 7

Leach's Petrel	1989	Collieston
Little Egret	1996	Ythan
Spoonbill	1970	Ythan
Spoonbill	1972	Ythan
Spoonbill	1991	Strathbeg
Spoonbill	1992	Strathbeg
American Wigeon	1989	North Esk

AUGUST 8

Cory's Shearwater	1995	Girdleness
Little Egret	1996	Ythan
Spoonbill	1970	Ythan
Spoonbill	1991	Strathbeg
Spoonbill	1992	Strathbeg
American Wigeon	1989	North Esk

AUGUST 9

Cory's Shearwater	1995	Girdleness
Great Shearwater	1977	Collieston
Leach's Petrel	1987	Peterhead
Little Egret	1996	Ythan

Spoonbill	1970	Ythan
Spoonbill	1991	Strathbeg
Spoonbill	1992	Strathbeg
American Wigeon	1989	North Esk
Red-crested Pochard	1985	Strathbeg

AUGUST 10

Cory's Shearwater	1989	Girdleness
Little Egret	1996	Ythan
Spoonbill	1970	Ythan
Spoonbill	1991	Strathbeg
Spoonbill	1992	Strathbeg
American Wigeon	1989	North Esk

AUGUST 11

Cory's Shearwater	1995	Collieston
Little Egret	1996	Ythan
Spoonbill	1970	Ythan
Spoonbill	1991	Strathbeg
Spoonbill	1992	Strathbeg
American Wigeon	1989	North Esk
Grey Phalarope	1989	Waulkmill, Ythan

AUGUST 12

Little Egret	1996	Ythan
Spoonbill	1970	Ythan
Spoonbill	1991	Strathbeg
Spoonbill	1992	Strathbeg
American Wigeon	1989	North Esk
Grey Phalarope	1989	Waulkmill, Ythan

AUGUST 13

Little Egret	1996	Ythan
Spoonbill	1970	Ythan
Spoonbill	1991	Strathbeg
Spoonbill	1992	Strathbeg
American Wigeon	1989	North Esk
Grey Phalarope	1989	Waulkmill, Ythan
Caspian Tern	1974	Strathbeg

AUGUST 14

Little Egret	1996	Ythan
Spoonbill	1970	Ythan
Spoonbill	1991	Strathbeg
Spoonbill	1992	Strathbeg

AUGUST 15

Cory's Shearwater	1995	Girdleness
Little Egret	1996	Ythan
Spoonbill	1970	Ythan
Spoonbill	1991	Strathbeg
Spoonbill	1992	Strathbeg
Lesser Yellowlegs	1992	Strathbeg
Icterine Warbler	1980	Girdleness

AUGUST 16

Spoonbill	1970	Ythan
Spoonbill	1991	Strathbeg
Spoonbill	1992	Strathbeg

AUGUST 17

Spoonbill	1970	Ythan
Spoonbill	1991	Strathbeg
Spoonbill	1992	Strathbeg
Icterine Warbler	1979	Girdleness

AUGUST 18

| Spoonbill | 1970 | Ythan |
| Spoonbill | 1991 | Strathbeg |

Spoonbill	1992	Strathbeg
Greater Sand Plover	1991	Donmouth
Icterine Warbler	1979	Girdleness

AUGUST 19

Great Shearwater	1976	Collieston
Spoonbill	1970	Ythan
Spoonbill	1991	Strathbeg
Spoonbill	1992	Strathbeg
Greater Sand Plover	1991	Donmouth
Pectoral Sandpiper (2)	1992	Strathbeg
Icterine Warbler	1979	Girdleness
Arctic Warbler	1979	Foveran

AUGUST 20

Mediterranean Shearwater	1982	Peterhead
Spoonbill	1970	Ythan
Spoonbill	1991	Strathbeg
Spoonbill	1992	Strathbeg
Pectoral Sandpiper (2)	1992	Strathbeg
Icterine Warbler	1979	Girdleness

AUGUST 21

Cory's Shearwater	1970	Collieston
Cory's Shearwater	1970	Rattray
Cory's Shearwater	1995	Girdleness
Great Shearwater (3)	1970	Collieston
Great Shearwater (3)	1970	Rattray
Great Shearwater	1981	Peterhead
Spoonbill	1970	Ythan
Spoonbill	1991	Strathbeg
Spoonbill	1992	Strathbeg
Pectoral Sandpiper	1977	Strathbeg
Pectoral Sandpiper	1992	Strathbeg

AUGUST 22

Spoonbill	1970	Ythan
Spoonbill	1991	Strathbeg
Spoonbill	1992	Strathbeg
Bonelli's Warbler	1980	Drums

AUGUST 23

Spoonbill	1970	Ythan
Spoonbill	1991	Strathbeg
Spoonbill	1992	Strathbeg
Greenish Warbler	1992	Girdleness
Bonelli's Warbler	1980	Drums
Common Rosefinch	1991	Girdleness

AUGUST 24

Cory's Shearwater	1981	Peterhead
Spoonbill	1970	Ythan
Spoonbill	1991	Strathbeg
Spoonbill	1992	Strathbeg
Avocet	1987	Cults
Greenish Warbler	1992	Girdleness
Greenish Warbler (2)	1994	Collieston
Greenish Warbler	1996	Rattray
Bonelli's Warbler	1980	Drums

AUGUST 25

Spoonbill	1991	Strathbeg
Spoonbill	1992	Strathbeg
Avocet	1987	Cults
Pectoral Sandpiper	1991	Kinloch
Greenish Warbler	1992	Girdleness
Greenish Warbler (2)	1994	Collieston

AUGUST 26

Cory's Shearwater	1990	Newtonhill
Cory's Shearwater	1991	Girdleness
Spoonbill	1991	Strathbeg
Spoonbill	1992	Strathbeg
Avocet	1987	Cults
Temminck's Stint (3)	1975	Meikle
Pectoral Sandpiper	1991	Kinloch
Greenish Warbler	1994	Collieston

AUGUST 27

Great Shearwater	1995	Girdleness
Spoonbill	1991	Strathbeg
Spoonbill	1992	Strathbeg
Avocet	1987	Cults
Pectoral Sandpiper	1991	Kinloch
Greenish Warbler	1994	Collieston

AUGUST 28

Great Shearwater	1976	Girdleness
Mediterranean Shearwater	1987	Peterhead
Spoonbill	1992	Strathbeg
Avocet	1987	Cults
Grey Phalarope (2)	1979	Ythan
Greenish Warbler	1994	Collieston

AUGUST 29

Great Shearwater (2)	1976	Girdleness
Great Shearwater	1976	Collieston
Great Shearwater	1995	Girdleness
Med. Shearwater (2)	1987	Peterhead
Spoonbill	1992	Strathbeg
Avocet	1987	Cults
Pectoral Sandpiper	1993	Strathbeg
Grey Phalarope	1960	Donmouth
Greenish Warbler	1994	Collieston

AUGUST 30

Mediterranean Shearwater	1981	Peterhead
Mediterranean Shearwater	1991	Girdleness
Spoonbill	1992	Strathbeg
Honey Buzzard	1992	Girdleness
Avocet	1987	Cults

AUGUST 31

Spoonbill	1992	Strathbeg
Honey Buzzard	1992	Strathbeg
Avocet	1987	Cults
White-rumped Sandpiper	1985	Ythan
Icterine Warbler	1994	Girdleness
Ortolan Bunting	1979	Girdleness

SEPTEMBER

The tempo of migration increases through the month with both Barred and Icterine Warblers, Wrynecks and Red-breasted Flycatchers regular. Seawatching still produces

Cory's and Great Shearwaters and September is the peak time for Long-tailed Skuas. Waders have been represented by Baird's Sandpiper, Pectoral Sandpiper and Buff-breasted Sandpiper.

SEPTEMBER 1

Cory's Shearwater	1976	Fraserburgh
Great Shearwater	1976	Fraserburgh
Pectoral Sandpiper	1990	Annachie
Red-necked Phalarope	1979	Donmouth
Greenish Warbler	1991	Collieston

SEPTEMBER 2

Great Shearwater	1976	Fraserburgh
Pectoral Sandpiper	1990	Annachie
Red-necked Phalarope	1979	Donmouth
Sabine's Gull	1984	Peterhead
Greenish Warbler	1991	Collieston
Arctic Warbler	1958	Forvie

SEPTEMBER 3

Cory's Shearwater	1995	Girdleness
Pectoral Sandpiper	1977	Meikle
Red-necked Phalarope	1979	Donmouth
Icterine Warbler	1974	Girdleness
Common Rosefinch	1987	Rattray

SEPTEMBER 4

Buff-breasted Sandpiper	1993	Strathbeg
Common Rosefinch	1987	Rattray

SEPTEMBER 5

SEPTEMBER 6

Cory's Shearwater	1996	Girdleness
Baird's Sandpiper	1990	Annachie

SEPTEMBER 7

Great Shearwater (2)	1977	Fraserburgh
Baird's Sandpiper	1990	Annachie
Sabine's Gull	1977	Fraserburgh
Icterine Warbler	1978	Drums
Firecrest	1975	Newburgh

SEPTEMBER 8

Mediterranean Shearwater	1985	Peterhead
Honey Buzzard	1980	Strathbeg
Baird's Sandpiper	1990	Annachie
Icterine Warbler (2)	1995	Girdleness
Icterine Warbler	1995	Newtonhill
Icterine Warbler	1995	Balmedie

SEPTEMBER 9

Baird's Sandpiper	1990	Annachie
Icterine Warbler (2)	1995	Girdleness
Icterine Warbler	1995	Newtonhill
Common Rosefinch	1990	Cruden Bay
Ortolan Bunting	1990	Cruden Bay

SEPTEMBER 10

Great Shearwater (3)	1976	Fraserburgh
Great Shearwater	1981	Peterhead
Honey Buzzard	1994	Drums
Baird's Sandpiper	1990	Annachie

Pectoral Sandpiper	1976	Meikle
Buff-breasted Sandpiper	1989	Ythan
Red-necked Phalarope	1976	Donmouth
Icterine Warbler	1995	Girdleness
Icterine Warbler	1995	Balmedie
Icterine Warbler	1995	Collieston
Common Rosefinch	1990	Cruden Bay

SEPTEMBER 11

Cory's Shearwater (2)	1989	Newtonhill
Black-winged Pratincole	1976	Strathbeg
Baird's Sandpiper	1990	Annachie
Buff-breasted Sandpiper	1989	Ythan
Hoopoe	1996	Newmacher
Icterine Warbler	1995	Collieston
Icterine Warbler	1995	Girdleness
Common Rosefinch	1990	Cruden Bay

SEPTEMBER 12

Mediterranean Shearwater	1994	Girdleness
White-rumped Sandpiper	1985	Ythan
Baird's Sandpiper	1990	Annachie
Buff-breasted Sandpiper	1989	Ythan
Hoopoe	1968	Strachan
Hoopoe	1969	Johnshaven
Hoopoe	1996	Newmacher
Icterine Warbler	1995	Collieston
Icterine Warbler	1995	Girdleness
Common Rosefinch	1990	Cruden Bay
Common Rosefinch	1993	Balmedie

SEPTEMBER 13

White-rumped Sandpiper	1985	Ythan
Baird's Sandpiper	1990	Annachie
Buff-breasted Sandpiper	1989	Ythan
Hoopoe	1969	Johnshaven
Hoopoe	1996	Newmacher
Icterine Warbler	1973	Cruden Bay
Icterine Warbler	1995	Girdleness
Common Rosefinch	1990	Cruden Bay

SEPTEMBER 14

Bewick's Swan	1975	Pitfour
Baird's Sandpiper	1990	Annachie
Buff-breasted Sandpiper	1989	Ythan
Red-necked Phalarope (2)	1991	Ythan
Hoopoe	1969	Johnshaven
Hoopoe	1996	Newmacher
Common Rosefinch	1990	Cruden Bay

SEPTEMBER 15

Baird's Sandpiper (2)	1990	Annachie
Red-necked Phalarope	1991	Ythan
Hoopoe	1969	Johnshaven
Common Rosefinch	1990	Cruden Bay

SEPTEMBER 16

Blue-winged Teal	1984	Sandhaven
Baird's Sandpiper (2)	1990	Annachie
Hoopoe	1969	Johnshaven
Icterine Warbler	1992	Girdleness
Common Rosefinch	1990	Cruden Bay

SEPTEMBER 17

Baird's Sandpiper (2)	1990	Annachie
Pectoral Sandpiper	1974	Strathbeg
Wilson's Phalarope	1984	Cotehill
Sabine's Gull	1987	Peterhead
Hoopoe	1983	Portsoy

| Icterine Warbler | 1992 | Girdleness |
| Common Rosefinch | 1990 | Cruden Bay |

SEPTEMBER 18

Great Shearwater	1971	Collieston
Baird's Sandpiper	1990	Annachie
Buff-breasted Sandpiper (3)	1977	Strathbeg
Wilson's Phalarope	1984	Cotehill
Grey Phalarope	1990	Strathbeg
Icterine Warbler	1992	Girdleness
Common Rosefinch	1990	Cruden Bay

SEPTEMBER 19

Blue-winged Teal	1984	Strathbeg
Honey Buzzard	1976	Methlick
Wilson's Phalarope	1984	Cotehill
Grey Phalarope	1990	Strathbeg
Sabine's Gull	1990	Peterhead
Icterine Warbler	1992	Girdleness
Common Rosefinch	1990	Cruden Bay

SEPTEMBER 20

Honey Buzzard	1980	Fowlsheugh
Wilson's Phalarope	1984	Cotehill
Grey Phalarope	1990	Strathbeg
Common Rosefinch	1990	Cruden Bay
Common Rosefinch	1993	Girdleness

SEPTEMBER 21

Honey Buzzard	1981	Donmouth
Pectoral Sandpiper	1973	Strathbeg
Pectoral Sandpiper	1982	Ythan
Wilson's Phalarope	1984	Cotehill
Grey Phalarope	1990	Strathbeg
Common Rosefinch	1993	Girdleness

SEPTEMBER 22

Pectoral Sandpiper	1973	Strathbeg
Wilson's Phalarope	1984	Cotehill
Grey Phalarope	1990	Strathbeg
Common Rosefinch	1992	Rattray
Common Rosefinch	1993	Girdleness

SEPTEMBER 23

| Pectoral Sandpiper | 1973 | Strathbeg |
| Grey Phalarope | 1990 | Strathbeg |

SEPTEMBER 24

| Pectoral Sandpiper | 1973 | Strathbeg |
| Grey Phalarope | 1990 | Strathbeg |

SEPTEMBER 25

Great Shearwater	1977	Collieston
Bewick's Swan (3)	1969	Strathbeg
Pectoral Sandpiper	1973	Strathbeg
Pectoral Sandpiper	1982	Meikle
Icterine Warbler	1982	Foveran

SEPTEMBER 26

Baird's Sandpiper	1982	Rattray
Pectoral Sandpiper	1982	Meikle
Hudsonian Godwit	1988	Slains
Sabine's Gull	1987	Girdleness
Ross's Gull	1987	Girdleness
White-winged Black Tern	1973	Ythan
Hoopoe	1967	Bridge of Don
Pied Wheatear	1976	Donmouth
Icterine Warbler	1982	Foveran
Firecrest	1977	Forvie

SEPTEMBER 27

Glossy Ibis	1986	Strathbeg
Pectoral Sandpiper	1982	Meikle
Pectoral Sandpiper	1996	Kinloch
Red-necked Phalarope	1980	Meikle
Ross's Gull	1987	Girdleness
Richard's Pipit	1991	Girdleness
Pied Wheatear	1976	Donmouth
Icterine Warbler	1965	Rattray
Icterine Warbler	1980	Drums
Icterine Warbler	1982	Foveran

SEPTEMBER 28

Glossy Ibis	1986	Strathbeg
Pectoral Sandpiper	1982	Meikle
Pectoral Sandpiper	1986	Ythan
Pectoral Sandpiper	1996	Kinloch
Red-necked Phalarope	1980	Meikle
Ross's Gull	1987	Girdleness
Siberian Stonechat	1991	Rattray
Pied Wheatear	1976	Donmouth
Icterine Warbler	1982	Foveran

SEPTEMBER 29

Great Shearwater	1975	Girdleness
Glossy Ibis	1986	Strathbeg
Pectoral Sandpiper	1982	Meikle
Pectoral Sandpiper	1996	Kinloch
Lesser Yellowlegs	1978	Rattray
Hoopoe	1976	Girdleness
Pied Wheatear	1976	Donmouth
Icterine Warbler	1982	Foveran

SEPTEMBER 30

Great Shearwater	1979	Collieston
Glossy Ibis	1986	Strathbeg
Honey Buzzard	1983	Strathbeg
Pectoral Sandpiper	1978	Donmouth
Pectoral Sandpiper	1996	Kinloch
Sabine's Gull	1990	Waulkmill, Ythan
Pied Wheatear	1976	Donmouth
Common Rosefinch	1993	Collieston

OCTOBER

In a good year the best month for rare and scarce migrants. Typically Yellow-browed Warblers, Firecrest and Pallas's Warblers appear in variable numbers. Barred, Icterine and Reed Warblers all peak at this time. Isabelline and Pied Wheatears have both been recorded in October along with 'Siberian' Stonechat. Big pipits are also well represented with

Richard's the commoner although Tawny and Pechora have been recorded in this month. Finches and buntings occur in small numbers with Rosefinch, Arctic Redpoll, Lapland Bunting and Little Bunting all recorded. Wintering and/or passage grebes start to appear along the coast.

OCTOBER 1

Great Shearwater (6)	1976	Collieston
Glossy Ibis	1986	Strathbeg
Pectoral Sandpiper	1996	Kinloch
Pied Wheatear	1976	Donmouth
Melodious Warbler	1993	Girdleness
Little Bunting	1992	Balmedie

OCTOBER 2

Glossy Ibis	1986	Strathbeg
Hoopoe	1993	Dunnotar Castle
Woodlark	1993	Girdleness
Pied Wheatear	1976	Donmouth
Icterine Warbler	1993	Girdleness
Firecrest	1976	Foveran
Common Rosefinch	1993	Cruden Bay

OCTOBER 3

Glossy Ibis	1986	Strathbeg
Hoopoe	1993	north of Donmouth
Richard's Pipit	1975	Drums
Richard's Pipit	1990	Donmouth
Pied Wheatear	1976	Donmouth
Pallas's Warbler	1992	Cruden Bay

OCTOBER 4

Bittern	1988	Strathbeg
Glossy Ibis	1986	Strathbeg
Temminck's Stint	1976	Donmouth
Richard's Pipit	1990	Donmouth
Pied Wheatear	1976	Donmouth
Pallas's Warbler	1992	Cruden Bay
Firecrest	1981	Foveran
Firecrest	1993	near Collieston

OCTOBER 5

Glossy Ibis	1986	Strathbeg
Long-billed Dowitcher	1995	St Cyrus
Bee-eater	1995	Belhelvie
Richard's Pipit	1990	Donmouth
Pied Wheatear	1976	Donmouth
Common Rosefinch	1982	Newburgh
Rustic Bunting	1986	Drums

OCTOBER 6

Glossy Ibis	1986	Strathbeg
Long-billed Dowitcher	1995	St Cyrus
Bee-eater	1995	Belhelvie
Richard's Pipit	1990	Donmouth
Pied Wheatear	1976	Donmouth

Icterine Warbler | 1994 | Mintlaw
Golden Oriole | 1968 | Seaton Park
Common Rosefinch | 1979 | Drums

OCTOBER 7

Glossy Ibis	1986	Strathbeg
Long-billed Dowitcher	1995	St Cyrus
Lesser Yellowlegs	1978	Ythan
Bee-eater	1995	Belhelvie
Richard's Pipit	1990	Donmouth
Pied Wheatear	1976	Donmouth
Radde's Warbler	1979	Cruden Bay

OCTOBER 8

Glossy Ibis	1986	Strathbeg
Long-billed Dowitcher	1995	St Cyrus
Hoopoe	1993	Portsoy
Richard's Pipit	1990	Donmouth
Pied Wheatear	1993	Donmouth
Pallas's Warbler	1993	Peterhead

OCTOBER 9

White-billed Diver	1988	Peterhead
Leach's Petrel	1988	Fraserburgh
Leach's Petrel	1988	Aberdeen
Glossy Ibis	1986	Strathbeg
Long-billed Dowitcher	1995	St Cyrus
Bee-eater	1995	Durris
Hoopoe	1993	near New Pitsligo
Richard's Pipit	1990	Donmouth
Siberian Stonechat	1982	Rattray
Pallas's Warbler	1982	Rattray
Little Bunting	1993	Girdleness

OCTOBER 10

Mediterranean Shearwater	1992	Fraserburgh
Glossy Ibis	1986	Strathbeg
Long-billed Dowitcher	1995	St Cyrus
Bee-eater	1995	Durris
Hoopoe	1993	near New Pitsligo
Richard's Pipit	1990	Donmouth
Richard's Pipit	1991	Rattray
Siberian Stonechat	1982	Rattray
Icterine Warbler	1993	Donmouth
Orphean Warbler	1982	Seaton Park
Pallas's Warbler	1982	Rattray

OCTOBER 11

Glossy Ibis	1986	Strathbeg
Long-billed Dowitcher	1995	St Cyrus
Bee-eater	1995	Durris
Hoopoe	1993	near New Pitsligo
Pechora Pipit	1993	St Fergus
Siberian Stonechat	1982	Rattray
Pallas's Warbler	1982	Girdleness
Radde's Warbler	1991	Girdleness

OCTOBER 12

Glossy Ibis	1986	Strathbeg
Bewick's Swan	1964	Pitfour
Long-billed Dowitcher	1995	St Cyrus
Bee-eater	1995	Durris
Hoopoe	1987	Wells of Ythan
Hoopoe	1993	near New Pitsligo
Siberian Stonechat	1982	Rattray
Pallas's Warbler	1982	Girdleness
Pallas's Warbler	1982	Strathbeg

OCTOBER 13

Glossy Ibis	1986	Strathbeg
Long-billed Dowitcher	1995	St Cyrus
Bee-eater	1995	Durris
Hoopoe	1987	Wells of Ythan
Hoopoe	1993	near New Pitsligo
Richard's Pipit	1979	Girdleness
Siberian Stonechat	1982	Rattray
Pallas's Warbler	1982	Cruden Bay
Pallas's Warbler	1982	Newburgh
Dusky Warbler	1988	Rattray

OCTOBER 14

Glossy Ibis	1986	Strathbeg
Black-winged Stilt	1984	Ythan
Long-billed Dowitcher	1995	St Cyrus
Bee-eater	1995	Durris
Hoopoe	1987	Wells of Ythan
Hoopoe	1993	near New Pitsligo
Siberian Stonechat	1982	Rattray
Pallas's Warbler	1982	Cruden Bay
Pallas's Warbler	1982	Newburgh
Firecrest	1990	Drums

OCTOBER 15

Glossy Ibis	1986	Strathbeg
Long-billed Dowitcher	1995	St Cyrus
Sabine's Gull	1978	Fraserburgh
Bee-eater	1995	Durris
Hoopoe	1993	near New Pitsligo
Siberian Stonechat	1982	Rattray
Pallas's Warbler	1982	Cruden Bay
Pallas's Warbler	1982	Drums
Lesser Grey Shrike	1952	Aberdeen

OCTOBER 16

Glossy Ibis	1986	Strathbeg
Black-winged Stilt	1984	Meikle
Long-billed Dowitcher	1995	St Cyrus
Bee-eater	1995	Durris
Hoopoe	1993	near New Pitsligo
Pallas's Warbler	1979	Girdleness
Pallas's Warbler	1982	Drums

OCTOBER 17

Leach's Petrel	1988	Aberdeen
Glossy Ibis	1986	Strathbeg
Black-winged Stilt	1984	Meikle
Long-billed Dowitcher	1995	St Cyrus
Hoopoe	1993	near New Pitsligo
Isabelline Wheatear	1979	Donmouth
Pallas's Warbler	1982	Drums

OCTOBER 18

Glossy Ibis	1986	Strathbeg
Black-winged Stilt	1984	Meikle
Long-billed Dowitcher	1995	St Cyrus
Sabine's Gull	1978	Fraserburgh
Hoopoe	1986	Wells of Ythan
Hoopoe	1993	Cairnbulg
Isabelline Wheatear	1979	Donmouth

OCTOBER 19

Leach's Petrel (2)	1991	Fraserburgh
Glossy Ibis	1986	Strathbeg
Black-winged Stilt	1984	Meikle
Long-billed Dowitcher	1995	St Cyrus

Alpine Swift	1984	Greg Ness
Richard's Pipit	1968	Girdleness
Isabelline Wheatear	1979	Donmouth
Pallas's Warbler	1988	Cruden Bay

OCTOBER 20

Glossy Ibis	1986	Strathbeg
Black-winged Stilt	1984	Meikle
Long-billed Dowitcher	1995	St Cyrus
Hoopoe	1986	Johnshaven
Olive-backed Pipit	1990	Cruden Bay
Isabelline Wheatear	1979	Donmouth
Pallas's Warbler	1988	Cruden Bay

OCTOBER 21

White-billed Diver	1974	Aberdeen
Glossy Ibis	1986	Strathbeg
Black-winged Stilt	1984	Meikle
Long-billed Dowitcher	1995	St Cyrus
Hoopoe	1986	Johnshaven
Richard's Pipit	1987	Foveran
Richard's Pipit	1987	Drums
Isabelline Wheatear	1979	Donmouth
Pallas's Warbler	1988	Cruden Bay
Pallas's Warbler	1990	Muchalls
Firecrest	1994	Balmedie

OCTOBER 22

Glossy Ibis	1986	Strathbeg
Black-winged Stilt	1984	Meikle
Long-billed Dowitcher	1995	St Cyrus
Sabine's Gull	1987	Rattray
Richard's Pipit (2)	1990	Balmedie
Isabelline Wheatear	1979	Donmouth
Pallas's Warbler	1968	Collieston
Pallas's Warbler	1988	Cruden Bay
Pallas's Warbler	1988	Drums
Pallas's Warbler	1990	Cruden Bay
Firecrest	1994	Balmedie

OCTOBER 23

Glossy Ibis	1986	Strathbeg
Black-winged Stilt	1984	Meikle
Long-billed Dowitcher	1995	St Cyrus
Richard's Pipit (2)	1990	Balmedie
Isabelline Wheatear	1979	Donmouth
Booted Warbler	1993	Newtonhill
Icterine Warbler	1994	Johnshaven
Pallas's Warbler	1968	Collieston
Rose-coloured Starling	1976	Braemar

OCTOBER 24

Leach's Petrel	1976	Forvie
Glossy Ibis	1986	Strathbeg
Bewick's Swan (4)	1990	Loirston
Black-winged Stilt	1984	Meikle
Long-billed Dowitcher	1995	St Cyrus
Richard's Pipit (2)	1990	Balmedie
Tawny Pipit	1987	Foveran
Siberian Stonechat	1990	Cruden Bay
Isabelline Wheatear	1979	Donmouth
Booted Warbler	1993	Newtonhill
Icterine Warbler	1993	Newtonhill
Pallas's Warbler	1968	Collieston
Rose-coloured Starling	1976	Braemar
Rose-coloured Starling	1993	Newburgh

OCTOBER 25

Glossy Ibis	1986	Strathbeg
Bewick's Swan (4)	1990	Loirston
Black-winged Stilt	1984	Meikle
Long-billed Dowitcher	1995	St Cyrus
Greater Yellowlegs	1957	Ythan
Richard's Pipit (2)	1990	Balmedie
Tawny Pipit	1987	Foveran
Isabelline Wheatear	1979	Donmouth
Booted Warbler	1993	Newtonhill
Icterine Warbler	1993	Newtonhill
Rose-coloured Starling	1976	Braemar
Rose-coloured Starling	1993	Newburgh
Common Rosefinch	1986	Rattray

OCTOBER 26

Glossy Ibis	1986	Strathbeg
Bewick's Swan (4)	1990	Loirston
Black-winged Stilt	1984	Meikle
Long-billed Dowitcher	1995	St Cyrus
Richard's Pipit (2)	1990	Balmedie
Isabelline Wheatear	1979	Donmouth
Booted Warbler	1993	Newtonhill
Icterine Warbler	1993	Newtonhill
Rose-coloured Starling	1976	Braemar
Rose-coloured Starling	1993	Newburgh

OCTOBER 27

Glossy Ibis	1986	Strathbeg
Bewick's Swan (4)	1990	Loirston
Black-winged Stilt	1984	Meikle
Long-billed Dowitcher	1995	St Cyrus
Richard's Pipit (2)	1990	Balmedie
Isabelline Wheatear	1979	Donmouth
Booted Warbler	1993	Newtonhill
Icterine Warbler	1993	Newtonhill
Rose-coloured Starling	1976	Braemar
Rose-coloured Starling	1993	Newburgh

OCTOBER 28

Glossy Ibis	1986	Strathbeg
Bewick's Swan (4)	1990	Loirston
American Wigeon	1995	Skene
Black-winged Stilt	1984	Meikle
Long-billed Dowitcher	1995	St Cyrus
Sabine's Gull	1976	Fraserburgh
Richard's Pipit (2)	1990	Balmedie
Isabelline Wheatear	1979	Donmouth
Booted Warbler	1993	Newtonhill
Icterine Warbler	1993	Newtonhill
Pallas's Warbler	1989	Cruden Bay
Rose-coloured Starling	1976	Braemar

OCTOBER 29

Glossy Ibis	1986	Strathbeg
Bewick's Swan (4)	1990	Loirston
Black-winged Stilt	1984	Meikle
Long-billed Dowitcher	1995	St Cyrus
Grey Phalarope	1991	Girdleness
Richard's Pipit (2)	1990	Balmedie
Richard's Pipit	1995	Rattray
Isabelline Wheatear	1979	Donmouth
Booted Warbler	1993	Newtonhill
Icterine Warbler	1993	Newtonhill
Pallas's Warbler	1989	Cruden Bay
Pallas's Warbler	1994	Girdleness

Firecrest	1989	Findon
Rose-coloured Starling	1976	Braemar

OCTOBER 30

Glossy Ibis	1986	Strathbeg
Black-winged Stilt	1984	Meikle
Long-billed Dowitcher	1995	St Cyrus
Hoopoe	1993	Tornaveen
Richard's Pipit	1977	Meikle
Isabelline Wheatear	1979	Donmouth
Booted Warbler	1993	Newtonhill
Icterine Warbler	1993	Newtonhill
Pallas's Warbler	1994	Girdleness
Rose-coloured Starling	1976	Braemar

OCTOBER 31

Great Shearwater	1970	Rattray
Glossy Ibis	1986	Strathbeg
Red-crested Pochard	1982	Strathbeg
Black-winged Stilt	1984	Meikle
Long-billed Dowitcher	1995	St Cyrus
Sabine's Gull	1977	Fraserburgh
Isabelline Wheatear	1979	Donmouth
Booted Warbler	1993	Newtonhill
Icterine Warbler	1993	Newtonhill
Pallas's Warbler	1994	Girdleness
Rose-coloured Starling	1976	Braemar

NOVEMBER

As wintering wildfowl begin to return searching should reveal small numbers of Bean Geese, Bewick's Swans and American Wigeon. Passage Shore Larks are expected to peak at this time though numbers are not usually high. Easterly and north easterly winds can still be expected to produce rarities such as Arctic Redpoll and Booted Warblers.

NOVEMBER 1

Glossy Ibis	1986	Strathbeg
Bewick's Swan	1979	Longside
Black-winged Stilt	1984	Meikle
Long-billed Dowitcher	1995	St Cyrus
Isabelline Wheatear	1979	Donmouth
Booted Warbler	1993	Newtonhill
Icterine Warbler	1993	Newtonhill
Pallas's Warbler	1994	Girdleness
Rose-coloured Starling	1976	Braemar

NOVEMBER 2

Cory's Shearwater (2)	1970	Rattray
Great Shearwater (4)	1970	Rattray

Glossy Ibis	1986	Strathbeg
Black-winged Stilt	1984	Meikle
Long-billed Dowitcher	1995	St Cyrus
Siberian Stonechat	1979	Foveran
Isabelline Wheatear	1979	Donmouth
Booted Warbler	1993	Newtonhill
Icterine Warbler	1993	Newtonhill
Rose-coloured Starling	1976	Braemar

NOVEMBER 3

Glossy Ibis	1986	Strathbeg
Black-winged Stilt	1984	Meikle
Long-billed Dowitcher	1995	St Cyrus
Siberian Stonechat	1979	Foveran
Isabelline Wheatear	1979	Donmouth
Booted Warbler	1993	Newtonhill
Icterine Warbler	1993	Newtonhill
Pallas's Warbler	1994	Cruden Bay
Pallas's Warbler	1994	Donmouth
Firecrest	1980	Newburgh
Rose-coloured Starling	1976	Braemar

NOVEMBER 4

Glossy Ibis	1986	Strathbeg
Ring-necked Duck	1989	Meikle Loch
Long-billed Dowitcher	1995	St Cyrus
Siberian Stonechat	1979	Foveran
Isabelline Wheatear	1979	Donmouth
Booted Warbler	1993	Newtonhill
Icterine Warbler	1993	Newtonhill
Pallas's Warbler	1994	Cruden Bay
Pallas's Warbler	1994	Collieston
Pallas's Warbler (5)	1994	Foveran
Pallas's Warbler (2)	1994	Drums
Pallas's Warbler (2)	1994	Hatterseat
Pallas's Warbler	1994	Newtonhill
Firecrest	1980	Cruden Bay
Rose-coloured Starling	1976	Braemar

NOVEMBER 5

Leach's Petrel	1985	Peterhead
Glossy Ibis	1986	Strathbeg
Bewick's Swan (5)	1990	Murcar
Long-billed Dowitcher	1995	St Cyrus
Isabelline Wheatear	1979	Donmouth
Booted Warbler	1993	Newtonhill
Icterine Warbler	1993	Newtonhill
Pallas's Warbler (5)	1994	Foveran
Pallas's Warbler (2)	1994	Hatterseat
Pallas's Warbler	1994	Newtonhill
Pallas's Warbler	1994	Drums Farm
Pallas's Warbler	1994	South Hatterseat
Pallas's Warbler	1994	Easter Muchalls
Pallas's Warbler	1994	Kineff Old Church
Pallas's Warbler	1994	Findon
Pallas's Warbler	1994	Balmedie
Firecrest	1994	Balmedie
Rose-coloured Starling	1976	Braemar

NOVEMBER 6

Glossy Ibis	1986	Strathbeg
American Wigeon	1994	Skene
Long-billed Dowitcher	1995	St Cyrus
Isabelline Wheatear	1979	Donmouth
Booted Warbler	1993	Newtonhill
Icterine Warbler	1993	Newtonhill

Pallas's Warbler (5)	1994	Foveran
Pallas's Warbler (2)	1994	Hatterseat
Pallas's Warbler	1994	Newtonhill
Pallas's Warbler (2)	1994	Strathbeg

NOVEMBER 7

Leach's Petrel	1985	Peterhead
Glossy Ibis	1986	Strathbeg
American Wigeon	1994	Skene
Long-billed Dowitcher	1995	St Cyrus
Isabelline Wheatear	1979	Donmouth
Booted Warbler	1993	Newtonhill
Icterine Warbler	1993	Newtonhill
Pallas's Warbler (5)	1994	Foveran
Pallas's Warbler (2)	1994	Hatterseat

NOVEMBER 8

Glossy Ibis	1986	Strathbeg
American Wigeon	1994	Skene
Steller's Eider	1970	Rattray
Long-billed Dowitcher	1995	St Cyrus
Siberian Stonechat	1994	Whinnyfold
Isabelline Wheatear	1979	Donmouth
Booted Warbler	1993	Newtonhill
Icterine Warbler	1993	Newtonhill

NOVEMBER 9

Glossy Ibis	1986	Strathbeg
Bewick's Swan (6)	1980	Strathbeg
American Wigeon	1994	Skene
Long-billed Dowitcher	1995	St Cyrus
Isabelline Wheatear	1979	Donmouth
Booted Warbler	1993	Newtonhill
Icterine Warbler	1993	Newtonhill

NOVEMBER 10

Glossy Ibis	1986	Strathbeg
Bewick's Swan (3)	1969	Strathbeg
American Wigeon	1994	Skene
Long-billed Dowitcher	1995	St Cyrus
Isabelline Wheatear	1979	Donmouth
Booted Warbler	1993	Newtonhill
Icterine Warbler	1993	Newtonhill
Pallas's Warbler	1994	Hatterseat
Hume's Warbler	1994	Bullers of Buchan

NOVEMBER 11

Glossy Ibis	1986	Strathbeg
American Wigeon	1994	Skene
Long-billed Dowitcher	1995	St Cyrus
Richard's Pipit	1994	Whinnyfold
Booted Warbler	1993	Newtonhill
Booted Warbler	1994	Sand Loch

NOVEMBER 12

Glossy Ibis	1986	Strathbeg
American Wigeon	1994	Skene
Red-crested Pochard	1982	Strathbeg
Richard's Pipit	1995	Girdleness
Booted Warbler	1993	Newtonhill
Booted Warbler	1994	Sand Loch

NOVEMBER 13

Glossy Ibis	1986	Strathbeg
Booted Warbler	1993	Newtonhill
Booted Warbler	1994	Sand Loch

NOVEMBER 14

Glossy Ibis	1986	Strathbeg

Bewick's Swan (4)	1990	Inverquhomery
Booted Warbler	1993	Newtonhill

NOVEMBER 15

Glossy Ibis	1986	Strathbeg
Bewick's Swan (4)	1990	Inverquhomery
American Wigeon	1992	Skene
Booted Warbler	1993	Newtonhill

NOVEMBER 16

Glossy Ibis	1986	Strathbeg
Bewick's Swan (4)	1990	Inverquhomery
American Wigeon	1992	Skene
Booted Warbler	1993	Newtonhill

NOVEMBER 17

Glossy Ibis	1986	Strathbeg
Bewick's Swan (4)	1984	Middlemuir
Bewick's Swan (5)	1990	Inverquhomery
Bewick's Swan (6)	1990	Longside
American Wigeon	1992	Skene
Sabine's Gull	1984	Peterhead
Red-rumped Swallow	1988	Kincorth
Booted Warbler	1993	Newtonhill

NOVEMBER 18

Glossy Ibis	1986	Strathbeg
Bewick's Swan (5)	1990	Inverquhomery
Bewick's Swan (6)	1990	Longside
American Wigeon	1992	Skene
Booted Warbler	1993	Newtonhill

NOVEMBER 19

Bittern	1994	Strathbeg
Glossy Ibis	1986	Strathbeg
Bewick's Swan (5)	1990	Inverquhomery
Bewick's Swan (6)	1990	Longside
American Wigeon	1992	Skene
Booted Warbler	1993	Newtonhill

NOVEMBER 20

Glossy Ibis	1986	Strathbeg
Bewick's Swan (5)	1990	Inverquhomery
Bewick's Swan (6)	1990	Longside
American Wigeon	1992	Skene

NOVEMBER 21

Glossy Ibis	1986	Strathbeg
Bewick's Swan (5)	1990	Inverquhomery
Bewick's Swan (6)	1990	Longside
American Wigeon	1992	Skene

NOVEMBER 22

Glossy Ibis	1986	Strathbeg
Bewick's Swan	1980	Strathbeg
Bewick's Swan (6)	1990	Longside
American Wigeon (2)	1992	Skene

NOVEMBER 23

Glossy Ibis	1986	Strathbeg
Bewick's Swan (6)	1990	Longside
American Wigeon	1992	Skene

NOVEMBER 24

Bewick's Swan (6)	1990	Longside
American Wigeon	1992	Skene

NOVEMBER 25

Bewick's Swan (2)	1980	Strathbeg
Bewick's Swan (6)	1990	Longside
American Wigeon	1992	Skene

NOVEMBER 26

Bewick's Swan (2)	1980	Strathbeg
Bewick's Swan (2)	1981	Strathbeg
Bewick's Swan (6)	1990	Longside
American Wigeon	1992	Skene

NOVEMBER 27

Bittern	1994	Strathbeg
American Wigeon	1992	Skene

NOVEMBER 28

American Wigeon	1992	Skene
Gyr Falcon	1992	Bennachie

NOVEMBER 29

American Wigeon	1992	Skene

NOVEMBER 30

Bewick's Swan	1983	Strathbeg
American Wigeon	1992	Skene

DECEMBER

Wintering Geese, wildfowl and gulls often dominate winter activities. Grey Phalaropes are sometimes present off Fraserburgh at this time. Surprises have occurred as with the American Robin in 1988.

DECEMBER 1

American Wigeon	1992	Skene

DECEMBER 2

Bewick's Swan	1981	Ythan
American Wigeon	1992	Skene

DECEMBER 3

American Wigeon	1992	Skene
Grey Phalarope	1978	Whitehills

DECEMBER 4

American Wigeon	1992	Skene
Avocet	1994	Ythan
Grey Phalarope	1978	Whitehills
Grey Phalarope	1988	Fraserburgh

DECEMBER 5

American Wigeon	1992	Skene
Avocet	1994	Ythan
Grey Phalarope	1978	Whitehills

DECEMBER 6

Bewick's Swan (8)	1990	Strathbeg
American Wigeon	1992	Skene
Avocet	1994	Ythan
Grey Phalarope	1978	Whitehills

DECEMBER 7

Bewick's Swan (8)	1979	Monymusk
Bewick's Swan (8)	1990	Strathbeg

American Wigeon	1992	Skene
Avocet	1994	Ythan
Grey Phalarope	1978	Whitehills

DECEMBER 8

Bewick's Swan	1975	Strathbeg
Bewick's Swan (8)	1990	Strathbeg
American Wigeon	1992	Skene
Avocet	1994	Ythan
Grey Phalarope	1978	Whitehills

DECEMBER 9

Bewick's Swan (8)	1990	Strathbeg
Bewick's Swan (3)	1993	Longside
American Wigeon	1992	Skene
Avocet	1994	Ythan
Grey Phalarope	1978	Whitehills

DECEMBER 10

Bewick's Swan (8)	1990	Strathbeg
Bewick's Swan (7)	1993	Longside
American Wigeon	1992	Skene
Avocet	1994	Ythan
Grey Phalarope	1978	Whitehills

DECEMBER 11

Bewick's Swan (8)	1990	Strathbeg
Bewick's Swan (3)	1993	Longside
Bewick's Swan	1994	Longside
American Wigeon	1992	Skene
Avocet	1994	Ythan
Grey Phalarope	1978	Whitehills

DECEMBER 12

Bewick's Swan (8)	1990	Strathbeg
Bewick's Swan (8)	1993	Longside
Bewick's Swan	1994	Longside
American Wigeon	1992	Skene
Avocet	1994	Ythan
Grey Phalarope	1978	Whitehills

DECEMBER 13

Bewick's Swan (8)	1990	Strathbeg
Bewick's Swan (3)	1993	Longside
Bewick's Swan	1994	Longside
American Wigeon	1992	Skene
Avocet	1994	Ythan
Grey Phalarope	1978	Whitehills

DECEMBER 14

Bewick's Swan (6)	1986	Blackhill
Bewick's Swan (3)	1993	Longside
Bewick's Swan	1994	Longside
American Wigeon	1992	Skene
Avocet	1994	Ythan
Grey Phalarope	1978	Whitehills

DECEMBER 15

Bewick's Swan (3)	1993	Longside
Bewick's Swan	1994	Longside
American Wigeon	1992	Skene
Grey Phalarope	1978	Whitehills

DECEMBER 16

Bewick's Swan (3)	1993	Longside
Bewick's Swan	1994	Longside
American Wigeon	1992	Skene
Grey Phalarope	1978	Whitehills

DECEMBER 17

Bewick's Swan (3)	1993	Longside
Bewick's Swan	1994	Longside
American Wigeon	1992	Skene
Grey Phalarope	1978	Whitehills

DECEMBER 18

Bewick's Swan (3)	1993	Longside
Bewick's Swan	1994	Longside
American Wigeon	1992	Skene
Grey Phalarope	1978	Whitehills

DECEMBER 19

Bewick's Swan (3)	1993	Longside
Bewick's Swan	1994	Longside
American Wigeon	1992	Skene
Grey Phalarope	1978	Whitehills

DECEMBER 20

Grey Phalarope	1978	Whitehills

DECEMBER 21

Grey Phalarope	1978	Whitehills

DECEMBER 22

Grey Phalarope	1978	Whitehills

DECEMBER 23

Grey Phalarope	1978	Whitehills

DECEMBER 24

Bewick's Swan	1994	Longside
Grey Phalarope	1978	Whitehills
American Robin	1988	Inverbervie

DECEMBER 25

Bewick's Swan	1994	Longside
Grey Phalarope	1978	Whitehills
American Robin	1988	Inverbervie

DECEMBER 26

Bewick's Swan	1994	Longside
Grey Phalarope	1978	Whitehills
American Robin	1988	Inverbervie

DECEMBER 27

Bewick's Swan	1994	Longside
Grey Phalarope	1978	Whitehills
American Robin	1988	Inverbervie

DECEMBER 28

Bewick's Swan	1994	Longside
Grey Phalarope	1978	Whitehills
American Robin	1988	Inverbervie

DECEMBER 29

Bewick's Swan	1994	Longside
Grey Phalarope	1978	Whitehills
Ivory Gull	1976	Westhill
American Robin	1988	Inverbervie

DECEMBER 30

Bewick's Swan	1994	Longside
Grey Phalarope	1978	Whitehills
Ivory Gull	1976	Westhill

DECEMBER 31

Bewick's Swan	1994	Longside
Grey Phalarope	1978	Whitehills
Ivory Gull	1976	Westhill

Appendices

Bibliography

The following *North East Scotland Bird Reports* were a primary source for bird records used in this book: 1974-1995

ADAMS, 1859 *The Birds of Banchory-Ternan.*

BAXTER, E.V. AND RINTOUL, L.J. 1953. *The Birds of Scotland.* Edinburgh: Oliver and Boyd.

BERRY, J. 1939. The Status and Distribution of Wild Geese and Wild Duck in Scotland. *International Wildfowl Inquiry*: Vol. 2. Cambridge University Press.

BUCKLAND, S.T., BELL, M.V. AND PICOZZI, N. 1990. *The Birds of North East Scotland.* Privately Published.

CRAMP, S. AND SIMMONS, K.E.L. (eds.) 1977. *The Birds of the Western Palearctic.* Vol. 1. Oxford.

CROOKE, C., DENNIR, R., HARVEY, M. AND SUMMERS, R. 1993. Population Size and Breeding Success of Slavonian Grebes in Scotland. In: Andrews, J. and Carter, S. 1993. *Britain's Birds in 1990-91: the conservation and monitoring review.* British Trust for Ornithology/ Joint Nature Conservation Committee.

DAVENPORT, D. 1992 The spring passage of Long-tailed and Pomarine Skuas in Britain and Ireland. *Birding World* 5: 92-95.

DRUMMOND-HAY, H.M. 1885-86 Report on the Ornithology of the East Coast of Scotland from Fife to Aberdeenshire inconclusive. *Scot. Nat.* 8: 1885-86.

DYMOND, J.N. AND THE RARITIES COMMITTEE. Report on Rare Birds in Great Britain in 1975. *British Birds* 69: 321-368.

DYMOND, J.N., FRASER, P.A. AND GANTLETT, S.J.M. 1989 *Rare Birds in Britain and Ireland.* Poyser.

EDWARD, T. 1860 A List of the Birds of Banffshire. *Zoologist* 18: 6968-70.

EDWARD, T. 1854-55 The Birds of Strathbeg. *The Naturalist* 1854-55.

EVANS, L.G.R. 1992 *Rare Birds in Britain 1991.* Privately Published.

EVANS, L.G.R. 1993 *Rare Birds in Britain 1992.* Privately Published.

EVANS, L.G.R. 1994 *Rare Birds in Britain 1800-1990.* Privately Published.

EVANS, L.G.R. 1995 *Rare Birds in Britain 1993.* Privately Published.

FORRESTER, R.W. 1995 Yellow-legged Gulls in Scotland. *Scottish Birds* 18: 95-100.

GIBBONS, D.W., REID, J.B. AND CHAPMAN, R.A. 1993 *The New Atlas of Breeding Birds in Britain and Ireland: 1988-1991.* Poyser.

HARBER, D.D. AND THE RARITIES COMMITTEE. Report on Rare Birds in Great Britain in 1962. *British Birds* 56: 393-409.

HARBER, D.D. AND THE RARITIES COMMITTEE. Report on Rare Birds in Great Britain in 1963. *British Birds* 57: 261-281.

HARBER, D.D. AND THE RARITIES COMMITTEE. Report on Rare Birds in Great Britain in 1964. *British Birds* 58: 353-372.

HARBER, D.D. AND THE RARITIES COMMITTEE. Report on Rare Birds in Great Britain in 1965. *British Birds* 59: 280-305.

HARRISON, P. 1983 *Seabirds: an identification guide.* Croom Helm, England.

HARVIE-BROWN, J.A. 1906 *A Fauna of the Tay Basin and Strathmore.* David Douglas, Edinburgh.

HOLLOWAY, S. 1996 *The Historical Atlas of Breeding Birds in Britain and Ireland 1875-1900.* Poyser.

HORN, W. 1878-80 Collected Notes on the Birds of Buchan, *Proc Nat Hist Soc of Glasgow*, Vol. 4.

INNES, M. The Movement of Divers and Grebes off Peterhead, Grampian. *North East Scotland Bird Report 1994.*

KNOX, A.G. 1983. The Crested Tit on Deeside. *Scottish Birds* 12: 255-258.

LACK, P.C. AND FERGUSON, D. 1986. *The Atlas of Wintering Birds in Britain and Ireland.* Poyser.

New Statistical Account of Scotland, 1845. Edinburgh: Blackwood.

OGILVIE, M. AND THE RARE BREEDING BIRDS PANEL. 1996 Rare Breeding Birds in the United Kingdom 1994. *British Birds* 89: 387-417.

O'SULLIVAN, J. AND THE RARITIES COMMITTEE. Report on Rare Birds in Great Britain in 1976. *British Birds* 70: 405-453.

MACGILLIVRAY, W. 1837-1852 *History of British Birds.*

MACGILLIVRAY, W. 1855 *The Natural History of Deeside and Braemar.*

MADGE, S. AND BURN, H. 1988 *Wildfowl: An identification guide to the ducks, geese and swans of the world.* Christopher Helm, London.

MAHOOD, A.E. 1917-18 Banffshire Birds. *Scot. Nat.* 1917-18.

NAYLOR, K.A. 1996 *A Reference Manual of Rare Birds in Great Britain and Ireland.*

PENNANT, T. 1772 *A Tour of Scotland.* Privately Published, Chester.

PYMAN, G.A. AND THE RARITIES COMMITTEE. Report on Rare Birds in Great Britain and Ireland in 1958. *British Birds* 53: 153-173.

PYMAN, G.A. AND THE RARITIES COMMITTEE. Report on Rare Birds in Great Britain and Ireland in 1959. *British Birds* 53: 409-431.

PYMAN, G.A. AND THE RARITIES COMMITTEE.
Report on Rare Birds in Great Britain in 1960.
British Birds 54: 173-200.

ROGERS, M.J. AND THE RARITIES COMMITTEE.
Report on Rare Birds in Great Britain 1977.
British Birds 71: 475-532.

ROGERS, M.J. AND THE RARITIES COMMITTEE.
Report on Rare Birds in Great Britain 1978.
British Birds 72: 503-549.

ROGERS, M.J. AND THE RARITIES COMMITTEE.
Report on Rare Birds in Great Britain 1979.
British Birds 73: 491-534.

ROGERS, M.J. AND THE RARITIES COMMITTEE.
Report on Rare Birds in Great Britain 1980.
British Birds 74: 453-495.

ROGERS, M.J. AND THE RARITIES COMMITTEE.
Report on Rare Birds in Great Britain 1981.
British Birds 75: 482-533.

ROGERS, M.J. AND THE RARITIES COMMITTEE.
Report on Rare Birds in Great Britain 1982.
British Birds 76: 476-529.

ROGERS, M.J. AND THE RARITIES COMMITTEE.
Report on Rare Birds in Great Britain 1983.
British Birds 77: 506-562.

ROGERS, M.J. AND THE RARITIES COMMITTEE.
Report on Rare Birds in Great Britain 1984.
British Birds 78: 529-589.

ROGERS, M.J. AND THE RARITIES COMMITTEE.
Report on Rare Birds in Great Britain 1985.
British Birds 79: 526-588.

ROGERS, M.J. AND THE RARITIES COMMITTEE.
Report on Rare Birds in Great Britain 1986.
British Birds 80: 516-571.

ROGERS, M.J. AND THE RARITIES COMMITTEE.
Report on Rare Birds in Great Britain 1987.
British Birds 81: 535-596.

ROGERS, M.J. AND THE RARITIES COMMITTEE.
Report on Rare Birds in Great Britain 1988.
British Birds 82: 505-563.

ROGERS, M.J. AND THE RARITIES COMMITTEE.
Report on Rare Birds in Great Britain 1989.
British Birds 83: 439-496.

ROGERS, M.J. AND THE RARITIES COMMITTEE.
Report on Rare Birds in Great Britain 1990.
British Birds 84: 449-505.

ROGERS, M.J. AND THE RARITIES COMMITTEE.
Report on Rare Birds in Great Britain 1991.
British Birds 85: 507-554.

ROGERS, M.J. AND THE RARITIES COMMITTEE.
Report on Rare Birds in Great Britain 1992.
British Birds 86: 447-540.

ROGERS, M.J. AND THE RARITIES COMMITTEE.
Report on Rare Birds in Great Britain 1993.
British Birds 87: 503-571.

ROGERS, M.J. AND THE RARITIES COMMITTEE.
Report on Rare Birds in Great Britain 1994.
British Birds 88: 493-558.

ROGERS, M.J. AND THE RARITIES COMMITTEE.
Report on Rare Birds in Great Britain 1995.
British Birds 89: 481-531.

SCOTT, M. 1995 The status and identification of
Snow Goose and Ross's Goose. *Birding World* 8:
56-63.

SERLE, W. 1895 The *Avi-Fauna of Buchan*, *Buchan
Field Club* Vol. 3.

SHARROCK, J.T.R. AND SHARROCK, E.M. 1976
Rare Birds in Britain and Ireland. Poyser, England.

SIM, G. 1903 *Vertebrate Fauna of Dee*. Wyllie,
Aberdeen.

SIMPSON, J. 1906-16 The Birds of Aberdeen Links
and Beach, *Trans Aberdeen Working Mens Natural
History Society* Vol. 2-3.

SMILES, S. 1893 *Life of a Scotch Naturalist*. John
Murray, London.

SMITH, F.R. AND THE RARITIES COMMITTEE.
Report on Rare Birds in Great Britain in 1966.
British Birds 60: 309-338.

SMITH, F.R. AND THE RARITIES COMMITTEE.
Report on Rare Birds in Great Britain in 1967.
British Birds 61: 329-365.

SMITH, F.R. AND THE RARITIES COMMITTEE.
Report on Rare Birds in Great Britain in 1968.
British Birds 62: 457-492.

SMITH, F.R. AND THE RARITIES COMMITTEE.
Report on Rare Birds in Great Britain in 1969.
British Birds 63: 267-293.

SMITH, F.R. AND THE RARITIES COMMITTEE.
Report on Rare Birds in Great Britain in 1970.
British Birds 64: 339-371.

SMITH, F.R. AND THE RARITIES COMMITTEE.
Report on Rare Birds in Great Britain in 1971.
British Birds 65: 322-354.

SMITH, F.R. AND THE RARITIES COMMITTEE.
Report on Rare Birds in Great Britain in 1972.
British Birds 66: 329-360.

SMITH, F.R. AND THE RARITIES COMMITTEE.
Report on Rare Birds in Great Britain in 1973.
British Birds 67: 310-348.

SMITH, F.R. AND THE RARITIES COMMITTEE.
Report on Rare Birds in Great Britain in 1974.
British Birds 68: 306-338.

SWAINE, C.M. AND THE RARITIES COMMITTEE.
Report on Rare Birds in Great Britain in 1961.
British Birds 55: 562-584.

The Statistical Account of Scotland 1791-99, ed Sir
John Sinclair.

THOM, V.M. 1986 *Birds in Scotland*. Poyser.

TUCKER, G.M. AND HEATH, M.F. 1994 *Birds in
Europe: Their Conservation Status*. Birdlife
International.

VOOUS, K.H. (1977) *List of Recent Holarctic Bird
Species*. British Ornithological Union, London.
(Originally published: 1973, 1977 in *Ibis*)

WILSON, A. AND SLACK, R. 1996 *Rare and Scarce
Birds in Yorkshire*. Privately Published.

YARRELL, W. 1871-85 *History of British Birds*, 4th
revised edition. Van Voorst, London.

Gazetteer

A			Bruckley Castle	NJ	911502	
Aberchirder	NJ	625525	Bucksburn	NJ	896094	
Aberdeen	NJ	941061	Bullers of Buchan	NK	111383	
Aboyne	NO	528984	Burnhervie	NJ	732195	
Aden Country Park	NJ	983482				
Alford	NJ	576161	**C**			
Annachie Lagoon	NK	107534	Cairnbulg	NK	038654	
Aquhythie	NJ	747184	Cairnbulg Castle	NK	015639	
Arbuthnott	NO	796756	Cairn O Mount	NO	649805	
Ardallie	NK	007391	Cairn Toul	NN	960970	
Ardlawhill	NJ	876623	Cairnwell	NO	134774	
Auchattie	NO	692946	Cammachmore	NO	906947	
Auchenblae	NO	726787	Castle Forbes	NJ	621192	
Auchleven	NJ	624243	Castle Fraser	NJ	723125	
Auchlossan	NJ	571021	Catterline	NO	868783	
Auchmacoy	NJ	992308	Chapel of Garioch	NJ	716240	
Auchnagatt	NJ	932417	Clola	NK	001436	
			Cock Bridge	NJ	257089	
B			Collieston	NK	040283	
Ballater	NO	368958	Cookney	NO	871933	
Balmedie	NJ	976180	Corby Loch	NJ	924144	
Balmoral Castle	NO	255949	Corrennie Forest	NJ	644103	
Banchory	NO	698955	Corrennie Moor	NJ	616098	
Banchory-Devenick	NJ	913022	Corgarff	NJ	275084	
Banff	NJ	685645	Cotehill Loch	NK	027293	
Barclay Castle	NJ	744438	Coull	NJ	513025	
Barthol Chapel	NJ	814341	Cove Bay	NJ	950015	
Belhelvie	NJ	946175	Craigmaud	NJ	887584	
Bellabeg	NJ	354132	Crathes Castle	NO	734968	
Ben Macdui	NN	989989	Crathie	NO	265949	
Bennachie (Mither Tap)	NJ	682223	Crimond	NK	052567	
Blackburn	NJ	828125	Crimmonmogate	NK	040587	
Blackdog	NJ	965140	Cross of Jackston	NJ	749326	
Blackhall Forest	NO	665955	Cruden Bay	NK	092363	
Blackhill	NK	074560	Cults	NJ	895033	
Blairs College	NJ	885008	Cults Reservoir	NJ	902027	
Boddam	NK	136423	Cuminestown	NJ	804504	
Boyndie	NJ	642639				
Boyndlie House	NJ	915620	**D**			
Braemar	NO	149914	Daviot	NJ	750282	
Braeroddach Loch	NJ	482003	Delnabo	NJ	303011	
Braes of Gight	NJ	825388	Den of Glasslaw	NJ	854593	
Brideswell	NJ	579393	Dinnet	NO	459987	
Bridge of Alford	NJ	562172	Donmouth	NJ	954095	
Bridge of Alvah	NJ	681611	Downies	NO	923951	
Bridge of Dee	NJ	929035	Drum Castle	NJ	795005	
Bridge of Feugh	NO	702951	Drumlithie	NO	785809	
Bridge of Muchalls	NO	895910	Drumoak	NO	785985	

Drums	NJ	998225
Duff House	NJ	691633
Duncanstone	NJ	580266
Dunecht	NJ	756091
Dunnottar Castle	NO	883839
Durno	NJ	716282
Durris Forest	NO	787928
Dyce	NJ	890126
Dykeside	NJ	725435

E

Echt	NJ	739056
Edzell Airfield	NO	632690
Ellon	NJ	956304

F

Fasque	NO	648755
Fedderate Reservoir	NJ	864523
Fetterangus	NJ	987508
Fettercairn	NO	651734
Fetteresso Forest	NO	772871
Findon	NO	937974
Finnygaud	NJ	604546
Fintry	NJ	756547
Forbestown	NJ	361129
Fordoun	NO	749758
Fordyce	NJ	556637
Forest of Birse	NO	525905
Forest of Deer	NJ	965508
Forest of Glen Tanar	NO	470940
Forgue	NJ	611451
Foveran Bushes	NK	004235
Fowlsheugh	NO	882830
Fraserburgh	NJ	995665
Fyvie	NJ	763376
Fyvie Castle	NJ	764393

G

Gairnshiel Lodge	NJ	293005
Gardenstown	NJ	800647
Gariochsford	NJ	674408
Garlogie	NJ	782053
Garmond	NJ	806520
Gartly	NJ	523324
Gartly Moor	NJ	565331
Gask	NJ	730473
Girdleness	NJ	973053
Glack	NJ	456275
Glenbervie	NO	769804
Glen Buchat	NJ	370168
Glen Buchat Lodge	NJ	333188
Glen Fenzie	NJ	323020

Glen Gairn	NO	342990
Glenkindie	NJ	438140
Glen Nochty	NJ	325157
Glen Shee Ski Centre	NO	139782
Glen Tanar House	NO	475956
Gordonstown	NJ	564565
Gourdon	NO	825707
Gowanwell	NJ	884419

H

Haddo House	NJ	868347
Hatterseat Bushes	NJ	988207
Hatton	NK	050372
Hatton Castle	NJ	758469
Hatton of Fintray	NJ	840162
Hazlehead	NJ	889052
Heugh-head	NJ	378115
Hillhead of Auchentumb	NJ	924586
Hill of Fare	NJ	688031
Howe of Teuchar	NJ	795470
Huntly	NJ	530400
Hythie	NK	007513

I

Insch	NJ	631282
Inverallochy	NK	044654
Inverbervie	NO	833725
Inverey	NO	086892
Inverkeithny	NJ	629470
Inverugie	NK	103484
Inverurie	NJ	774216

J

| Johnshaven | NO | 796671 |

K

Kemnay	NJ	733160
Kincardine O'Neil	NO	592995
Kingswells	NJ	868065
Kinloch	NK	097506
Kinnaird Head	NJ	999676
Kinneff (Old Church)	NO	856748
Kennethmont	NJ	539288
Kildrummy	NJ	468172
Kildrummy Castle	NJ	455165
Kintore	NJ	793163
Kirkhill Forest	NJ	849126
Kirkton of Alvah	NJ	678603
Kirkton of Auchterless	NJ	714415
Kirkton of Culsalmond	NJ	645327
Kirkton of Durris	NO	773961
Kirkton of Glen Buchat	NJ	378151

Kirkton of Logie Buchan	NJ	989297	Milltown of Kildrummy	NJ	471164
Kirkton of Maryculter	NO	857992	Milton of Cushnie	NJ	522113
Kirkton of Oyne	NJ	682257	Mintlaw	NK	000483
Kirkton of Skene	NJ	803076	Monkshill	NJ	796409
Knock Hill	NJ	537552	Montgarrie	NJ	576177
			Monymusk	NJ	684153
L			Mormond Hill	NJ	981569
Largue	NJ	636413	Moss Maud	NO	627993
Laurencekirk	NO	718716	Muchalls	NO	902921
Leochel-Cushnie	NJ	529106	Muir of Fowlis	NJ	563123
Leslie	NJ	597247	Muir of Kinellar	NJ	809132
Linn of Dee	NO	062906	Murcar GC	NJ	959120
Linn of Quoich	NO	115913			
Loch Callater	NO	184840	**N**		
Loch Davan	NJ	443006	Netherley	NO	854933
Lochhead of Leys	NO	697978	New Aberdour	NJ	884632
Loch Kinnord	NO	442995	Newburgh	NJ	999252
Loch of Aboyne	NO	537997	New Byth	NJ	822540
Loch Muick	NO	290830	New Deer	NJ	885468
Lochnagar	NO	250855	New Leeds	NJ	996547
Loch of Skene	NJ	785075	Newmacher	NJ	886195
Loch of Strathbeg	NK	074590	New Pitsligo	NJ	883560
Logie Coldstone	NJ	435044	Newtonhill	NO	914933
Loirston Loch	NJ	938011	North Esk Mouth	NO	743628
Longhaven	NK	109397	North Kirkton	NK	107508
Longmanhill	NJ	740624	North Rayne	NJ	695317
Longside	NK	037473			
Lonmay	NK	015586	**O**		
Lumphanan	NJ	584045	Old Aberdeen	NJ	936085
Lumsden	NJ	474218	Old Deer	NJ	977476
Lyne of Skene	NJ	764105	Old Kinernie	NJ	725095
			Oldmeldrum	NJ	809273
M			Old Rayne	NJ	674284
Macduff	NJ	705645	Ordie	NJ	453015
Mains of Drumtochty	NO	699800	Oyne	NJ	673261
Mains of Glen Buchat	NJ	395147			
Mains of Leask	NK	031332	**P**		
Mains of Towie	NJ	742442	Park House	NO	780976
Mar Lodge	NO	100900	Peathill	NJ	933661
Marykirk	NO	686657	Pennan	NJ	845655
Marywell	NO	581961	Peterculter	NJ	840005
Maud	NJ	924480	Peterhead	NK	133464
Meikle Loch	NK	029308	Philorth House	NK	003641
Meikle Wartle	NJ	721309	Phingask Bay	NJ	975670
Memsie	NJ	971624	Pitcaple	NJ	721254
Methlick	NJ	857373	Pitmedden	NJ	893274
Midmar	NJ	677073	Pitsligo Castle	NJ	937670
Midmar Forest	NJ	700047	Port Elphinstone	NJ	778201
Migvie	NJ	437067	Port Erroll	NK	094356
Mill Maud	NJ	570068	Portlethen	NO	922967
Mill of Glenbervie	NO	762803	Portsoy	NJ	590660
Milltimber	NJ	855013	Potterton	NJ	940157

Q

Quilquox	NJ	904386

R

Raemoir Hotel	NO	695995
Rathen	NK	003607
Rattray Head	NK	110577
Red Loch	NJ	990627
Redmoss	NJ	825318
Rhynie	NJ	498272
Rickarton	NO	816892
Roadside of Kinneff	NO	845767
Rora	NK	060505
Rosehearty	NJ	932675
Rothienorman	NJ	721356
Roughpark	NJ	343111
Ruthven	NJ	506469

S

St Combs	NK	054634
St Cyrus	NO	747648
St Fergus	NK	097520
St Katherines	NJ	784345
Sandend	NJ	555663
Sandhaven	NJ	963675
Sand Loch	NK	034284
Sauchen	NJ	699110
Savoch	NK	046588
South Fornet Farm	NJ	787108
South Quilquox	NJ	895376
Starnafin	NK	056582
Stirling	NK	127423
Stonehaven	NO	874856
Stoneywood	NJ	897108
Strachan	NO	672923
Strichen	NJ	945554
Strathdon	NJ	351129
Stuartfield	NJ	973459

T

Tap O'North	NJ	484294
Tarland	NJ	482046
Tarves	NJ	867312
The Bin Forest	NJ	520430
Tifty	NJ	775407
Tillyfourie	NJ	644123
Tillypronie Lochs	NJ	420084
Tipperty	NJ	968267
Tore of Troup	NJ	833625
Tornaveen	NJ	619060
Torphins	NJ	624017
Towie	NJ	439128

Troup Head	NJ	825674
Tullynessle	NJ	558196
Turriff	NJ	725500
Tyrie	NJ	924625

U

Udny Green	NJ	880264
Udny Station	NJ	908244
Upper Boddam	NJ	622306

V

W

Waterside	NJ	366119
Westhill	NJ	830070
Whinnyfold	NK	081332
Whitehills	NJ	655655
Whitehouse	NJ	622146
Woodhead	NJ	790384

X

Y

Ythanbank	NJ	905342
Ythanwells	NJ	634384

Z

Index of species' scientific names

Index of species' English names

Systematic checklist

This checklist includes all species recorded in the North East Scotland region, accompanied by their British Ornithological Union category banding. The regions list at time of publication totals 340 species.

Species	Category	Species	Category
☐ Red-throated Diver	A	☐ Snow Goose	A
☐ Black-throated Diver	A	☐ Canada Goose	A
☐ Great Northern Diver	A	☐ Barnacle Goose	A
☐ White-billed Diver	A	☐ Brent Goose	A
☐ Pied-billed Grebe	A	☐ Shelduck	A
☐ Little Grebe	A	☐ Mandarin Duck	C
☐ Great Crested Grebe	A	☐ Wigeon	A
☐ Red-necked Grebe	A	☐ American Wigeon	A
☐ Slavonian Grebe	A	☐ Gadwall	A
☐ Black-necked Grebe	A	☐ Teal	A
☐ Fulmar	A	☐ Mallard	A
☐ Cory's Shearwater	A	☐ Pintail	A
☐ Great Shearwater	A	☐ Garganey	A
☐ Sooty Shearwater	A	☐ Blue-winged Teal	A
☐ Manx Shearwater	A	☐ Shoveler	A
☐ Mediterranean Shearwater	A	☐ Red-crested Pochard	A
☐ Storm Petrel	A	☐ Pochard	A
☐ Leach's Petrel	A	☐ Ring-necked Duck	A
☐ Gannet	A	☐ Ferruginous Duck	A
☐ Cormorant	A	☐ Tufted Duck	A
☐ Shag	A	☐ Scaup	A
☐ Common Bittern	A	☐ Common Eider	A
☐ American Bittern	B	☐ King Eider	A
☐ Little Bittern	B	☐ Steller's Eider	A
☐ Night Heron	A	☐ Long-tailed Duck	A
☐ Little Egret	A	☐ Common Scoter	A
☐ Great White Egret	A	☐ Surf Scoter	A
☐ Grey Heron	A	☐ Velvet Scoter	A
☐ Purple Heron	A	☐ Goldeneye	A
☐ White Stork	A	☐ Smew	A
☐ Glossy Ibis	A	☐ Red-breasted Merganser	A
☐ Spoonbill	A	☐ Goosander	A
☐ Mute Swan	A	☐ Ruddy Duck	A
☐ Bewick's Swan	A	☐ Honey Buzzard	C
☐ Whooper Swan	A	☐ Black Kite	A
☐ Bean Goose	A	☐ Red Kite	A
☐ Pink-footed Goose	A	☐ White-tailed Eagle	A
☐ White-fronted Goose	A	☐ Marsh Harrier	A
☐ Greylag Goose	A	☐ Hen Harrier	A

Species	Category	Species	Category
☐ Montagu's Harrier	A	☐ Sanderling	A
☐ Goshawk	A	☐ Little Stint	A
☐ Sparrowhawk	A	☐ Temminck's Stint	A
☐ Common Buzzard	A	☐ Least Sandpiper	A
☐ Rough-legged Buzzard	A	☐ White-rumped Sandpiper	A
☐ Spotted Eagle	B	☐ Baird's Sandpiper	A
☐ Golden Eagle	A	☐ Pectoral Sandpiper	A
☐ Osprey	A	☐ Curlew Sandpiper	A
☐ Lesser Kestrel	B	☐ Purple Sandpiper	A
☐ Kestrel	A	☐ Dunlin	A
☐ Red-footed Falcon	A	☐ Broad-billed Sandpiper	A
☐ Merlin	A	☐ Buff-breasted Sandpiper	A
☐ Hobby	A	☐ Ruff	A
☐ Gyr Falcon	A	☐ Jack Snipe	A
☐ Peregrine	A	☐ Common Snipe	A
☐ Red Grouse	A	☐ Great Snipe	B
☐ Ptarmigan	A	☐ Long-billed Dowitcher	A
☐ Black Grouse	A	☐ Woodcock	A
☐ Capercaillie	C	☐ Black-tailed Godwit	A
☐ Red-legged Partridge	C	☐ Hudsonian Godwit	A
☐ Grey Partridge	A	☐ Bar-tailed Godwit	A
☐ Quail	A	☐ Eskimo Curlew	B
☐ Pheasant	C	☐ Whimbrel	A
☐ Water Rail	A	☐ Curlew	A
☐ Spotted Crake	A	☐ Spotted Redshank	A
☐ Corncrake	A	☐ Common Redshank	A
☐ Moorhen	A	☐ Marsh Sandpiper	A
☐ Coot	A	☐ Greenshank	A
☐ Common Crane	A	☐ Greater Yellowlegs	B
☐ Little Bustard	B	☐ Lesser Yellowlegs	A
☐ Houbara Bustard	B	☐ Green Sandpiper	A
☐ Oystercatcher	A	☐ Wood Sandpiper	A
☐ Black-winged Stilt	A	☐ Common Sandpiper	A
☐ Avocet	A	☐ Turnstone	A
☐ Black-winged Pratincole	A	☐ Wilson's Phalarope	A
☐ Little Ringed Plover	A	☐ Red-necked Phalarope	A
☐ Ringed Plover	A	☐ Grey Phalarope	A
☐ Killdeer	A	☐ Pomarine Skua	A
☐ Kentish Plover	A	☐ Arctic Skua	A
☐ Greater Sand Plover	A	☐ Long-tailed Skua	A
☐ Dotterel	A	☐ Great Skua	A
☐ American Golden Plover	A	☐ Mediterranean Gull	A
☐ Golden Plover	A	☐ Little Gull	A
☐ Grey Plover	A	☐ Sabine's Gull	A
☐ Lapwing	A	☐ Black-headed Gull	A
☐ Knot	A	☐ Ring-billed Gull	A

Species	Category	Species	Category
☐ Common Gull	A	☐ Hoopoe	A
☐ Lesser Black-backed Gull	A	☐ Wryneck	A
☐ Herring Gull	A	☐ Green Woodpecker	A
☐ Iceland Gull	A	☐ Great Spotted Woodpecker	A
☐ Glaucous Gull	A	☐ Short-toed Lark	A
☐ Great Black-backed Gull	A	☐ Woodlark	A
☐ Ross's Gull	A	☐ Skylark	A
☐ Kittiwake	A	☐ Shore Lark	A
☐ Ivory Gull	A	☐ Sand Martin	A
☐ Caspian Tern	A	☐ Swallow	A
☐ Sandwich Tern	A	☐ Red-rumped Swallow	A
☐ Roseate Tern	A	☐ House Martin	A
☐ Common Tern	A	☐ Richard's Pipit	A
☐ Arctic Tern	A	☐ Tawny Pipit	A
☐ Forster's Tern	A	☐ Olive-backed Pipit	A
☐ Bridled Tern	A	☐ Tree Pipit	A
☐ Little Tern	A	☐ Pechora Pipit	A
☐ Black Tern	A	☐ Meadow Pipit	A
☐ White-winged Black Tern	A	☐ Rock Pipit	A
☐ Guillemot	A	☐ Water Pipit	A
☐ Razorbill	A	☐ Yellow Wagtail	A
☐ Black Guillemot	A	☐ Grey Wagtail	A
☐ Little Auk	A	☐ Pied Wagtail	A
☐ Puffin	A	☐ Waxwing	A
☐ Pallas's Sandgrouse	B	☐ Dipper	A
☐ Rock Dove	A	☐ Wren	A
☐ Stock Dove	A	☐ Dunnock	A
☐ Woodpigeon	A	☐ Robin	A
☐ Collared Dove	A	☐ Thrush Nightingale	A
☐ Turtle Dove	A	☐ Nightingale	A
☐ Cuckoo	A	☐ Bluethroat	A
☐ Barn Owl	A	☐ Black Redstart	A
☐ Scop's Owl	B	☐ Redstart	A
☐ Snowy Owl	A	☐ Whinchat	A
☐ Hawk Owl	B	☐ Stonechat	A
☐ Little Owl	C	☐ Isabelline Wheatear	A
☐ Tawny Owl	A	☐ Northern Wheatear	A
☐ Long-eared Owl	A	☐ Pied Wheatear	A
☐ Short-eared Owl	A	☐ White's Thrush	A
☐ Tengmalm's Owl	B	☐ Ring Ouzel	A
☐ Nightjar	A	☐ Blackbird	A
☐ Swift	A	☐ Eye-browed Thrush	A
☐ Alpine Swift	A	☐ Fieldfare	A
☐ Kingfisher	A	☐ Song Thrush	A
☐ European Bee-eater	A	☐ Redwing	A
☐ Roller	A	☐ Mistle Thrush	A

Species	Category	Species	Category
☐ American Robin	A	☐ Magpie	A
☐ Grasshopper Warbler	A	☐ Nutcracker	B
☐ Sedge Warbler	A	☐ Jackdaw	A
☐ Marsh Warbler	A	☐ Rook	A
☐ Reed Warbler	A	☐ Carrion Crow	A
☐ Great Reed Warbler	A	☐ Raven	A
☐ Booted Warbler	A	☐ Starling	A
☐ Icterine Warbler	A	☐ Rose-coloured Starling	A
☐ Melodious Warbler	A	☐ House Sparrow	A
☐ Subalpine Warbler	A	☐ Tree Sparrow	A
☐ Orphean Warbler	A	☐ Chaffinch	A
☐ Barred Warbler	A	☐ Brambling	A
☐ Lesser Whitethroat	A	☐ Greenfinch	A
☐ Whitethroat	A	☐ Goldfinch	A
☐ Garden Warbler	A	☐ Siskin	A
☐ Blackcap	A	☐ Linnet	A
☐ Greenish Warbler	A	☐ Twite	A
☐ Arctic Warbler	A	☐ Redpoll	A
☐ Pallas's Warbler	A	☐ Arctic Redpoll	A
☐ Yellow-browed Warbler	A	☐ Common Crossbill	A
☐ Hume's Warbler	A	☐ Scottish Crossbill	A
☐ Radde's Warbler	A	☐ Common Rosefinch	A
☐ Dusky Warbler	A	☐ Bullfinch	A
☐ Bonelli's Warbler	A	☐ Hawfinch	A
☐ Wood Warbler	A	☐ Lapland Bunting	A
☐ Chiffchaff	A	☐ Snow Bunting	A
☐ Willow Warbler	A	☐ Yellowhammer	A
☐ Goldcrest	A	☐ Ortolan Bunting	A
☐ Firecrest	A	☐ Rustic Bunting	A
☐ Spotted Flycatcher	A	☐ Little Bunting	A
☐ Red-breasted Flycatcher	A	☐ Reed Bunting	A
☐ Pied Flycatcher	A	☐ Corn Bunting	A
☐ Bearded Tit	A		
☐ Long-tailed Tit	A		
☐ Willow Tit	B		
☐ Crested Tit	A		
☐ Coal Tit	A	☐ Brünnich's Guillemot	D3
☐ Blue Tit	A	☐ Greater Flamingo	Dl
☐ Great Tit	A	☐ Lesser white-fronted Goose	Dl
☐ Treecreeper	A	☐ Bar-headed Goose	Dl
☐ Golden Oriole	A	☐ Ruddy Shelduck	Dl
☐ Red-backed Shrike	A	☐ Eagle Owl	Dl
☐ Lesser Grey Shrike	A	☐ Long-tailed Rosefinch	Dl
☐ Great Grey Shrike	A		
☐ Woodchat Shrike	A	Black-browed Albatross, *offshore of region*	
☐ Jay	A	Little Shearwater, *pended*	